The Consumer's Guide to
Understanding
and Using
the Law

Daniel Johnson

BETTERWAY BOOKS

CINCINNATI, OHIO

The purpose of this book is to provide the reader with basic legal principles and terminology. This information is intended to be educational in nature. The material herein is not to be used or interpreted as a substitute for professional legal advice.

The pronouns *he*, *his* and *him* as used in this book are not intended to denote masculine gender exclusively, rather they are used to avoid awkward or redundant grammar.

98 97 96 95 94   5 4 3 2 1

Library of Congress Cataloging-in-Publication Data

Johnson, Daniel L.
   The consumer's guide to understanding and using the law / by Daniel L. Johnson. — 1st ed.
       p.   cm.
   Includes index.
   ISBN 1-55870-332-2
   1. Law — United States — Popular works. I. Title.
KF387.J58   1994
349.73 — dc20
[347.3]

K F
3 8 7
. J 5 8
1 9 9 4
P A P

93-47213
CIP

Edited by Mary L. Sproles
Designed by Paul Neff

To my parents,
Bill and Eloyse Johnson,
with loving gratitude.

ABOUT THE AUTHOR

A partner in the law firm of Latenser and Johnson, P.C., Daniel L. Johnson is the author of *Legal Aspects of Buying, Owning and Selling a Home*. He and his wife Susan live in Omaha, Nebraska, with their two children, Rachel and Mark.

ACKNOWLEDGMENTS

Acknowledgment and sincere appreciation to Mary Sproles for her editorial expertise and to Audrey Aken for her professional secretarial service and support. Many thanks to my wife, Susan, for getting our children (Rachel and Mark) to bed on those nights when I worked on this book. I would also like to acknowledge the following individuals and entities whose help and inspiration contributed in some manner to this book:

Justice Frank E. Henderson
Professor Thomas Cleary
Lee Magnuson
Jim Krause
Kal Lausterer
Belvedere Elementary School
Dan and Blanche Henry
Verl and Ardeth Bodenhamer

Albin and Ethel Johnson
Merle and Ethel Amundson
University of South Dakota
Ruth Christensen
David Latenser
Jim Londay
Curt Iwen
Rocky Balboa

INTRODUCTION

Justice, Sir, is the great interest of man on earth.
—*Daniel Webster*

Your five-year-old son has a friend who often plays with rocks and sticks. On previous occasions, he has scraped or bruised your son while playing. You have mentioned this to the parents of your son's playmate, but they have done little to keep this type of activity from recurring. One day your son runs into the house screaming and crying with his hand over his eye. The damage looks more than superficial and you rush him to the hospital. Eventually, you find out that he may have a permanent loss of vision in one eye. Can your son be legally compensated for the loss of his eyesight? Is your son's playmate responsible? Are his parents?

Your mother owns several hundred acres of farmland that she rents out and receives a portion of the crop proceeds on an annual basis. Lately, she has acted very confused and does not seem able to manage her own affairs, either personally or with regard to the farm. The situation worsens and you decide that she must leave the farm and move in with you. By this time, she is incapable of managing or overseeing her farm in any capacity. All the property remains solely in her name. What, if anything, can be done to allow you to have the legal authority to manage her personal and business affairs?

During the summer, you sign a one-year lease that states that the landlord is to provide you with air-conditioning and heating for the apartment. Everything goes fine until winter sets in. Your landlord refuses to keep the temperature above sixty degrees, despite your constant complaining to him that the apartment is too cold. The lease itself makes no mention of a specific temperature for the winter months. Can you refuse to pay your rent until the landlord provides you with more heat? Can you "break the lease" and leave without being responsible for the lease payments?

These situations are examples of how anyone can find themselves involved in the legal system. The question in each case becomes: "What can I legally do?" or "Do I have any legal recourse?"

There is no shortage of law books in this country, but most of them are geared toward lawyers and judges. They are much more complicated than the average person needs to become acquainted with our system of justice. This book is designed to provide you with a legal compass to steer you toward what remedies and procedures are available to protect or enforce your rights.

I have not attempted to provide you with a comprehensive source of legal rights, nor should the book be considered an absolute synopsis of American law. Such an undertaking would, I believe, negate the purpose of this book, which is to focus on the areas of law that will most likely affect the average citizen.

The material in this book will serve as a long-term legal guide for the consumer. Although the law is a dynamic and ever-changing animal, every effort has been made to focus on the basic legal principles and concepts that will, in all likelihood, stand the test of time.

Keep in mind that this book is not a substitute for a formal legal education, nor is it designed to act as a guide for legal self-representation. It will, however, provide you with a smooth and convenient path to the door of our legal system. I hope that once I explain the principles of American law, you can understand and use them to your advantage.

Chapter One

The Legal System

They have no lawyers among them, for they consider them as a sort of people whose profession it is to disguise matters.
— Sir Thomas Moore

The law is a sort of hocus-pocus science.
— Charles Macklin

Joe Client: "So . . . what's the latest with my lawsuit?"

Larry Lawyer: "Well, the defendant has demurred to our petition, which is good and bad; the delay could cause an increase in specials, but if his motion is sustained, we will have to move to amend from negligence to *res ipsa*. The court may require a detailed brief unless we can stipulate otherwise."

Joe Client: "Oh."

If the response to Joe Client's question made no sense to you, you are in the majority. Often, it seems that people regularly involved in the legal system not only have their own special terms and language, but can use everyday words in a fashion that leaves the layperson completely in the dark about what is going on. The average person will probably be involved in a lawsuit or have dealings with an attorney more than once during his lifetime. Before reviewing the various areas of the law in the following chapters, you must understand the legal arena and its players. This chapter will be divided into four sections: a discussion of lawyers and law firms and how they operate and deal with clients; the court system on which the American system of jurisprudence is based; the various sources of the law itself; and a discussion of the rules and procedures that come into play when a case goes to trial.

LAWYERS AND LAW FIRMS

This section will review the different methods of law practice, including a discussion of the different types of fee arrangements that can be agreed on. The general duties that every attorney has toward his client will also be reviewed.

Attorney Qualifications

Each state has its own requirements concerning what type of education, experience and testing is necessary to become an attorney. In most states, a college degree coupled with a postgraduate degree from an accredited law school is necessary to take the bar exam. Each state has its own bar exam section dealing with local law. Many states also use the multistate bar exam, which is the same throughout the country and tests areas of the law that are uniform from state to state.

If the bar exam is passed and the other educational experience requirements are met, the person is sworn in as a member of that state's bar association. Usually, becoming a member of a state bar association does not entitle an attorney to practice law in any other state without meeting that state's bar requirements. After several years, most attorneys can "motion" in other states' bar associations without having to take another formal bar examination.

Types of Law Practice

After becoming a member of the bar, some attorneys become solo practitioners, meaning that they are the only attorney in their office and, aside from support staff such as secretaries or law clerks, they run the office. Although many solo practitioners have a general practice, others focus their practice in a specific area of the law.

Some attorneys join in partnership arrangements and create law firms. A law firm can include anywhere from two to several hundred attorneys. Usually, a partner owns or has an ownership interest in the assets of the partnership. The partners often hire *associate attorneys* who are employees of the firm rather than partners. Typically, after several years, an associate is reviewed by the other partners to determine whether he can become a partner in the firm.

Sometimes, attorneys set up their partnerships as professional corporations or *PCs*. A professional corporation standing may give the firm certain tax advantages over a partnership. It does not change any of the inherent duties that firm members have toward their clients. In this regard, it generally makes no difference whether the law firm is a partnership or a professional corporation.

Often, there will be hybrids of partnerships and professional corporations involved in the same office. That is, some attorneys are themselves professional corporations, and these solo professional corporations can become partners with other solo professional corporations. Most of these arrangements are chosen for the tax advantages they provide for the lawyers involved and do not diminish the professional obligation of the attorney toward his client.

Often, solo practitioners will enter into an office-sharing arrangement with other independent attorneys. They may use a common secretarial pool, library and office machinery to maximize their income and minimize their overhead. Do not assume that a group of attorneys sharing a secretary and office space is a law firm. Often, an office-sharing arrangement looks like a law firm, but it is merely a sharing of office space and expenses. Attorneys cannot hold themselves out to be a law firm if, in fact, their only connection is the joint use of an office.

Many attorneys do not enter into private practice. Some are employees of the federal, state or city government; others enter politics; and others enter one of the many administrative or business professions that do not directly entail the practice of law or representation of clients. Some examples of government employee attorneys who do practice law (usually criminal law) include district or county attorneys, public defenders and federal prosecutors.

Selecting an Attorney

One of the most common problems that most people have is selecting a lawyer. Many people ask friends or family members to recommend an attorney they have used in the past. Most bar associations have a lawyer referral service (you can contact them through the telephone book). This is a service of bar associations that provides names of local attorneys that practice in the area in which you have an interest. If you are limited in funds, sometimes a legal aid society or legal service corporation can provide free or reduced-fee legal assistance if you meet certain low-income guidelines. These types of services are generally related to civil cases, while indigent individuals who need criminal defense representation will usually be assigned an attorney through the public defender's office or be given a court-appointed attorney.

Another useful source for locating suitable attorneys is your telephone book. Many lawyers advertise their experience in a specific area. Usually, the local bar association makes no guarantee that an attorney who advertises knowledge or experience in a certain area is in fact an expert, although some states do provide a specialization or expert designation for attorneys. If the attorney is in fact a specialist or has been certified as a specialist in his field, and such a certification has the backing of the applicable bar association, that attorney will generally provide more focused and specific representation in that area.

Aside from any specialization or certification by the attorney, you should also consider the lawyer's reputation in the community, his experience in this area of law, and his ability to clearly and satisfactorily explain how he intends to handle your legal problem. Another factor that needs to be considered is the fee that he will charge. Attorney fees will be discussed at greater length later in this chapter.

Obligations to the Client

Once you have decided to hire a particular attorney or law firm, that attorney is said to have a *fiduciary duty* toward the client. This means that the attorney must put the client's interest above his own and ensure that no information the client divulges is passed to any third party without the client's express consent, regardless of whether that information is damaging. This is called the *duty of confidentiality* and pertains not only to the attorney with whom the client is dealing directly, but to any other attorneys or employees working in his office or firm.

When an attorney is hired, he is entrusted to protect your legal interests to the best of his ability. This generally requires an initial conference between you and the attorney. This initial meeting allows the attorney to discern the particular problem or desired goal involved. The attorney must also analyze all the available facts pertaining to the situation and do whatever is necessary to gather such facts.

If a trial or hearing in court is involved, the attorney is responsible for procuring or preparing all necessary documents and for making legal arguments in court. In most situations where litigation is involved, the attorney also has a duty to negotiate a settlement if possible, but he cannot agree to any settlement terms without your express consent. The attorney also has an obligation to keep you informed of the status and progress of your case. You must understand that no attorney can guarantee to win the case in a contested matter that proceeds to court. The attorney can give his opinion on the chances of succeeding, but this is merely a prediction, not a guarantee.

It is important to note that you, as the client, have certain inherent obligations to the attorney. You must be honest in relating all the facts concerning the legal problem involved. Any dishonesty or failure to divulge such facts may have a direct and severe bearing on the result of the case.

Attorney Fees

At the initial meeting, a fee should be agreed upon. There are several different types of fee arrangements, ranging from an hourly rate to a flat fee to a percentage of settlement won. Some attorneys advertise or state that there is no charge for the initial consultation. Usually, this type of claim pertains to potential personal injury or contingent fee arrangements. However, if you wish to confer with an attorney on a specific real estate question, the attorney probably will not give any free advice. Rather, the initial free consultation is for the attorney to determine whether your case interests him. It is also an opportunity for you to decide if he is the right attorney to represent you.

The fee the attorney charges for work performed depends upon several things. First, and probably foremost, is the amount of time or anticipated time spent on the problem. If a simple will is desired, the attorney will know almost exactly how much time and effort will be required on his part and can quote a specific fee for having the will drafted and executed. However, if the client hires an attorney to help obtain custody of his minor child, the attorney will find it difficult to quote a set fee, since it would be impossible to determine how much time would be involved in a custody case. The case could be settled relatively simply without a trial, or, if a trial is necessary, it is impossible to know how much work would be involved in preparing for the trial plus the court time itself.

Generally, when the attorney quotes a fee, he considers not only the time likely to be spent on the legal problem, but also his expertise (if any) in the area involved, the complexity of the case, etc. The lawyer's fee also includes the cost of his secretarial and clerical support, including library materials and office space. In effect, the client is hiring the attorney's entire office or firm to work for him.

Hourly Rate. One of the most common methods of determining a fee is the hourly rate. In this situation, you give the attorney a specific legal problem or goal; the attorney tracks the time spent to reach that goal and charges the client periodically for the cost of accrued time. A divorce (at the most advantageous financial terms) is often billed at an hourly rate. Usually, the more experienced and specialized an attorney is, the more he will charge per hour. The complexity of the case may also increase the hourly charge. Most people are surprised at the variety of hourly rates that are charged within the same community. While some simple matters can be handled at anywhere from $40 an hour or less, some lawyers or law firms will charge several hundred dollars per hour. Obviously, you should shop before determining which lawyer will give you the most bang for the buck.

Flat Fee. Attorneys will sometimes charge a flat fee for what usually amounts to a routine service or document. A bankruptcy proceeding, an uncontested divorce or the drafting of a will or trust lend themselves to flat fee quotes. Keep in mind, though, that if a very low price for a legal product is quoted, the result may not be the best.

Contingent Fee. Another fairly typical fee arrangement is the *contingent fee*. Here, the attorney receives a percentage of any money recovered on your behalf. Generally, if no money is recovered, you're not responsible for any attorney fees. If the attorney has to pay a fee to file a lawsuit, pay a court reporter to take depositions of witnesses, or pay for the serving of summonses, these expenses ultimately remain your responsibility. An attorney cannot pay for these expenses on your behalf; by doing so, he would be buying a lawsuit from you instead of representing your legal interests.

Contingent fee arrangements are advantageous if you would not otherwise be able to afford an attorney to protect your legal interests. Contingent fees are most often used in personal injury lawsuits and in cases attempting to collect a debt. In both situations, the attorney is representing you in doing whatever is necessary to obtain the best settlement, judgment and collection of money available. In personal injury claims, the fee can vary between 20 and 40 percent, and will depend on the amount of effort required to obtain the desired result. For instance, if the attorney settles the case to your satisfaction without ever having to file a lawsuit, the contingent fee may be 25 percent. However, if suit is filed, a trial required and an appeal filed following the trial, the contingent fee may escalate to 33⅓ to 40 percent.

Retainer. Another type of fee arrangement is the *retainer*. This can be handled in one of two ways. First, you can agree on a sum at the initial representation stage, and future billings by the attorney (usually at an hourly rate) are credited against the retainer. The retainer in this situation ensures that the attorney receives timely payments. Many attorneys require a retainer in certain legal matters they anticipate will require a great deal of time or effort.

Second, you, as an individual or corporation, pay an attorney an agreed on sum (retainer) on a periodic basis, such as monthly, and during that time the attorney is obligated to handle any legal problems or interests that may arise for you. This allows the attorney a steady source of income in exchange for providing you with complete and constant legal representation. This type of retainer situation is becoming more and more rare, however, as most clients would rather pay as they go for specific work done on problems as they may arise.

Put It in Writing. If possible, get the fee agreement in writing. Written fee agreements are encouraged and sometimes mandated by local bar associations. (See the appendix for samples of fee agreements.) In one type of fee agreement, the attorney agrees to provide you with legal representation on a certain matter or issue. The fee is stated, with a provision that if additional issues arise, the agreement may be modified. You agree to pay a certain amount on a specified time basis, and the attorney makes it clear that if you don't pay the attorney will no longer represent you.

A contingent fee agreement bases the amount of fee on the amount of work required by the attorney. Note that the agreement requires you to remain responsible for all court costs and expenses incurred by the attorney in representing your legal interests.

One final statement about written fee agreements. If a written fee agreement is entered into, the client is always entitled to a copy. If there are any questions about the agreement, ask the lawyer to explain it to you and make sure that all the terminology and legalese is understood. The Attorney Code of Professional Responsibility states that attorneys "should not charge more than a reasonable fee" for the matter involved. In determining what constitutes a reasonable fee, consider the time and labor required, the type of issues involved and the customary fee in your area. The fee may also depend on the results obtained and experience and reputation of the lawyer. Nevertheless, if you have any questions about your attorney's billing methods or amounts, address them immediately rather than waiting to bring it to the attorney's attention.

Pro Bono and Pro Se. You should understand *pro bono* and *pro se* as we talk about attorney's fees and representation. *Pro bono* means that the attorney will represent you for free. Attorneys are encouraged to represent clients on a nonfee basis if they have a legitimate claim and are simply unable to pay the fee that would otherwise be charged. The client does remain responsible for any court costs and expenses. It is up to the individual attorney or firm to take on as much *pro bono* work as they believe is prudent or necessary. Some bar association referral services routinely assign *pro bono* cases.

Pro se means representing yourself in court — which is not illegal — even if an attorney represents the party against you. Obviously, there may be some difficulties in dealing with the rules of evidence and procedure, but every citizen has the right to represent himself. *Pro se* applies to individuals; in many jurisdictions a corporation cannot be represented by a corporate officer or board of directors and must have an attorney represent its interests in court.

American Rule. When you are involved in a trial or litigation, the question often arises concerning who is responsible for attorney fees. In this country, the courts generally follow what is called the *American Rule*. This means that each party in the lawsuit is responsible to his attorney for his own legal fees, regardless of the outcome of the lawsuit. This is different from the *English Rule*, where the loser of the lawsuit is responsible for paying the attorney fees of the other party.

There are several exceptions to the American Rule regarding attorney fees. Several federal acts, as well as many local statutes, require the payment of attorney fees to the winning side's attorney. A few of these are as follows: Fair Credit Billing Act, Fair Credit Recording Act, Freedom of Information Act, Federal Tort Claims Act, Age Discrimination and Employment Act, Fair Housing Act, and Title VII of the Civil Rights Act of 1964. The court will determine the amount of attorney fees awarded. Generally, the court will look at the time and labor involved, the difficulty or complexity of the issues presented, and the amount of skills required to perform the legal services correctly.

Tax Exemption. Generally, attorney fees are not tax deductible. But business legal fees are deductible if they are ordinary and necessary business expenses. There are certain exceptions to the nondeductibility of personal attorney fees, but these are somewhat rare and the Internal Revenue Service will undoubtedly require any taxpayer to prove the deductibility of attorney fees. A qualified accountant will be able to answer any questions you might have about this issue.

Terminating the Attorney-Client Relationship

Sometimes you no longer want to have the attorney you originally hired continue to represent you. There are three primary reasons for wanting to fire or switch attorneys: dollars, distrust and delay.

As mentioned before, the fee arrangement between the attorney and the client should be agreed on at the beginning of the attorney-client relationship. If you and the attorney agree on the fee arrangement, and the attorney later does not abide by the agreement or you believe that the attorney is dragging out the case in an attempt to increase the fee, you may advise the attorney to take no further action with the matter at hand. Other times you can simply no longer afford the attorney and will terminate the relationship to avoid incurring further fees. If such termination is desired, it should be made in writing so the attorney can keep a written record of when his employment ended.

If for whatever reason you have lost faith in your attorney and do not believe that your best interest is being served, or if the attorney is simply not responding effectively to your inquiries, you may also fire the attorney. Again, this should be done in writing to protect the interests of both parties.

One of the most common complaints against attorneys is the delay in responding or achieving the desired results. Although many lawsuits or legal matters take several months or longer to reach their ultimate conclusion, there are instances in which the attorney is simply not diligent in pursuing your claim. If you find it more and more difficult to communicate directly with your attorney, the inherent delay and frustration may lead you to terminate the relationship.

If an attorney is representing you in a matter that has proceeded to court, the attorney will generally have to file a motion to withdraw as attorney of record. The court will usually allow you sufficient time to find another attorney before the case proceeds. Most attorneys will withdraw representation if you are not paying on a timely basis, or if they are not able to communicate with or obtain feedback from you, which allows for ineffective representation.

If you believe an attorney has breached his duty or has not fulfilled his obligation of solving your legal concerns, you may want to make a formal complaint to the local bar association. The bar association will get the attorney's side of the story and determine whether formal charges need to be filed. Often, the bar association will contact the state supreme court if it believes that a violation has occurred. The potential penalty to the offending attorney range from a short probation period, to public censure, to total disbarment.

THE COURT SYSTEM

This section provides a brief overview of the American court system, including the different types of courts and the jurisdictions they have.

Federal Courts

The federal government has created a system of courts composed of the U.S. District Courts, eleven U.S. Courts of Appeals (which handle appeals from the District Courts) and the U.S. Supreme Court. Each state has at least one U.S. District Court, and many states have several, depending on their population. Each state also has a bankruptcy court that operates under the federal court system and handles all bankruptcies and disputes or lawsuits pertaining to a filed bankruptcy. Other federal courts include the U.S. Court of Customs and Patent Appeals, the U.S. Court of Claims, the Tax Court of the United States, the U.S. Customs Court and the U.S. Court of Military Appeals. As their names indicate, most of these courts have jurisdiction over specialized or specific cases.

The federal courts generally handle cases involving the U.S. Constitution; interpretation of the laws of the United States and its treaties; disputes involving ambassadors, admiralty and maritime jurisdictions; and cases in which the United States is a named party to the lawsuit. Also, controversies between two or more states, or between a state and a citizen of another state, invoke federal jurisdiction. Similarly, lawsuits involving citizens of different states or between citizens of foreign nations may also be subject to federal jurisdiction.

State and Local Courts

Each state court system has its own structure at the state and local level. Many states have local courts called county courts or courts of limited jurisdiction. These courts generally handle misdemeanor criminal cases, including traffic and municipal ordinance violations, preliminary hearings of felony criminal cases and civil cases involving disputes of a lesser monetary amount. Often, the county court will be responsible for estate or probate matters, and may also hear all juvenile offenses, if a specific juvenile court doesn't exist. The county courts may double as small claims courts, which will be discussed later.

The next level above these local courts are the courts of general jurisdiction, often called district courts. Depending on the population of the state, one area may have several district courts, while other areas may have just one. The district court, in general, can hear any type of civil matter, including domestic relation cases, that may be brought before it. Sometimes, the controversy involved must reach a certain dollar amount (for instance, $10,000 or more) before a district court has jurisdiction. The district courts are often responsible for handling the major criminal offenses not otherwise heard in a lower court.

States in which there are a large number of cases being appealed will generally have one or more courts of appeal to alleviate the load on the state supreme court. Any appeals from a lower court may be heard by a court of appeals rather than a direct appeal to the state supreme court. Most of the time, an adverse ruling at the appeal court will allow the party to appeal once again to the state supreme court. These appeal courts usually consist of three or more judges or justices.

Generally, each state will have a supreme court to hear appeals from lower courts. In certain circumstances, however, the supreme court may have authority to be the *court of original jurisdiction* (the supreme court will be the first court to hear that particular case). Often, this entails a matter in which the state or an agency of the state is a party to the lawsuit, usually involving a matter of major economic or tax policy.

A state supreme court may also be primarily responsible for the regulation of the practice of law. This includes the appointment of attorneys to serve on committees and may also act as the final authority on discipline or professional responsibility. It is not unusual for the supreme court to be responsible for the admission of individuals to the state bar association. However, the primary responsibility of the supreme court will be to hear appeals from other various courts, whether they are civil or criminal in nature. The supreme court generally consists of a chief judge or justice with several associate judges or justices. The rulings of this court are almost always a formal written opinion and serve as a guide for future legal questions.

Specialty Courts. There are various specialty courts in many state court systems. For instance, many states have a workers' compensation court that hears only cases involving claims for workers' compensation benefits for injuries or illnesses on a job. Some states also have specialized domestic relations or divorce courts. These courts hear divorce cases, custody dispute cases, or cases involving modification of a divorce decree.

Juvenile courts are designed solely to hear cases involving minors who are charged with criminal offenses. These specialty courts generally provide the offender with viable options in the event of a conviction, especially in sentencing. Many juvenile court records are sealed and are not subject to public review and, thus, do not become a part of the juvenile's public record.

It should be noted, however, that minors charged with a crime are not automatically placed in juvenile court. Generally, a motion to transfer the case to juvenile court from the regular criminal docket must be made. Also, the prosecuting attorney may argue that the defendant, although a minor, should stand trial or face charges as an adult due to the offense involved and any prior criminal record of the juvenile. The judge decides whether the case should be transferred to juvenile court or remain on the regular criminal docket.

Another specialty court is the *small claims court* or *people's court*. Most counties or cities have a division of their court where individuals can settle legal disputes that involve a lesser monetary amount, usually less than a few thousand dollars. Court procedure and rules of evidence are informal, and, in most cases, attorneys are not allowed to represent individuals in this type of court. Disputes in small claims courts often involve landlord-tenant disputes, minor automobile accidents, and faulty service or merchandise. Sometimes a case will be transferred out of small claims court at the request of one of the parties, if he believes that he would receive a better chance in another court or wishes to have an attorney represent him.

Whenever you have a legal dispute or problem that entails filing a court action, the attorney you hire decides which court would best suit your particular case. Often, the type of dispute dictates the court the attorney will use, but sometimes the lawsuit will lend itself to a particularly favorable court.

SOURCES OF THE LAW

No matter which court an individual may find himself in, its primary duty is to apply the law to the facts at hand. This next section will discuss the various sources from which our law arises.

Constitutional Law

The legal system in the United States starts with the *U.S. Constitution*. This document sets forth the minimum standards that all laws must meet. The Constitution consists of seven articles and twenty-six amendments. The first ten amendments to the Constitution are also known as the *Bill of Rights*. Some of the more well-known amendments affecting the average citizen are as follows:

- Amendment One: Congress shall make no law respecting an establishment of religion, or prohibiting the free exercise thereof; or abridging the freedom of speech, or of the press; or the right of the people peaceably to assemble, and to petition the government for a redress of grievances.

- Amendment Four: The right of the people to be secure in their persons, houses, papers and effects, against unreasonable searches and seizures, shall not be violated, and no warrant shall issue, but upon probable cause, supported by oath or affirmation, and particularly describing the place to be searched, and the persons or things to be seized.

- Amendment Five: No person . . . shall be subject for the same offense to be twice put in jeopardy of life and limb; nor shall be compelled in any criminal case to be a witness against himself, nor to be deprived of life, liberty, or property, without due process of law; nor shall private property be taken for public use, without just compensation.

- Amendment Six: In all prosecutions, the accused shall enjoy the right to a speedy and public trial, by an impartial jury of the state and district wherein the crime shall have been committed, which district shall have previously ascertained by law, and to be informed of the nature and cause of the accusation; to be confronted with the witnesses against him; to have compulsory process for obtaining witnesses in his favor, and to have the assistance of counsel for his defense.

- Amendment Eight: Excessive bail shall not be required, nor excessive fines imposed, nor cruel and unusual punishments inflicted.

- Amendment Fourteen: All persons born or naturalized in the United States, and subject to the jurisdiction thereof, are citizens of the United States and of the state wherein they reside. No state shall make or enforce any law which shall abridge the privileges or immunities of citizens of the United States; nor shall any state deprive any person of life, liberty, or property, without due process of law; nor deny to any person within its jurisdiction the equal protection of the laws.

• Amendment Sixteen: The Congress shall have power to lay and collect taxes on incomes, from whatever source derived, without apportionment among the several states, and without regard to any census or enumeration.

• Amendment Nineteen: The right of citizens of the United States to vote shall not be denied or abridged by the United States or any state on account of sex.

• Amendment Twenty-Six: The rights of citizens of the United States, who are eighteen years of age or older, to vote shall not be denied or abridged by the United States or by any state on account of age.

Each state bases its law on a constitution. State constitutions must, of course, abide by the provisions of the U.S. Constitution and the laws enacted thereunder.

The U.S. Constitution can be amended by either a two-thirds vote of the members of both houses of Congress, or by two-thirds of the states making application to Congress. Any changes in the U.S. Constitution must be ratified by three-fourths of the states.

Statutory Law

Another source of the law is statutes—laws passed by legislatures. The U.S. Congress is the legislative body of the federal government. In addition, each state has a legislature that enacts statutes for its state. Local county and municipal governments may also have statutory enacting power. The courts, in reviewing any statute or applying any statute to a specific controversy, may declare a statute unconstitutional, which means that it no longer binds citizens.

Administrative Law

Administrative laws are passed by administrative agencies created by a legislative body. For instance, a state may create a real estate commission to govern the conduct of real estate brokers. The state may also grant the agency the right to create and enforce its own administrative laws. Thus, the administrative agency acts as its own legislature in drafting and compiling specific rules and regulations pertaining to its particular area.

Whenever a controversy arises over a particular administrative agency's jurisdiction, the agency enforces its own laws. It should be noted that the authority of these administrative agencies always returns to the particular federal or state legislature from which it was created.

Municipal Codes

A municipality may pass legal codes (ordinances) dealing with specific offenses involved within its geographic boundaries. As long as these municipal codes are not in violation of or inconsistent with previously passed statutes, they enforce the laws of the municipality. These types of laws will generally revolve around the day-to-day workings of a city, including animal licensing, traffic infractions and so on.

APPLYING THE LAW

When the application of a statute, administrative law or municipal ordinance is challenged, the courts will be called on to interpret the statutes based on the factual situation at hand. These statutory court interpretations or applications are recorded and serve as legal precedents for future court cases.

For instance, a statute may state that "no motorist may operate his automobile in an unreasonable or unsafe manner on a state highway." A set of facts is presented to the judge where an individual drove the maximum speed limit on a rainy night, lost control of his vehicle, and struck a pedestrian who filed suit for damages. Even though the driver did not exceed the speed limit, the court must determine whether that individual was driving in an "unreasonable or unsafe manner" and in violation of the statute.

Over time, these decisions are compiled and studied by attorneys and judges, who look for situations where similar facts pertain to the statutes invoked. They will then cite those cases as legal authority, as the basis for their decision. This principle is called *stare decisis*. Often when an attorney is doing research on a particular case, he looks for case authorities to find similar factual scenarios that substantiate his client's position. So, it is not only the particular written law (statute or administrative rules) that affects the outcome, but also any earlier interpretation of these laws by the courts.

It should be noted that not every court writes a formal written opinion on its decision; rather, an appellate or supreme court, whether state or federal, most likely issues a written opinion based on a case that has been appealed to it. Generally, the trial court's opinions, if any, are not retained for future use by the legal community.

Several terms and concepts need to be understood whenever an individual becomes involved in a trial or lawsuit.

Jurisdiction

Recognize that a case must be heard in a court that has *jurisdiction* over the subject matter. That is, it would be improper to file a divorce action in small claims court, a bankruptcy action in a state district court, and so on. As mentioned before, attorneys can readily determine which court the particular lawsuit needs to be filed in. If there is a choice between two courts, an attorney can decide which court would best serve his client's interests.

The lawsuit is generally filed in the county or area in which the cause of action (facts surrounding the dispute) arose, or in which the defendant (the person who is being sued) resides.

Judges

In smaller communities, the attorney will know who the judge will be even before filing the lawsuit, because in some areas only one judge is assigned to the court in which the lawsuit is filed. However, in larger communities, any one of several judges may be assigned to a particular case. In almost all circumstances, it will not be possible for the attorney to choose which judge will be assigned. Rather, the judge assigned to the case is chosen at random. This obviously prevents an attorney from shopping for a judge he believes would be more sympathetic to his case.

Sometimes, different areas invoke different methods of selecting a judge. In the federal system, judges are appointed by the President for life. In most state systems, the governor will appoint a judge, who may run for retention every few years. The governor will usually receive a list of qualified individuals from a judicial nominating committee that reviews applicants and narrows them down before presenting the names to the governor. In some states, however, judges may be elected as in other political offices.

Each state will have its own minimum requirements before a person can be appointed a judge. These requirements will involve a minimum age, minimum years of practice of law as an attorney (including prior service as a judge), requirements of residency, etc. Often, these requirements will vary depending on which type of judicial appointment is being sought. Lawyers who become judges come from many backgrounds, including private practice, government employment, or as corporate counsel to a private company.

The function of a judge (when a jury is not involved) is to rule on various pretrial motions, conduct the trial, including rulings on evidence that may come up during the trial, render a judgment based on the evidence, and often render a written opinion substantiating his judgment. In essence, a judge needs to rule on the various controversies brought to his court on the particular cases assigned to him. Without a jury, the judge becomes the interpreter of the law as well as the finder of fact on the case.

The Jury

Often a jury is used in the trial process. The jury consists of a number of impartial individuals from the community at large that are called on to listen to and review the evidence presented by both sides of a controversy and render a decision. The jury is instructed in the law that applies to the case, but the jury will render a verdict. The jury does not rule on evidence questions, but can put as much weight as it deems appropriate on any evidence that is admitted.

Jurors are generally picked from a jury pool. Many individuals are questioned by the respective attorneys and judge assigned to the case. The attorneys will ask to disqualify any juror who has either an obvious conflict with the parties or issue at hand, or cannot render an impartial decision based solely on the evidence presented.

Most states have laws prohibiting employers from discharging or penalizing an employee who is required to serve on jury duty. Most jurors will be compensated for their time, in the neighborhood of $20 to $50 a day, plus mileage to and from the court house.

It is important to note that jury duty as described above is not the same as a grand jury. A grand jury is a select group of citizens called to review evidence on a specific issue to decide whether or not further criminal prosecution is necessary. If the grand jury believes that sufficient evidence exists to proceed with criminal prosecution, it will return an indictment against the individual for the charges involved. Generally, a district attorney or attorney general will have the power to call a grand jury if he believes one is necessary.

Statute of Limitations

Whenever an individual first meets with an attorney regarding a potential lawsuit, one of the initial determinations is whether the *statute of limitations* has run out. The client's cause of action, whether it be an automobile accident, breach of contract or malpractice lawsuit, must be filed within a certain time after the cause of action first occurred. Once the individual has the right to sue, he must file suit within a specified period of time. If that period of time has already passed, his lawsuit may be dismissed for noncompliance with the statute of limitations. The statute of limitations can run from two to ten years, depending on the type of lawsuit.

Many criminal offenses also have statute of limitations. However, the more serious the crime, the longer the statute of limitations will be. Many felonies, for example, do not have any statute of limitations attached to them.

Court Costs

A primary court cost is the filing fee paid to the clerk of the court to initiate the lawsuit. Filing fees range from $5 to $10 for filing a small claims case, to several hundred dollars for filing a federal court lawsuit.

Aside from the filing fee, court costs also include the amount of money paid to the local sheriff, constable or federal official who serves the summons on the defendant. These charges vary widely and should be discussed between you and your attorney at the time that the lawsuit is contemplated.

Also, in many fee agreements, *court costs* refers not only to the filing fee and summons delivery costs, but to any costs incurred by the attorney in taking depositions, procuring documents, mileage, postage, etc. If the fee agreement between you and your attorney refers simply to the court costs, you should insist on knowing what that specifically includes. This should prevent unpleasant surprises when you write the check later.

Pleadings

Often attorneys discuss or mention the *pleadings* of a case. Pleadings are the written documents that declare the respective parties' positions. When a civil lawsuit is filed, the party filing the suit, usually called the *plaintiff* or *petitioner*, files a statement of fact and a request for relief — typically a judgment or a court order requiring another party to stop a particular activity or to comply with a previous court order. Often this initial pleading is called a *petition* or *complaint*.

When a criminal lawsuit is filed, the charges must be set forth in the *complaint* (sometimes called an *information*) to allow the defendant (the party charged with a crime) to understand the specific charges against him and the evidence of the charges.

Once a defendant is advised that a lawsuit has been filed against him (usually by service of a summons with a copy of the petition or complaint), he may file various motions. The pretrial motions may include modifying the petition, questioning the jurisdiction of the court, striking portions of the petition as being irrelevant, etc. The defendant will ordinarily have to file a written response to the petition within a certain period of time (thirty days is average) or be in default. The defendant may explain the reasons why he does not feel liable, responsible or guilty of the particular allegations being made, and in a civil case, the defendant may file a *counterclaim* against the plaintiff, or even a *cross-claim* against a third party as long as the subject matter of the lawsuit remains basically the same. Once these written documents setting forth the various parties' positions, defenses and allegations are made, the parties are deemed *at issue*.

The Discovery Process

Once the plaintiff's and defendant's positions are outlined in their respective pleadings, the matter does not usually go to trial immediately. Rather, the *discovery* stage comes next. During this time, the attorneys attempt to find out as much information as possible about the merits of the other's position. This information gathering is designed to uncover the facts of the allegations as set forth in the pleadings. Discovery entails taking the testimony (*deposition*) of witnesses under oath, written questions to the opposing side (*interrogatories*) and requests to produce documents relating to the subject matter of the lawsuit.

The discovery rules are designed to work on a somewhat voluntary basis. If one party deems it necessary, however, a court order can be obtained mandating that the other party comply with the discovery process. Sometimes the opposing party objects to some aspect of the discovery procedure, and the court will rule on whether the information requested falls within legal parameters.

Often, if the facts weigh greatly in favor of one of the parties, he will move the court for a *summary judgment*. This means that he has established to the satisfaction of the court that there is no material basis for the lawsuit. Accordingly, he is entitled to a favorable judgment as a matter of law. A summary judgment renders a trial unnecessary.

Trial

Once the discovery process has been completed, including pretrial motions and rulings, the matter can then be set for trial. At this stage, the decision is made whether the trial will be a jury trial or trial to the judge, also known as a *bench trial*. Some lower courts automatically take each case as a bench trial, unless one of the parties specifically requests a jury trial. In other courts, a jury trial will be granted automatically, unless the parties agree to try the case before the judge.

In criminal trials, the right to a jury trial is guaranteed, except for very minor criminal or traffic offenses. The jury in a criminal trial determines whether the defendant is guilty or innocent, and often the degree of guilt (such as first-degree murder, second-degree murder or manslaughter). In civil trials, not only will the jury determine the liability of one party to the other, but it is sometimes required to determine the amount of a financial award.

In a jury trial, even though the jury determines the ultimate verdict or judgment, the presiding judge is responsible for ensuring that the attorneys comply with all rules of evidence. The judge will also make sure that the jury is instructed correctly on the law to apply to the facts. It is his job, in general, to see that the trial is conducted in an orderly and procedurally correct fashion.

One of the most important functions of an attorney at a trial is to abide by the rules of evidence. The rules of evidence set forth what type of evidence (testimony, documents, and tangible evidence) will be allowed into court.

In most trials, attorneys will object to various attempts to have certain testimony or physical evidence introduced on several different grounds. As mentioned previously, the judge will determine whether the evidence in question can be considered (legally admissible) in determining the result of the case.

Although the above steps in proceeding toward a trial seem fairly simple on the surface, months or even years can pass from the time a lawsuit is filed until it actually reaches the courtroom. Depending on the complexity of the case, the discovery process alone can often take several months or longer as each party will generally have thirty days or more to respond to the request for information by the opposing party. Other times, the case is ready for trial, but the court is too backed up to call the trial for quite some time. In criminal trials, the defendant has a right to a speedy trial and, accordingly, the court system will accommodate criminal cases much more efficiently than civil ones.

Many courts have recently adopted case progression standards that mandate how long a case can remain alive before it is dismissed by the court for lack of prosecution. If the case is dismissed for lack of prosecution, it is usually *without prejudice*. The plaintiff may refile the lawsuit if he so chooses, if the statute of limitations has not run out.

Sometimes, at the conclusion of a bench trial, the judge will request *briefs* from the attorneys involved. Briefs are written arguments, citing specific authorities to support their arguments. The briefs are submitted to and considered by the judge to assist him in deciding the case. In some jurisdictions, attorneys can submit briefs without being requested by the judge, if the attorney believes that a written argument would further enhance his client's position. The opposing party would have an opportunity to file a responsive brief.

Appeal

After trial, the losing party may file an appeal. Generally, an appeal occurs when the loser of the trial believes the court either committed an error in applying the law to the case, or the jury (or judge) did not rule fairly based on the evidence presented.

When an appeal is made, the case is not retried in another court. Instead, written appellate briefs are submitted to the superior court indicating why the verdict or judgment in the lower court was in error. Applicable statutes and cases are cited to substantiate the appealing party's position. The party appealing the verdict or judgment is called the *appellant*, while the party responding to the appeal is called the *appellee*.

Besides the submission of written briefs on appeal, the appellate court will usually grant the parties on appeal an opportunity to argue their case orally. No witnesses are called and no further evidence is received; the attorneys argue the case based on the evidence submitted at the trial court and the law that applies. Although appellate standards vary from jurisdiction to jurisdiction, the lower court will be deferred to on questions of fact due to its first-hand observation of the witnesses at the time of trial. The party appealing the verdict must show that there was some type of legal error or clear abuse of discretion by the lower trial court to have a verdict or judgment reversed on appeal.

Depending on the backlog in the appellate court, an appeal can be heard several months or years after the judgment or verdict is rendered by the trial court. The appellate court may also have the option of remanding the case to the lower court to enter a verdict or judgment consistent with the appellate court's ruling. Also, the appellate court may order that the case be completely retried.

Chapter Two

Family Law

Draw up the papers, lawyer, and make 'em good and stout, for things at home are crossways, and Betsey and I are out.
   — *William McKenree Carlton*

T his chapter will review the various topics that commonly fall under family law. These will include marriage, divorce, legal separation, child custody and other issues affecting these general themes. Although most general practitioners involve themselves to a certain degree with some aspect of family law, many attorneys devote their entire practice to this area and consider it a specialty, especially the areas of divorce and child custody.

MARRIAGE
A legal marriage is contractual in nature. It is a legally binding and enforceable contract between two individuals. As sanctioned by the state, certain minimum requirements must be met by individuals entering into marriage before a license is issued. These requirements will vary from state to state.

Most states require that each party must have reached a minimum age before they can enter into a marriage. Without parental consent, an individual usually must be at least eighteen years old before he or she can enter into marriage. Some states require a minimum age of nineteen or twenty-one. If the minimum age is not met, the express consent of the individual's parents must be obtained. This age requirement is lowered somewhat when parental consent is obtained. Some states allow a male to get married at sixteen, while other states have lowered their minimum age to fourteen for females, again assuming that parental consent is granted.

The majority of states require a blood test before a marriage license can be issued. The majority of states require the marriage license be used within thirty to sixty days after the blood test. A few states have no such minimum period of time. The purpose of the blood test is to screen for venereal disease, although testing for AIDS is also a recent concern. Many states have a three-to-five-day waiting period before a marriage license can be issued even after a blood test is made. The majority of states also require that an authorized person, usually a judge or applicable church official, conduct the marriage ceremony.

Validity of a Marriage

To determine the validity of a marriage, both parties must possess sufficient mental capacity to agree to the creation of marital status; that is, *knowledgeable consent* to the marriage contract is a necessary element of a valid marriage. The general test used by most courts to determine the validity of a marriage is whether either party had sufficient mental capacity to appreciate the nature of the marriage contract and its inherent implications and responsibilities.

Generally, intoxication (drug or alcohol induced) at the time of the marriage vows will create a situation where the marriage may be later voided. Certain other types of physical defects or disabilities such as impotency, sterility, or the pregnancy of the woman by a man other than the husband may be sufficient for legally voiding a marriage.

Common Law Marriage

Many states honor *common law marriage*, in which two people act as husband and wife for an extended period of time without the benefit of any formal ceremony or marriage license. The period of time that must pass before a common law marriage exists will vary from state to state, but several years is not uncommon.

Some states do not recognize common law marriages, even if they are legal in a state where the couple previously lived. Other states take a middle-of-the-road approach and honor common law marriages if they are recognized in other states, but will not allow a common law marriage to be created within its borders.

For a common law marriage to exist, as with a state-sanctioned marriage, the parties must live together for a certain period of time, must be legally competent and have the capacity to enter into the marital condition. Another general requirement is that the individuals have agreed to be husband and wife. It is usually a factual question as to whether or not the individuals desiring to live by common law marriage have held themselves out as husband and wife to the rest of the world.

Once a common law marriage is deemed legal, the inherent rights and responsibilities of a state-sanctioned marriage (including laws of inheritance), go into effect. So, common law marriages do effect the couple's property rights despite the lack of a formal marriage license or ceremony.

Breach of the Marriage Promise

In some jurisdictions a person can sue for the recovery of damages for the breach of a promise to marry. The aggrieved party must prove that a promise to marry was made, the promise was not fulfilled, and there was no justifiable reason for not fulfilling the promise.

Often, even though the cause of action may exist, the element of damages (how the party was hurt) becomes a difficult question to answer. If, however, the aggrieved party can prove to the satisfaction of the judge or jury that he or she has suffered economic or physical/emotional damages, a judgment for damages may be awarded.

ANNULMENT OF MARRIAGE

An *annulment* proceeding is where the court declares that no valid marriage ever existed between a couple and, accordingly, no marital relationship ever existed. Since marriage is a legal contract, many of the grounds for annulling a marriage are based on contract law.

Grounds for Annulment

A marriage entered into by fraud or deceit can be annulled, provided that the fraud substantially affects the very essence of the marriage. That is, not every kind of marriage fraud results in an annulment. But, the fact-based frauds proven to cause a marriage annulment include concealing a prior marriage, failing to change one's religion after pledging such religious adherence in a ceremony, and withholding impotency or infertility problems.

If one of the parties can show that the marriage was entered into under duress (not by free will), an annulment may also be granted. However, this type of annulment is not generally favored by the courts unless it clearly appears that the party requesting the annulment was unable to exercise his or her free will throughout the marriage ceremony.

As with other contracts, the lack of mental capacity to consent to the marital agreement is also grounds for annulment. Generally, the court will determine whether the individual requesting the annulment had the ability to understand the nature of the marriage contract and its inherent duties and responsibilities. Extreme intoxication by alcohol or drugs at the time the marriage contract was entered into may constitute grounds for annulment.

Undisclosed impotency, sterility or infertility (which can prevent consummation of the marriage) may serve as viable grounds for annulment. But premarital sex or an undisclosed illegitimate child will not usually be considered grounds for annulment. Sometimes, if the wife is pregnant at the time of marriage by someone other than her husband, an annulment may be granted. The courts have, however, typically denied annulment requests of a husband based on his claim that he would not have otherwise married the woman if it were not for her false claims of pregnancy.

Defense to Annulment

One of the most common defenses to an annulment action is the post-marriage conduct of the parties. If the annulment request is made several months or years after the marriage occurred, the courts will generally not annul the marriage because the passage of time indicates compliance or acquiescence to the marriage. This is true even though the marriage was entered into by fraud or under duress.

ANTENUPTIAL CONTRACT (PRENUPTIAL AGREEMENT)

As mentioned earlier, one of the factors involved in any divorce or legal separation is the property settlement. On occasion, couples anticipating marriage will enter into a *prenuptial agreement* (legally known as an *antenuptial agreement*). The prenuptial agreement *contract* discloses the complete financial status and condition of each person before marrying. The disclosure can include ownership rights and probable future inheritance rights. The couple enters into a mutually binding agreement outlining the division of their property in the event of a legal separation or divorce. The agreement can also state the rights of the parties to any property acquired during the marriage, including future support rights and obligations.

Jurisdictions vary widely in their interpretation of prenuptial agreements. Some courts have ruled that these agreements are against public policy and do not place any weight on them in determining the property settlement. Other courts require complete and total disclosure between the parties at the time the contract is entered into, or it will not carry any weight whatsoever in determining the property settlement of the parties. Some courts find these agreements valid and will rely on them a great deal in dividing the property in a divorce or legal separation.

DIVORCE

A *divorce* legally dissolves the marriage contract at the request of one or both of the parties and determines all issues involved in a marriage, such as child custody and support, alimony and property division. Each divorce case will revolve around the facts of the particular marriage being terminated. Divorce cases are always heard by a judge, not a jury.

Couples seeking what they consider an amicable divorce sometimes attempt to obtain the services of one attorney to represent both people in the divorce. As stated in chapter one, an attorney is charged with pursuing his client's best interests. Even though a couple may be in total initial agreement to the terms of the divorce, an attorney who attempts to represent both spouses is in essence representing neither party effectively. Many jurisdictions disallow the representation of both divorce clients by one attorney. In any event, it is not a recommended practice and ideally each person should be represented by separate counsel. Of course, there is no legal prohibition against representing yourself in a divorce.

The divorce procedure begins when a spouse files a petition

or complaint against the other, allowing him to respond as in any other type of lawsuit. By this time both parties should be represented by separate counsel. (An example of a divorce petition is included in the appendix.)

Attorneys representing the parties usually enter into a pretrial discovery period that allows them to become acquainted with the history and facts of the marriage, which will in turn allow them to determine the best interests of the client. Often, there is much negotiation back and forth between attorneys representing divorcing parties, and settlements are often reached out of court. During this interim period, the court will usually enter an order for some type of temporary support (alimony or child support) and may also issue an order directing the parties not to abscond with any marital assets that may be subject to the property settlement of the divorce.

No Fault Divorce

A major difference lies between states that recognize *no fault divorce* and states that require specific grounds for divorce. In a no fault divorce state, a divorce will be granted if the couple has demonstrated that the marriage is irretrievably broken or that they have irreconcilable differences or incompatibility. Some states require proof that a reconciliation has been attempted. In fact, some courts have domestic relations referees or conciliation courts that the divorce judge can order the parties to see on an individual or joint basis. The referee reports to the court and advises whether he believes the standard is met for a no fault divorce to be granted. The court presumes that a divorce should only be granted if all else fails, as it is in the interest of the community and general public policy that the marriage survive if at all possible.

Grounds for Divorce

In other states, specific grounds (legal basis) for divorce must be alleged and proven. The following categories are examples of sufficient grounds for a divorce:

- Adultery
- Mental and/or physical cruelty
- Desertion

- Alcoholism or drug addiction
- Impotency
- Nonsupport by husband

In states that require one of these specific grounds for absolute divorce, there will be potential defenses to these grounds. One is collusion—an agreement between the spouses to obtain a divorce by having the accused spouse appear to commit an act that constitutes grounds for divorce. Collusion is considered a corrupt arrangement between the spouses in an attempt to obtain an otherwise unobtainable divorce.

Condonation is a type of defense that arises by one spouse relieving the other of his or her marital duties. Usually, it involves the acquiescence or forgiveness of an act that would otherwise constitute grounds for divorce.

Alimony

Alimony is the money paid from one spouse to another (usually husband to wife) for support and maintenance while living apart. It may be permanent or temporary, depending on the history of the marriage. Alimony was historically set up to prevent divorced wives from becoming wards of the state. It was deemed best that the ex-husband continue to support his ex-wife to allow her to find other means of support.

Many factors go into the court's ruling whether alimony is justified. The financial condition of the parties, their age and station in life, and their respective earning capacities and abilities (both present and future), are all matters considered by the court in determining whether alimony is awarded, and, if so, how much. If the wife's economic position is bolstered by outside sources of income, this may also be a factor that the court takes into consideration.

In recent years, alimony awards have decreased or been omitted altogether in divorce decrees as women advance in the workplace and enjoy increased economic independence from their spouses. It should also be noted that in states that require specific grounds for divorce, alimony, permanent or temporary, will usually not be awarded to a wife when the husband obtained a divorce on the grounds of her marital misconduct.

Property Settlement

Aside from any award of alimony, the court will also divide all the property owned by the divorcing couple. This division of assets covers all tangible property and can include future pension assets, retirement funds, stock options, etc. This includes payment of all existing debts and obligations. Even if the couple agrees as to the division of their property, in most jurisdictions, the court still must review the agreement to ensure that it is fair and contains no illegal conditions.

If real estate is owned by the parties, the court will often order the transfer of interests to the party awarded the real estate, including the obligation to continue any payments (including taxes). Often, the parties will have several ongoing debt payments. Based on the division of property and other equitable considerations, the court will usually require one of the divorcing spouses to continue paying periodic obligations.

Understand that a divorce decree and accompanying property settlement is only a court order affecting the divorcing parties. For example, if one party is awarded to pay a particular creditor, and those payments are not made, the creditor is not bound by the divorce decree and may legally pursue both individuals. The divorce decree and property settlement is like a contract between the two parties. Since the parties' creditors have not agreed to its terms, they are not bound by them and will likely pursue both parties of a joint debt.

The only remedy the person not required to pay the debt may have is to bring that fact to the court's attention in an attempt to require the delinquent party to pay the debt. This usually entails some type of formal hearing prior to entering such an order, which often takes the shape of contempt of court charges for failure to abide by the terms of the decree. A copy of a typical divorce decree can be found in the appendix.

Community Property

Mention should be made at this point of the concept of *community property*. As of this writing, there are eight states that recognize community property rights. The theory of community property is as follows: Any property (including earnings) acquired by either spouse during the marriage becomes property equally owned by both. This does not include any property acquired by either spouse by gift or inheritance, any property that was owned prior to the marriage, any cash or proceeds that are realized from the sale of property not under the community property rule.

The co-ownership of any and all property coming into the marriage, as set forth above, will necessarily have an affect on the division of property in the property settlement of the divorce decree.

Divorce Decree

When a divorce decree is entered, it becomes a court order like any other verdict or judgment rendered by a court. Given that, it may be appealed by either or both parties if they believe that the court rendered an unfair decision. As in other appeals, however, the appellate court will generally defer to the discretion of the lower court unless some type of clear abuse of discretion or misapplication of the law is proven.

It should also be noted that many states have a provision that, once the divorce decree is entered, the divorce still is not final for several months. If one of the parties wants to apply to the court to have the divorce decree voided, in the event they decide to stay married, the divorce will never have become final and the parties will remain married. Also during this time, neither party may remarry since the divorce is not yet legally final. Similarly, if one of the parties should happen to die in the interim period between entering and finalizing the decree, the divorce may not be legally effective.

Legal Separation

Often, a married couple wants to live apart without the formal dissolution of the marriage. A legal separation will generally entail all of the issues involved in a typical divorce, such as alimony, child custody and support, and even property settlement.

Rather than apply for a divorce, one of the couple files a lawsuit and requests a legal separation from the other. As in the case of divorce, some states require a showing of fault to allow the legal separation, while other states have a no fault policy. As a practical matter, a formal legal separation with its divorce-like factors is a prerequisite to a formal divorce. However, since many states have a minimum residency requirement that must be met before a divorce can be granted, many couples will file for a formal legal separation until such time as the residency requirements are met. Once these residency requirements are met, generally the legal separation can be modified to a divorce action.

Modification of a Divorce Decree

When a couple divorces, the terms of the decree are based on the current facts. Later, the factual basis of the decree can change. For example, one person may have a substantial increase or decrease in income, or may remarry, or a child may have a change of heart about which parent to live with, and so on.

If the income of the alimony recipient increases substantially, there is a chance the court may order the alimony reduced or eliminated earlier than originally planned. Also, any substantial increase or decrease in the income of a custodial or noncustodial parent may effect the amount of child support payments.

If one party believes a decree modification is appropriate, an application must be filed with the court, presumably to the benefit of the party making the application. Understand that minor deviations or changes will usually not support modifying the decree. Rather, a *material change of circumstances* must be shown. This discourages the parties in a divorce from continually returning to court to request minor adjustments in the decree.

With regard to child custody, the court will continue to maintain authority over the children until they reach the age of majority or are otherwise emancipated. Again, unless a significant or material change in the circumstances of the custodial or noncustodial parent can be shown, the custody and visitation provisions will remain as set forth in the original decree.

Since these types of issues are very factual in nature, an attorney can determine the reasons why a change in custody, alimony or child support is viable, and if a substantial chance of modifying the decree exists. Usually, the less time that has passed since the original divorce decree was entered into, the less willing a court will be to modify it.

Enforcement of Property Settlement

On occasion, the divorce decree's property division and alimony payment provisions may need to be enforced. Generally, the party attempting to require the delinquent party to comply with the divorce decree will have a hearing in court to prove that the other party is not abiding by the terms of the decree. The noncomplying party will be served with what amounts to an order to show cause and will be entitled to respond to the allegations and advise the court why the divorce decree provisions have not been complied with.

If the court finds that there is no justifiable reason why the divorce decree is not being complied with, it may find the non-complying party in contempt of court and issue a fine or even jail time. Typically, the court will order the party to comply with the property settlement or alimony provision within a specific period of time. Otherwise, a contempt of court citation or bench warrant may be issued.

CHILD CUSTODY

In any divorce or legal separation action involving minor children, one of the prime considerations will be the custody and support of the children. As you might expect, some of the most bitter disputes in divorce cases revolve around the custody and support of children.

Best Interests Test

It is a general legal maxim that in determining the custody of any children, the court will always focus on what is in the best interests of the child. Since both parties to the divorce may be arguing that he or she is the best or most proper person to retain custody of the child, the court will often appoint an individual, called a *guardian ad litem*, to make a recommendation to the court as to what he believes would be in the best interest of the child.

Aside from determining what is in the best interests of the child, the court will normally try to allow each parent, assuming they are fit and proper, to maintain as normal a relationship with the child as possible and to allow that parent to contribute substantially to the child's care and upbringing. The party who is awarded custody of the child is called the *custodial parent*, while the parent who does not have physical custody is called the *noncustodial parent*. In many divorce situations, the divorcing couple will agree on the custody arrangement of the children between themselves. The court may only accept this agreement if it believes it is in the best interests of the children.

If the custody issue proceeds to trial, the judge must consider several issues in making his final ruling. In almost every state, the judge is not to give any deference to either parent based on the sex of the parent or the sex of the child involved, and no presumption is made that either parent, regardless of sex, is more fit than the other to have custody. All parents start from an equal position in determining which parent would be the most beneficial to the child in a custody dispute.

Typically, the court will consider the following factors in reaching its decision of custody:

- Which parent appears to have the closest relationship with the child
- Which parent appears to be responsible for the day-to-day care of the child
- The stability of the parent on a daily basis
- The particular child's age and degree of maturity
- The health, both mental and physical, of the child's parents
- Any potential disruptive effect of the child's life in choosing one custodian over the other
- The parents' and child's respective life styles, including educational, religious, and neighborhood considerations

A judge may also take into consideration what the child wants. There is generally no particular age at which the judge may or may not consider the child's wishes. Generally, if the children are of sufficient age to understand the issue involved, the judge may take their desires into consideration or apply whatever weight he believes their desires should have. The child is usually not required to testify in court, but the judge will discuss the matter with the child in his office.

Guardian Ad Litem. As mentioned earlier, if a custody issue is involved in a divorce case, many states require that a *guardian ad litem* be appointed to represent the interests of the child. The duties of the *guardian ad litem* include making a report, either oral or written, to the judge describing the child's living situation and relationship with his parents. The *guardian ad litem* may also recommend one or the other of the parents to the judge. The judge is usually not bound by any recommendation that the *guardian ad litem* may make.

Aside from the *guardian ad litem*, the judge may request a psychologist to evaluate the child and his home environment and report which parent he believes would best suit the child. Again, the judge is usually not bound by this recommendation.

Joint Custody

Many states have an arrangement called joint custody, where both parents are given custody of the child and, theoretically, are involved equally in the daily decisions concerning his care. Joint custody is sometimes accompanied by shared physical custody — the child may live at both the residence of his mother and father for an equal period of time during the year.

A joint custody situation does not necessarily negate the need for child support, however. In most situations, the divorcing parties must indicate a strong willingness to cooperate completely in seeing that the best interests of the child are protected. Only when the court is satisfied that the divorcing parties are willing and able to meet such an objective, will joint custody be granted.

Move of the Custodial Parent

In most areas of the country, the custodial parent must obtain court permission before moving (with the child) out of state or outside the jurisdiction of the court. In several states, the court requires that the noncustodial parent agree to the move before such permission is granted.

If the custodial parent should die before the child reaches the age of majority, a court will, in most circumstances, give custodial preference to the surviving natural parent, assuming that he or she wants custody. The court's decision will override any custodial request the deceased parent made in his or her will.

VISITATION

When one of the divorcing parties obtains custody of the child, the noncustodial parent is usually entitled to visitation rights. In many situations, the parties will agree to liberal or general visitation rights without having to specify what particular days, months or hours the noncustodial parent will be entitled to visit.

As long as the divorcing couple remains amicable about the situation, the court does not necessarily mandate specific visitation dates and times. However, if an amicable agreement does not appear possible, the court may be as specific as it believes necessary to ensure that the noncustodial parent has certain days and times to exercise visitation rights.

Typically, a court-ordered visitation schedule will allow the noncustodial parent to have the child live with him every other weekend and perhaps one day during the week. Holidays may also be alternated between the parents, with the noncustodial parent having the child for an extended period of time during the year, such as two weeks or more during the summer months. The goal of visitation of the noncustodial parents is to try and ensure that a parental relationship with the child continues despite the divorce of the parents.

Visitation schedules can generally be informally modified by the parents without court intervention. However, if such modifications in the visitation schedule cannot be worked out, the court may be asked to create a specific modified schedule of visitation after hearing both parents' arguments on why or why not such a schedule, in their opinion, would be workable.

Rights of Grandparents

In some states and in some instances, grandparents of the child can be awarded visitation rights. This will often depend on the particular circumstances of the child's parents, such as whether one may have died after the divorce decree was entered, or if the grandparents can establish a significant beneficial relationship with the child. Some states have passed laws guaranteeing grandparents the right to ask the court for visitation rights. Again, as with most custody situations, the visitation rights of a grandparent will depend on the particular facts of the parties involved. The court will also try to determine if grandparent visitation could potentially interfere with the child's relationship with his parents.

Modification and Termination of Visitation

Typically, when the custodial parent moves out of state or away from the noncustodial parent, visitation rights must be modified accordingly. Usually, the noncustodial parent will have the child visit him on several occasions throughout the year for extended periods of time. The travel costs will also have to be worked out and, if the parties can't agree, specifically ordered by the court.

Rarely will a parent's right to visitation not be granted in some way. If the court questions whether the noncustodial parent is fit (or can be trusted) to spend time alone with the child, the court may order the visitation supervised by a third party. This is a consideration when the noncustodial parent has either a history of abuse, neglect, or criminal behavior.

Before complete termination of visitation rights, the court will almost always require limited or supervised visitation. Only when the court is convinced that there would be no benefit to the child, or the potential harm to the child is too great, will visitation rights be totally removed.

CHILD SUPPORT

Directly related to child custody is the issue of child support. Child support is paid by the noncustodial parent to the custodial parent in an attempt to share the burden of the cost of raising the child.

Determination of Amount

Many states have set schedules to determine the amount of child support the noncustodial parent is required to pay. As a general principal, set formulas and rules dictate how much the noncustodial parent is required to pay in child support based on the respective net incomes of each parent. As in most divorce case issues, the amount of child support paid to the custodial parent is based on the economic facts and circumstances.

As the divorce process begins, the court may issue a temporary order of child support and custody. These temporary orders will be in effect until the final divorce decree, which permanently sets child support and custody arrangements.

In most states, child support payments go through the court. They are not paid directly to the custodial parent but to the clerk of the court that retains jurisdiction over the divorce case. This creates a permanent objective record of the status of the payments in the event a dispute later arises.

Many states have laws that require a custodial parent receiving ADC (aid for dependent children) to execute an assignment giving all rights to their child support monies to the local department of social services to help repay the cost of ADC payments.

Termination of Child Support

Generally, the obligation to pay child support will continue until there is a specific legal reason to discontinue payment. The most common reasons for the termination of child support include the child reaching the age of adulthood or enlisting in the military (emancipation), the marriage of the child, the death of the child, or any other legal emancipation.

In most situations, child support payments will terminate once the child reaches the age of majority. In some situations, however, the divorce decree may provide that the obligation to pay child support will continue even after the child becomes of legal age.

In most states, child support cannot be automatically stopped by the noncustodial parent without court approval. A court order authorizing the discontinuation of child support payment must be obtained. Similarly, if the child's parents informally agree that the noncustodial parent no longer has to pay child support, this informal agreement is not binding on the court. Rather, the parties should apply to the court for an order terminating the child support obligation if that is the desired result.

Medical Care

The divorce decree may also provide for health insurance or payment of medical bills for the minor child. In most situations, if one of the parents has health insurance provided through his place of employment, the court will order that coverage be kept on the minor child even if the parent providing the coverage does not have custody. Either parent may be required to maintain health insurance over the child, depending largely on which parent currently maintains adequate health insurance. Often any extra cost of maintaining health insurance for the child is taken into consideration relative to the amount of child support paid.

Nonpayment Issues

One of the more difficult aspects of child custody is the failure to pay child support. When a noncustodial parent fails to make the required child support payments, he is in violation of a court order. Although local rules governing delinquent child support vary widely, as a rule of thumb, legal proceedings to enforce past due child support have a tendency to be one of the more frustrating aspects of the judicial system.

In some areas, the county attorney attempts to collect past due child support. Other areas use primarily private practice attorneys. Many jurisdictions allow the parent to decide whether they desire to go through the county attorney's office or use a private attorney in an attempt to collect past-due child support.

Several methods can be attempted to collect past-due child support payments. Often a court garnishes wages or bank accounts of the delinquent parent. The percentage of money allowed to be taken from the nonpaying parent's paycheck is usually greater than would otherwise be allowed in more typical types of debt collection. Some jurisdictions have a procedure that creates a *continuing lien* over the nonpayor's wages so the garnishment will be in effect until the back-due child support is paid in full. This is also known as a child support wage withholding order and requires the employer to withhold a specific amount of the paycheck and forward the money to the court as the money is earned. The court will, in turn, see that the custodial parent receives the collected money.

Sometimes the Internal Revenue Service can attempt to collect past-due child support. If the nonpaying parent is owed a tax refund, a court order can intercept these tax refunds and pay them directly to the court for the benefit of the custodial parent.

The obligation to pay child support, whether past due or current, will almost always constitute an automatic lien on any real estate in the name of the payor. If the parent is current on his child support, the lien will be released by the court or with the acquiescence of the custodial parent. However, if the child support is delinquent, and the nonpaying parent attempts to sell, transfer or refinance a loan on the real estate, the lien will block such a transaction until the past-due child support is paid.

As with other types of judgments, past-due child support payments may be collected through the execution of a judgment. This means that the local constable or sheriff will seize and sell any nonexempt personal property of the nonpaying parent. Local procedures and exemptions in this regard vary quite a bit. It is recommended that an attorney be consulted if this route is taken.

Since paying child support is mandated by a civil court order, if child support is not paid, an order to show cause why the nonpaying parent should not be held in contempt of court may be issued. This would usually entail serving a notice of hearing to the nonpaying parent, which may not always be easy to do if his or her location is unknown. At such a show-cause hearing, the nonpaying parent will have an opportunity to tell the court why he or she has not paid child support, and if no justifiable reason exists, the court will have the option to order a fine, jail sentence or a combination.

If the parent charged with making child support payments declares bankruptcy, this obligation will not be *discharged* (declared legally void). Also, a bankruptcy will not discharge any past-due child support, nor does it discharge any future obligation to pay child support.

Collecting past-due child support when the nonpaying parent has moved out of state is difficult. Every state has enacted the Uniform Reciprocal Enforcement of Support Act (URESA) that allows reciprocal enforcement of court-ordered support between the states. The upshot of URESA is to simplify implementing the sanctions previously discussed against the parent not making required child support payments.

Visitation and Child Support

One question that comes up on a regular basis about child support and visitation is whether the custodial parent can refuse the noncustodial parent visitation rights if the noncustodial parent has not paid child support. In almost every jurisdiction, the answer to this question is no. This is based on the fact that the order to pay child support and the order to allow visitation are two separate court orders and are not contingent to or dependent on one another.

On occasion, the noncustodial parent becomes concerned that the money being paid for child support is not being spent with the best interests of the child in mind. Similarly, the noncustodial parent may be concerned that the parent who has custody is not raising the child in a generally acceptable manner, or is raising the child in an environment the noncustodial parent does not approve of.

Although courts are hesitant to get involved in what would otherwise be family arguments regarding the upbringing of a child, they will become involved if it can be shown that the custodial parent's conduct is contrary to the best interests of the child. The court may require that the custodial parent provide an accounting or financial history of how the money is being spent for the child if the use is questioned. Again, the noncustodial parent bears the burden of proving to the court that the child support money is not being directed toward the child but to the custodial parent's personal interests. Only where such an abuse is extreme will the court enter an order either reducing child support or requiring that the custodial parent regularly show the court that the money is being spent for its intended purpose.

TAX CONSEQUENCES AND ENFORCEMENT OF THE DECREE

A couple's income tax situation will change when the divorce is decreed.

Alimony and Child Support

The recipient of an alimony award must declare this money as income on his tax return. The party making the alimony payment may deduct the alimony payment from his tax return. However, any child support money that is received is not considered taxable income and, accordingly, the child support money that is paid by the noncustodial parent is not deductible on his tax return.

Interest Deductions

Other tax issues that come up in a divorce may be which party, if any, retains the right to declare mortgage interest and property tax deductions on real estate held in both parties' names after the divorce. This can be outlined in the divorce decree. If the divorcing couple owns a closely held business, the tax effects of business ownership may also be provided for in the decree, such as credits, deductions, etc.

Dependency Exemptions

Any divorce decreed after January 1, 1985, allows the custodial parent to claim the child as a dependent for income tax purposes. But the decree can specifically provide that the noncustodial parent claim the child as a dependent. The custodial parent is required to sign a waiver of his or her right to claim the child as a dependent, which is attached to the noncustodial parent's income tax return.

The court does not necessarily become involved in the issue of whether the custodial or noncustodial parent is allowed to claim the child as a dependent. Often this will be determined by the I.R.S. through requirement tests or investigation.

PATERNITY

Most states have laws requiring the payment of child support when a child is born out of wedlock. In a situation where the man is denying that he is the father, the child's mother may be required to file a paternity action. This type of lawsuit asks the court to require the alleged father to subject himself to a test (blood and/or genetic) to determine whether he is indeed the father.

Proof of Paternity

The mother is usually allowed to testify as to the identity of the child's father, and why she believes he is the child's father. If the man is denying paternity, the woman's testimony alone is generally not enough to allow the court to rule that the man is the father of the child without some corroborative evidence.

Effect of Paternity

If the court enters a judgment ruling that the named defendant is the father, the court will enter an additional order requiring child support payments. As in a custody dispute in a divorce action, the father may be given visitation rights or, possibly, even be awarded custody of the child even though the parties have never been married. An example of a paternity lawsuit petition is located in the appendix.

If the father alleges that the mother stated that she was on birth control at the time of conception, this will not be considered a legal defense to being held responsible for supporting the child and making child support payments. Even if the father is a minor, the court may order child support. In some cases, the parents of the minor father of the child will be required to pay child support, at least for a limited period of time.

Surname of the Child

The last name of the child will be the mother's last name unless both parents agree to have the child take the father's last name. If the defendant is determined to be the father of the child, it is possible the court will require the child's last name be changed to the father's. Even though it is probably in the best interest of the mother to establish paternity as early as possible to take full advantage of any potential court-ordered child support payments, in most states a paternity action can be brought any time before the child reaches the age of majority.

CHANGE OF NAME

Often a wife will assume the last name of her husband upon marrying. By law, however, a woman is not required to take her husband's name and may retain her maiden name. By the same token, upon divorcing, the decree may provide that the woman's maiden name be restored. This is generally done only if the woman so requests it. However, some courts may be reluctant to restore the woman's maiden name if minor children are involved.

If an individual wishes to change his name, for whatever reason, a change of name lawsuit needs to be filed with the court. Many states require that any interested persons be formally notified of the lawsuit (usually by way of a summons) so they may voice their objections, if any, to the change of name request. Also, many states require the change of name application be published in a local newspaper to provide notice to the public at large. If no one objects, the court will usually grant any application for a name change as a matter of course without regard to the reason for the request.

Finally, if a woman desires to return to her maiden name after the divorce decree has been signed, a separate change of name lawsuit is generally required.

ADOPTION

Adoption severs the legal relationship between a biological or natural parent and his child and establishes a parental relationship between a child and a person or couple who is not the child's parents. Each state has laws governing the steps required to legally adopt a child.

General Requirements and Procedures

Most states require that the individual applying to adopt a minor child be a legal adult and a resident of the state in which the adoption proceedings are brought. In some states, an adult may adopt another adult. Unless a specific statute or law exists to the contrary, a family relationship between the child and the adoptive parent is not a reason to reject the adoption request. That is, an uncle may adopt a nephew, a cousin may adopt a cousin, and so forth. Once an adoption order or decree is entered, all other states are generally required to recognize the decree as valid and legally enforceable.

Although most states require the adoption proceeding to be filed in the court of proper jurisdiction, some states do permit adoption by contract. An individual or couple who is otherwise legally competent to adopt a child may enter into a legally binding contract to do so, and, unless a legal prohibition contradicts it, the contract will be upheld unless otherwise breached. Most states, though, only allow a contract adoption to take place when the particular procedural and substantive requirements are met.

Parental Consent and Notice

The adoption terminates the parental rights of the natural parents and substitutes the adoptive parents as the legal parents of the child. If the child's natural parents do not give their formal consent to the adoption, they must be formally notified of the application and date and time of the hearing so they can present to the court reasons why the adoption should not take place.

In many states, if a judge determines that one or both of the natural parents has abandoned the child, the consent to the adoption may not be necessary. If the mother and/or father have voluntarily relinquished parental rights by turning the child over to a state agency, this also will negate their right to protest the adoption application. If the father has not acknowledged paternity of an illegitimate child, or refused the marriage to the child's mother after the birth, the consent of the father may not necessarily be required.

If the child's natural parents are divorced, the court involved in the adoption proceeding must review the custody provisions of the divorce decree. Some states require that only the custodial parent be given notice of the adoption proceedings, although many states require that both parents be given notice and their consent to the adoption proceeding is required.

If a third party, such as a guardian, *guardian ad litem* or state child care agency or orphanage, has legal authority over the child, most states require the consent of the institution or individual before the adoption takes place.

State law varies substantially as to whether a natural parent can withdraw consent to the adoption after the adoption has been computed. Often, the validity of the consent withdrawal will depend on the facts of the particular case. However, absent some extraordinary circumstances, the courts have generally held in favor of the adoptive parents in determining whether to allow withdrawal of a previously granted consent.

As in most court proceedings involving a child's future, the best interests of the child will govern the court's ruling. In an adoption proceeding, if the adoption is not consented to by all the parties involved, including any agencies, *guardian ad litems*, natural parents and the like, the court hears testimony and other evidence about why the adoption should or should not take place, always with an eye toward what will be in the long-term best interests of the child. The rights of natural parents, however, will also be given great consideration by the court if it involves a situation where the natural parents are objecting to the adoption application made by a third party or couple.

Effect of Adoption

As a general rule, the adoptive parents of a child will assume the rights and duties of natural parents. They will have the right to custody and control, and the relationship to that child, on a legal basis, will be the same as if the child were their own. The relationship created by the adoption is permanent and will continue after the child reaches the age of majority, and will generally not be affected by the death of one or both of the adoptive or natural parents. Once the adoption has occurred, any legal obligation the natural parents might have otherwise had to the child are terminated.

Sometimes the question arises whether the phrase "my children" or "my child" in a parent's will includes the adoptive child as well as their natural children, if any. While the prime consideration of the court will be the intent of the individual signing the will, state laws will usually provide that all legally adopted children will inherit as if they were natural children. If no controlling law exists, however, some states exclude an adopted child from taking property under the adoptive parent's estate if the terms "children" or "heirs" are referred to in the will without further clarification as to intent of including adopted children.

If the adopted child should die without a surviving spouse or children, the adoptive parent generally takes over his estate, to the exclusion of the natural parents. Also, in most states, if an adoptive parent dies without a will and has both adopted and natural children, the law will provide that there be no distinction between adopted or natural children, and the estate will be divided up accordingly.

Furthermore, most states also provide that when an adopted child dies before his adoptive parents, and the adopted child has had children (grandchildren of the adopted parents), these children will be regarded as the legal grandchildren of the adoptive grandparents. Thus, they are entitled to represent their parents and receive from their grandparents' estate any bequest made to their parent by his adoptive parents.

TERMINATION OF PARENTAL RIGHTS
Most states have laws governing termination of parental rights.

Grounds for Termination
A lawsuit is filed by the state against the natural parent or parents alleging specific acts that, under state law, constitute grounds for the termination of parental rights. Generally, one or more of the following needs to be shown before such a lawsuit is filed:

• Abandonment of the child for a certain period of time, usually several months.

• Substantial and continuous neglect of the child, including the refusal to give the child necessary parental care and/or protections.

• Willful neglect to provide the child with necessary sustenance, education, or to care for the child's morale, health or welfare.

• Parental unfitness because of habitual use of alcohol or

drugs, or lewd and lascivious behavior, which the court finds to be seriously detrimental to the health, morals or well-being of the child.

• Inability of the parents to fulfill their parental responsibilities due to mental illness or mental deficiency, if these conditions are likely to exist for a prolonged period of time.

Most states have a department of social services that deals with child protection issues. Typically, based on complaints of neighbors, teachers or relatives, a social caseworker will research or review the factual circumstances surrounding the parents' relationship with the child, taking into consideration the aforementioned factors. The social worker will then make a report to the district attorney describing the facts of the child's environment. The district attorney will decide whether to proceed with formal charges for the termination of parental rights.

As with a criminal action, if the natural parents are unable to afford an attorney to represent them in contesting the application to terminate their parental rights, an attorney will be appointed for them at the state's cost. Most courts are reluctant to terminate the rights of a parent without proof that there is very little or no opportunity the parents will be able to turn their lives around and provide an environment that does not violate the state's requirements for fitness of a parent. Once again, the court will focus on the best interests of the child, keeping in mind the threshold position that a parent has the inherent legal right to remain parent of his child, unless the state can provide to the court's satisfaction that one or more of the necessary conditions for the termination of parental rights exists.

Rehabilitation Plans

Rather than the complete termination of parental rights, the court sometimes orders a rehabilitation plan the parents must abide by for a certain period of time. If the parent does not follow this plan, the parental rights are terminated. Often, the courts will temporarily terminate parental rights until the parent has satisfied the court that the rehabilitation plan (usually involving drug or alcohol rehabilitation and gainful employment), has been successful.

Failing to follow the rehabilitation plan will be sufficient grounds for the permanent termination of parental rights. Some states require that before any termination can occur, the parent must have had at least one opportunity to correct the unacceptable condition or behavior.

Effect of Termination

If a court order for termination of parental rights is entered, the child will usually become a ward of the state and, if not adopted, be placed in a foster home or with the state department of social services or similar state agency. Most states will provide that an order terminating the parent-child relationship remove all legal rights, privileges and duties between the parent and the child.

SPOUSAL LAW

Sometimes there are civil lawsuits filed between spouses. Historically, a husband and wife could not sue each other for any reason because the law considered them one legal entity. Many states have modified their laws to extend the right of spouses to sue each other or recover from a third party a loss of spousal companionship.

Loss of Consortium

Some states also provide that a husband may sue a third party who wrongfully injures his wife and thereby causes him expense or *loss of consortium* (spousal companionship and comfort). Other states have ruled or passed laws that specifically limit a husband to only expenses incurred by him because of his wife's injury. An increasing number of states now permit a wife to sue a negligent third party when her husband has been injured.

Alienation of Affection and Criminal Conversation

Both alienation of affections and criminal conversation are based on the theory that one of the fundamental rights of a husband in a marriage relationship is that the wife shall have intercourse only with him, and any act by a third party in committing adultery with the wife, or enticing her to, is considered a legally actionable invasion of the husband's rights. An action for alienation of affections involves the husband filing suit against a third party, alleging that the third party is enticing his wife away from him, to his detriment. An action for criminal conversation is where the husband alleges that a third party is seducing his wife, again to the detriment of the husband. Both of these actions are based upon the theory of *loss of consortium*.

Most of these types of lawsuits will request that a court order direct the third party to cease and desist any alleged actions causing these losses. A separate action can be brought for money damages the husband may be able to prove or convince the factfinder that he is entitled. Many states have abolished these types of lawsuits in recent years.

Chapter Three

Real Estate and Housing

The first man who, having fenced in a piece of land, said, "This is mine," and found people naive enough to believe him, that man was the true founder of civil society.

    —Jean Jacques Rousseau

This chapter will focus on the area of law concerning housing, both the purchasing and leasing of a household. During the typical consumer's lifetime, one of his largest dollar transactions will be the purchase or lease of a home. The transaction and factors involved in purchasing or leasing a home are often complex and easily misunderstood. This chapter will focus on the information that a consumer should have regarding the legal aspects of purchasing or leasing a home.

THE PURCHASE OR SALE OF A HOME

When a residence is being sold, often the seller will hire a real estate agent. However, to avoid the payment of a commission or fee to the real estate agent, many individuals will attempt to sell their home themselves—a sale by owner. Whether or not to list the home with a real estate agent is an individual choice, and often depends upon the expertise or experience of the seller and the necessity of saving the money owed on a commission. If a homeowner decides to sell the home himself, there are certain obligations that he must meet. The legal obligations of real estate agents will be discussed shortly.

Misrepresentation

Any homeowner attempting to sell his home must deal in an honest manner with any potential buyer. This means that any fraud committed on a buyer about the condition of the home may be grounds for the buyer to rescind (legally cancel) the purchase agreement and sue for any resulting damages. Whether or not any particular intentional misrepresentation by the seller constitutes grounds for recision will revolve around the following question: Did the homeowner deliberately misrepresent a fact on which the buyer had reasonably relied and which caused the buyer injury? If the buyer suffered a loss due to misrepresentation, the seller (and possibly his real estate agent) can be held legally responsible.

Disclosure of Defects

Beyond intentional misrepresentation, the seller of a home may be held legally responsible if he fails to disclose to a buyer any type of defect that is not readily apparent. And if this defect is material in nature, as opposed to a minor defect, the buyer may be able to rescind the contract and sue for damages. These types of defects, known as *latent defects*, must be disclosed by the seller regardless of whether the buyer asks about any such condition. The general rule is that if a nonexpert would be unable to discover an existing defect, the seller, if aware of the defect, must inform the buyer of this fact.

A *material defect* is one that a reasonable person would consider a factor in deciding whether or not to purchase the home. An example of a material latent defect would be previous water in the basement, which a buyer would not be able to detect by walking through the house.

Dangerous defects must also be disclosed to the buyer. These are defects that may make the property dangerous to the buyer, who would otherwise be unaware of the defect until after the home was purchased. Faulty electrical wiring is an example of this type of defect.

In many real estate purchase agreements, the buyer agrees to purchase the property *as is*. However, most states have ruled that even with this *as is* provision in the contract, the seller has a duty to point out any latent or dangerous defects to the buyer to absolve himself of any potential future liability.

A *patent defect* is one considered legally and readily apparent to the buyer. If a defect is patent in nature, the homeowner is not legally required to disclose these defects to the buyer. Outwardly apparent defects such as a crumbling foundation or standing water in the basement are examples of patent defects. Because notice of these defects is considered legally apparent, the seller has no duty to further and otherwise disclose these to a buyer.

Many states have adopted a *buyer's questions* rule. This means that if a buyer asks any specific question about any aspect of the home, the seller (or his agent) must answer the question truthfully. However, if the condition that was questioned has changed before the property is transferred, the seller must notify the buyer of the change in condition. If he does not notify the buyer of this change, the buyer may have a legal basis for rescinding the purchase of the home.

Despite the rules of disclosure incumbent on the seller, *caveat emptor* applies to a buyer wanting to rescind a purchase agreement on the basis of nondisclosure of a defect in the home. Caveat emptor is a legal term meaning let the buyer beware. That is, the law will make it incumbent on the buyer to protect his own interests and do what is necessary to inspect the property before agreeing to purchase it. And, as mentioned above, not all types of defects need to be disclosed. The buyer should always inspect the home to his satisfaction, regardless of any disclosures by the seller, to protect himself from disputes or legal problems arising from defects in the home, disclosed or otherwise.

Real Estate Agents

Most sellers will hire a real estate agent to sell their homes. A real estate agent is an individual who has obtained a state license to sell, transfer or lease real estate on behalf of another, usually for compensation. Most states have laws and administrative rules that regulate the professional conduct of real estate agents. Although many states differentiate between real estate agents and real estate brokers, usually dependent on the amount of experience or the degree of license obtained, for purposes of this book we use only the term real estate agents.

When a homeowner sells his home through a real estate agent, he will enter into a written contract, called a *listing agreement*. This agreement specifically gives the real estate agent the authority to use his expertise in attempting to sell the home at a predetermined price. Typically, when the house sells, the listing agent agrees to receive a certain percentage of the sale price as compensation. The commission or compensation earned is not set by law, but is always a matter of negotiation between the seller and the real estate agent, although anywhere between 5 and 8 percent is not uncommon.

Listing Agreements. The agreement between the homeowner and the real estate agent can take several forms. There are three specific types of listing agreements: the nonexclusive listing agreement, the exclusive agency listing agreement and the exclusive right to sell listing agreement.

A nonexclusive listing agreement (also called an open listing agreement) can be entered into between the homeowner and any number of listing real estate agents. The listing agent who closes the sale will receive the commission. All the agents who enter into a nonexclusive listing agreement are aware that other agents may also be attempting to procure a buyer for a commission. Also, if the homeowner sells the home to another without any effort or help by any of the agents involved, a commission will not be paid or owed to any agent.

The second type of listing agreement is the exclusive agency listing agreement. This type of listing gives the real estate agent the authority to sell the home to the exclusion of all other agents. However, this listing agreement does allow the homeowner to sell the home on his own and, if he does, he would not be liable to the listing agent for any such commission. The homeowner must show that it was his efforts, and his efforts alone, that sold the home. Otherwise, the listing agent will be entitled to receive a sales commission.

The third type of listing agreement is an exclusive right to sell listing. This listing gives the real estate agent the exclusive and sole right to sell the home for a certain period of time. Even if the homeowner procures an acceptable buyer without any effort whatsoever on behalf of the listing agent, a commission will still be owed that listing agent.

Only one agent at a time can enter into an exclusive right to sell listing agreement for a particular piece of property. Once the exclusive right to sell agreement has been entered into, the homeowner will have to pay the agreed-on commission to the listing agent if the home is sold, even though the eventual buyer may have been procured without any effort or assistance by the listing agent. The appendix contains a sample exclusive right to sell listing agreement.

If a homeowner knows of an individual who may be interested in purchasing his home prior to the execution of an exclusive right to sell listing, most agents will allow a specific exclusion for that person. However, the agent may not want to enter into the listing agreement at all if he believes that such a person may in fact buy the property and, accordingly, negate the agent's efforts and chance of obtaining a commission.

The length of time that a listing agreement is entered into is totally between the homeowner and the real estate agent. Generally, anywhere between 60 and 120 days is considered standard.

Cooperative Real Estate Agents. In addition to the listing agent, other real estate agents who are not directly connected with the listing agent are involved in the sale of the home. A particular agent may be assisting a potential buyer in looking for the right home by showing various homes that are listed with other agents. These agents are called cooperative agents or subagents. They are, in effect, extensions of the listing agent and have the same legal duties and obligations to the seller as the listing agent. If a cooperative agent is involved in the eventual sale of the home, the commission earned (as stated in the listing agreement) will be divided between the listing agent and the cooperative agent. How much of the commission goes to the cooperative agent and how much goes to the listing agent usually will depend on local practice, rules or custom.

Duties of the Real Estate Agents. Any listing agent or cooperative agent has a *fiduciary duty* to the seller during the period of the listing. This means that these agents must put the seller's interest above their own in attempting to market and sell the home.

There are three main rules regarding the fiduciary duty owed the seller:

1. The agents must disclose all information to the seller about the sale of the home, including any offers whatsoever on the property.

2. The agents must account to the seller for all proceeds from the sale of the home. Further, the agent cannot use accessible funds such as escrow deposits, earnest money and the like as his

own because of his relationship to the seller.

3. The agent must obey his seller. Although the agent may have a level of knowledge and expertise to advise the seller about the sale of the home, it will be the seller, and not the real estate agent, who has the ultimate authority in making any decisions affecting the sale of the home.

Also, all listing agents and cooperative agents must act honestly with the buyer, but not disclose any information that they are not otherwise required that may harm the seller's interest in attempting to sell the home at the highest price possible. For instance, if an agent involved advises a potential buyer that the seller is desperate for an offer on the home, this may cause the buyer to offer a lesser price on the home than he would otherwise have made. Although it is sometimes difficult to prove how this type of information may have harmed the seller, it should be stressed that the fiduciary duty from the real estate agent to the seller also entails nondisclosure of any information that may harm the seller's ability to sell the home for the highest price possible. Of course, any latent or dangerous defects in the property known by the agent must be disclosed to a buyer.

Buyer Representation. In some areas, there are real estate agents that act as representatives of the buyer. That is, they have fiduciary duty to the buyer, and not the seller, in attempting to locate a suitable home for the buyer. Since listing agents and cooperative agents owe their allegiance to the seller, it is generally the seller's commission as provided for in the listing agreement that provides their compensation. However, a buyer's agent will usually be compensated directly by the buyer, and not the seller.

Buyer representation by real estate agents has been slow in catching on because most potential buyers are unwilling to pay a separate fee to be legally represented by a real estate agent, instead of dealing with agents who have their allegiance to the seller.

Dual Agency. At this point, mention needs to be made of a fairly recent phenomenon known as dual agency. As the name suggests, dual agency involves one real estate agent representing both the buyer and the seller. Currently allowed in some states, dual agency must be agreed on between both the seller and the buyer. The agent acts as a neutral party and legally can favor neither the buyer nor the seller but in essence works as a match-maker to bring an acceptable buyer together with an appropriate seller.

Dual agency does have its critics, however. Since a buyer is trying to obtain a house for the lowest acceptable amount while the seller is trying to obtain the highest sale price possible, complete neutrality is nearly impossible. It has been said that a dual agent has no strict master and must walk the finest of tightropes to ensure that neither the buyer nor the seller is prejudiced by the dual agency relationship.

Another problem arises with regard to the compensation to the dual agent. Since the commission earned is generally paid by the seller, as stated in the listing agreement, if an agent is representing both the buyer and the seller, a seller may not be willing to pay a commission to an agent who does not totally represent his interests. Obviously some of the practical details of dual agency are still being worked out, and a buyer or seller who hires a dual agent must be aware of the precise allegiances that this type of agency encompasses.

Multiple Listing Service. Once a home is listed with a real estate agent or agency, it generally becomes part of a local *multiple listing service*. This is a listing of all the homes for sale in a geographic area at any given time. Any house that is listed by a real estate agency that belongs to the multiple listing service will have the home listed in the service to provide information to any potential cooperative agents who may be searching for a home for a potential buyer. In certain areas, only exclusive rights to sell listing agreements are automatically included in the multiple listing service.

Generally, the multiple listing service book is updated every few weeks to include any new listings or cancellation or sales of previous listings. The multiple listing service is a valuable tool to real estate agents in trying to match buyers with sellers and serves as a marketing device used by members of the multiple listing service to expose listed homes to the widest market base possible.

THE PURCHASE AGREEMENT

A contract between a buyer and a seller for the purchase of the home is called a *real estate purchase agreement*. It is a legally binding contract that states, sometimes in great detail, the terms and conditions of the sale of the home. There are two types of real estate purchase agreements, the *cash for deed* contract and the *land installment sales contract*.

First of all, recognize that any type of contract for the sale of real estate must be in writing to be enforceable. All states have a body of law called the *statute of frauds*. These laws provide that certain contracts must be in writing to be enforceable. Although some very limited exceptions to this rule exist, an oral contract for the sale of real estate is unenforceable. Thus, the first rule of a real estate purchase agreement is to make sure that the contract is in writing, or at least evidenced by a writing.

On a related note, if the written purchase agreement contains confusing language and the intent of the parties cannot be ascertained by reading the contract, a court will allow oral testimony to discern what the parties meant. However, if the contract is clear and unambiguous, any oral promises not contained within the agreement will not be enforceable.

Cash for Deed Purchase

A cash for deed purchase agreement is where the seller agrees to transfer title to the buyer when the buyer pays the purchase price in full. The buyer often is required to obtain a loan for the entire purchase price. This is different from a land installment sales contract, where the buyer makes periodic payments to the seller, often for several years, until the purchase price is paid. Land installment sales contracts will be discussed later in the chapter (see page 69).

Offer and Acceptance

Usually when a house is for sale, a potential buyer will learn what the asking price is and make an offer, either at the asking price or at a price that is somewhat less. If there are no contingencies in the offer and the seller accepts it, the signature of the buyer and the seller on a piece of paper indicating the purchase price, and probably various other terms, will create a binding contract for the sale of real estate.

If, however, the seller receives an offer to purchase his home and agrees to the offer, yet changes some of the terms of the offer, such as the purchase price, an acceptance has not occurred. Rather, a counteroffer exists, which the potential buyer must agree to before a binding contract is created. Offers and counter-offers can go back and forth several times before the final contract terms are agreed upon by both parties.

Whenever an offer is made on a home, the potential buyer should specifically state the date of the offer and how much time the seller has to respond to it. This way, it will remain clear how long the offer to purchase the home remains open. Without a specific time frame in this regard, the seller will have a reasonable time to respond. Obviously, this "reasonable time" is open to interpretation. It is in the potential buyer's best interest to specify a date by which reply must be made.

Both the buyer and the seller need to execute (sign) the contract for an enforceable real estate purchase agreement to exist. There are some exceptions to this rule, usually involving one of the parties granting a third person the legal right to sign on his behalf. Signatures must be notarized in some states, but not all. The notary process merely lends an element of validity to the signatures in case a question later arises as to whether or not the seller and/or the buyer actually signed the agreement.

Earnest Deposit

To ensure that a buyer is serious about purchasing the home under the terms of the purchase agreement, some form of earnest deposit is required. An earnest deposit is a percentage of the purchase price, usually 1 or 2 percent, that accompanies the offer to show the seller that the buyer is serious in wanting to purchase the home.

If the purchase is consummated, the earnest deposit is applied to the purchase price. If, for no valid reason, the buyer does not purchase the home, the earnest deposit is usually retained by the seller as damages. If a real estate agent is involved in the sale, he will usually hold the earnest deposit until title to the home is transferred.

Financing Contingency

The real estate purchase agreement should also contain a statement about how the buyer is going to obtain the necessary funds to purchase the property. Obviously, the obligation to purchase the property will be contingent on the buyer getting a loan. The terms and amount of the loan should be specifically stated in the purchase agreement. If the buyer makes a good faith effort to obtain a loan and is unable to, any earnest deposit will be refunded to him and the buyer will no longer be bound to purchase the property.

Possession Date

The possession date of the home should also be specifically provided for in the purchase agreement. In most cases, the possession date will be the date of closing; that is, the date that the ownership of property actually changes hands from the seller to the buyer.

However, if for whatever reason the buyer desires to take possession of the property before closing, the parties can enter into an "early occupancy agreement" where the buyer is allowed to take possession of the home before becoming the owner. Usually the buyer will pay the seller a specified amount on a per day, per week or per month basis until the actual closing has occurred. An example of an early occupancy agreement is located in the appendix.

Similarly, if the seller needs or desires to stay in the home after closing, and the buyer is agreeable, a *post-closing occupancy agreement* can be executed. In a post-closing occupancy agreement, the seller remains in possession of the home for a certain period of time after transferring ownership to the buyer. The seller will compensate the buyer for possession of the home, at whatever terms and payment amount they may agree on.

Proration of Liabilities

The purchase agreement should also provide for the proration of real estate taxes and utilities on the home. That is, absent a preclosing or postclosing occupancy agreement, generally the seller will pay all utility costs up to the time of closing, with the buyer assuming any liability for the utilities on the property thereafter. Similarly, real estate taxes on the home will usually be assessed on an annual or semiannual basis; hence, they must be prorated between the buyer and the seller up to the date of closing.

Personal Property

Often there is a misunderstanding between the buyer and the seller as to certain items of personal property that may or may not be considered part of the home. Generally, any item of personal property that is permanently attached to the home is considered a fixture and will stay with the home at sale unless otherwise agreed. The question is always what is and what is not a fixture.

If there is any question about what types of personal property stay with the home, they should be specified in the purchase agreement. Consider the following items and decide whether you would consider them a fixture to stay with the home upon its sale:

- a concrete bird bath sitting on top of the ground
- a full length mirror bolted into the wall in the home's entry-way
- a built-in microwave oven

In each of the above examples, the buyer and the seller could easily have a dispute about whether the items stay with the home. Instead of courting a dispute, anything that is potentially debatable should be specifically provided for in the agreement, clarifying to both parties which items are to be retained when the home is sold. Most real estate agents are very helpful in determining what items would be considered a fixture in residential real estate.

Property Description

A specific description of the property being sold should also be contained in the agreement. The street address and the legal description of the property should both be used. The *legal description* of a home usually refers to the specific lot, subdivision, city and county in which the property is located. Usually a local title company can look up the legal description to the property if it is not otherwise known.

Role of Attorneys

Often attorneys are used when a real estate transfer is being made. An attorney who represents the buyer is generally concerned about the buyer receiving everything that is bargained for—that the property is in the shape that it appears to be, with no latent or undisclosed defects, and that the title being transferred does not lead to problems later of questioning the buyer's ownership rights to the home.

An attorney who represents the seller, however, is usually there just as a parachute. If purchase agreement or title transfer problems arise, the seller's attorney will attempt to correct them to facilitate the closing. An example would be to clear up potential or objectionable title defects that may exist on the property. Either the buyer or the seller's attorney may be involved in the drafting or reviewing of the purchase agreement.

Other Contingencies

Other contingencies that may be contained in the purchase agreement include situations where the buyer is not legally obligated to purchase the property until he has sold his existing home. Also, the buyer or the seller may put a provision in the contract that unless the agreement is specifically approved by the attorney for one or both of the parties, the contract can be declared nonenforceable.

The purchase agreement should also contain the specific date that the parties desire to close on the home. If the buyer is attempting to procure a loan to purchase the house, the closing would generally be six to eight weeks after the purchase agreement is finalized.

If the closing does not occur on the specified date, this is not necessarily fatal to the purchase agreement. Unless the key phrase, "time is of the essence," is contained in the agreement, the closing date is considered merely a target date and any delays will not automatically allow one of the parties to rescind the agreement without other circumstances involved.

Closing Costs

Specific mention should also be made in the agreement regarding payment of closing costs. Closing costs usually entail the various filing fees, discount points of the loan the buyer may obtain, costs of title insurance or updating of the abstract of title or attorney's opinion, escrow costs, etc. Local custom or negotiation will generally dictate which party pays for these items or if the cost is to be divided. The liability for closing costs should be specifically set forth in the agreement so that no later dispute can arise in this regard.

A typical residential real estate purchase agreement is in the appendix.

Forms and Addendums

A few other terms need to be mentioned concerning real estate purchase agreements for a home. In most situations, a preprinted form will suffice in containing provisions for all the necessary terms for a typical home sale contract. Recognize, however, that trying to use a form agreement where the terms of the sale may be somewhat unique is like trying to place a square peg in a round hole: The fit will not be good — even with the assistance of real estate agents. Sometimes attorneys draft purchase agreements that specifically include all the necessary elements and desired aspects of the agreement.

If the original signed agreement contains a clause that needs to be clarified or modified, the buyer and the seller can draft and sign an *addendum* to modify the original agreement.

DEEDS

The agreement to purchase should also state the type of deed transferred from the seller to the buyer at the time of closing. When a home is sold, the document that transfers ownership is called the deed. There are several different types of deeds that are used to transfer real estate: warranty deeds, quit claim deeds, bargain and sale deeds, estate deeds, sheriffs' deeds, and a variety of less common deeds.

Warranty Deed

Most buyers of residential real estate will only accept a warranty deed for the transfer of ownership. A warranty deed conveys title to the home and implies that the seller is the property owner and has legal authority and ability to make the transfer. If some type of title defect arises later, the buyer can pursue the seller for any damages suffered because the warranty deed in essence guarantees (by the seller) good and valid title. The appendix contains an example of a warranty deed.

Quit Claim Deed

A quit claim deed, however, merely transfers whatever interests the seller may have in the property without making any promises, guarantees or warranties. In fact, an individual transferring property by way of a quit claim deed is not liable whatsoever for any future title defects. A quit claim deed only transfers whatever interest, if any, the seller may have, and, if no interest is held at the time of the transfer, the buyer is simply out of luck.

Other Deeds

Other types of deeds used in the transfer of real estate usually involve certain specific situations, like buying real estate at a foreclosure auction, at the sale of property to satisfy creditors or through an estate proceeding. The type of deed that is used to transfer the property should always be specified in the purchase agreement.

EVIDENCE OF TITLE

The purchase agreement should also refer to *evidence of title*, which means the seller must demonstrate that he is in fact the owner of record and that the property is unencumbered (no liens, mortgages, etc.). Usually, this evidence of title is shown by way of *title insurance*, or an attorney's opinion on the home's *abstract of title*.

Abstract of Title

An abstract of title (or title search) is a summary of the conveyances, transfers or other facts of evidence of the seller's ownership in the property. An abstract will also include any other documents of public record that may affect the title to the property. Generally, a title company or attorney will review all of the past documents that make up the history of the property being sold and determine if the property is without any outside encumbrances that may be detrimental to the buyer. However, an abstract of title without an opinion being rendered on it does not necessarily guarantee good and valid title. Rather, it is merely a recorded history that needs to be interpreted to decide whether the seller has sufficient title rights to the property.

Title Insurance

Another method of assuring that the buyer is obtaining valid title to the property is a *title insurance* policy. Title insurance is where an insurance company guarantees and insures that the property being sold is not subject to any outside interest to the detriment of the buyer.

If the buyer incurs a loss due to any type of insured title defect, the title insurance company will be required to reimburse him. Title insurance has replaced, for the most part, attorneys' opinions and abstract review as the most common and preferred method of guaranteeing valid title to property. Even though a warranty deed is used for the transfer, title insurance should also be obtained to provide extra assurance that no problems later arise concerning ownership rights to the home.

LAND INSTALLMENT SALES CONTRACT

A *land installment sales contract* (or land contract) is different from a cash for deed purchase, because the deed to the home is not transferred to the buyer until several installment payments are made to the seller. The entire purchase price is not paid all at once, but rather the seller acts as the lender for the buyer in accepting payments over an extended period of time, often many years, before the seller is obligated to transfer the deed.

In most states, the following elements must be included in a land contract before it can be legally enforceable:

- Names of the buyer and the seller
- Description of the home being sold
- Purchase price
- Method of payment, including the down payment and the periodic payment schedule

The amount of interest, if any, being charged by the seller needs to be stated. It is best if an amortization schedule is attached to the land contract so that the buyer and the seller are both clear on the amount of each payment split between principal and interest. Many land installment sales contracts require a balloon payment at the end of the payment period. The buyer makes installment payments over a period of time and, at the end of the installment period, pays the balance of the purchase price.

Escrow Agent

Many land contracts are negotiated by an escrow agent, who acts as an intermediary between the parties.

During the life of the contract, which may extend many years, the escrow agent holds two separate deeds. One deed is signed by the seller transferring title to the buyer, and the other deed is signed by the buyer transferring his interest in the property to the seller. Once the buyer makes all the necessary payments, the escrow agent files (in the appropriate public office) the deed previously executed by the seller. If the buyer should default, however, the escrow agent will file the deed from the buyer to the seller to negate any effect the land contract may have on the seller's title rights to the property. This is especially important if the contract has been recorded.

Title Rights

During the life of the land contract, the buyer is said to have *equitable title*, while the seller is said to have *legal title*. Usually possession of the property is granted to the buyer, and this should be stated in the contract itself. If the buyer is not in possession of the property, he should make sure that a statement of existing contract, if not the contract itself, is filed in the appropriate local public office to provide notice to third parties that he is in the process of purchasing the property. This will keep an unscrupulous seller from selling the property to another person and creating an ownership rights dispute of the home and/ or land.

Often a potential buyer wants to enter into an option to purchase agreement. An option to purchase is a real estate contract between a homeowner and a potential buyer where the potential buyer pays for the right to possibly purchase the property within a specified period of time. By granting an option to purchase, the seller is in effect precluding anyone else from buying the home during the option period without the option holder's consent.

Generally, an option to purchase must be supported by valid consideration. This means that a homeowner cannot give someone an option to purchase; rather, the person receiving the option must pay for it in some fashion. Only in this way will the person receiving the option have enforceable rights to the first opportunity to purchase the home within the time frame that the option allows.

Some states require that the terms of the sale also be contained in the option agreement. This way, if and when the option is exercised, a valid purchase agreement and all its necessary terms will immediately exist. If the terms of the sale are not agreed upon in the option, the exercise of the option only allows the seller and the buyer to further negotiate the specifics of the purchase. So, an option to purchase is sometimes not a true option, but only an option to make an offer on the property to the exclusion of others.

THE CLOSING

A closing on a real estate transaction refers to the actual date when the seller transfers the property deed to the buyer in exchange for the purchase price.

Seller's Obligations

Although the specific requirements of a closing may depend somewhat on the terms of the purchase agreement, in most cases the seller is obligated at or prior to the time of closing to do the following:

1. Provide evidence of title—that is, assure the buyer, by whatever means described in the purchase agreement, that the seller has the legal right and authority to transfer the property being sold.

2. If any objections to the title have previously been made, to prove to the buyer that these objections (such as liens or other title encumbrances) have been removed.

3. If the purchase is contingent upon some type of repair being made on the property, the seller should be prepared to prove to the buyer that these repairs or improvements have been made.

4. If any lease exists on the property between the seller and a tenant, the seller needs to execute a mutually acceptable assignment of leasehold interest to the buyer.

5. The seller will usually be required to sign a *lien waiver affidavit*. This is a document indicating that there have been no permanent improvements on the property to allow a third party to file a lien on the title after closing.

6. Sellers will almost always have to have some form of certificate indicating that a termite inspection has been done, and that no infestation has been found, or that the infestation was treated to the satisfaction of the buyer.

7. The seller needs to make sure that an acceptable deed is

executed in the name of the buyer, which will be transferred to the buyer at the time of closing.

Buyer's Obligations

The buyer is usually required to satisfy the following elements:

1. Provide the entire purchase price, usually in certified funds, at the time of closing.
2. Have inspected the property immediately prior to closing.
3. Supply a property survey that indicates specifically that the perceived boundary lines of the home are in fact the correct boundary lines so that there is no mistake as to the property that is actually being transferred.
4. See that premises and hazard insurance are in place at the time of closing, so that if anything happens to the home immediately after transfer of ownership he will be protected.

Once the deal closes, the deed the buyer receives should be immediately recorded in the appropriate form to provide public notice of the transfer of ownership. Also, the utilities need to be transferred over to the buyer's name, as well as transfers of keys, garage door openers, etc.

Land Installment Sales

In a land installment sales contract, there are really two closings. The first occurs when the land contract is executed and the buyer commences his periodic payments. Then, when the periodic payments have all been made and the deed is actually transferred from the seller to the buyer, the second closing is deemed to have occurred.

Escrow Closings

In many areas of the country, home sales are handled by an *escrow closing*. A deed is usually deposited by the seller with an escrow agent. The deed is later delivered to the buyer when the payment of the purchase price has been paid to the escrow agent.

For a legally enforceable escrow closing to exist, the following requirements must be met:

- There must be a valid purchase agreement.

- There must be a valid deed from the seller to the buyer.
- This deed must be delivered to the escrow agent.
- An escrow agent must be appointed with the power to handle the escrow closing.
- There must be a separate escrow agreement.

The prime advantage of an escrow closing is that it affords a certain amount of protection from intervening liens on the title to the home. The escrow agent will typically record the deed immediately upon receipt of the purchase price to minimize any risk that creditors or other potential lien holders of the seller encumber the title to the property. Escrow closings also minimize the risk of either the seller or the buyer changing their minds and preventing the closing from occurring.

REAL ESTATE SETTLEMENT PROCEDURES ACT

The Real Estate Settlement Procedures Act is a body of federal law that mandates that mortgage companies, banks or lenders of money must disclose certain information about a home loan to buyers, as well as prohibiting lenders from certain practices.

Applicability

The Real Estate Settlement Procedures Act (RESPA) is applicable to first mortgage loans made for residential real estate, including duplexes, triplexes, quadplexes, cooperatives, condominiums and possibly even mobile homes. The provisions of RESPA only apply to lenders involved in federally related mortgage loans. However, the term *federally related* is usually very broadly defined and includes any type of lender whose funds are federally insured or regulated. The basic premise behind RESPA is that a potential homeowner/borrower needs to have all information made clear to him regarding the terms and conditions of the loan. This allows him to make an educated and informed decision about whether the loan is in his best interests.

Settlement Cost Booklet

All RESPA lenders must provide a potential borrower with a settlement cost booklet that includes information concerning the real estate purchase process and various terms and factors involved in a loan obtained for the purchase of a home.

The lender must also provide the buyer with a good faith estimate of all settlement charges that the buyer may have to pay in obtaining the loan. As with the settlement costs booklet, this good faith estimate of the cost of the loan must be provided to the potential borrower at the time the loan application is made, or within three business days. The charges estimated to the buyer will include any loan origination fees, credit report fees, appraisal fees, title search fees, surveys and document preparation charges.

Uniform Settlement Statement

RESPA also requires the lender to make available to a potential borrower a uniform settlement statement. This is a summary of the buyer's loan and purchase transaction and itemizes and includes all the charges (debited and credited) of the loan and sale of the home. Within three business days after closing, the lender must provide the buyer/borrower an itemized list of all charges for the services provided, as set forth in the uniform settlement statement.

NEW HOME CONSTRUCTION

If a home buyer is having a new home built, the process differs somewhat from the purchase of an existing home.

Purchase Agreement

Specifications and blueprints approved by both the buyer and the builder need to be attached as part of the purchase agreement. This makes it clear what specifically is to be built and leaves no room for error regarding exactly what is being contracted for. If changes are to be made in the home after construction begins, this will often involve an extra charge to the homeowner and a "change order" will be attached to the blueprints and specifications to keep them as complete as possible before construction starts.

Permits

The builder is usually responsible for obtaining all necessary building permits and seeing that applicable zoning requirements are met. The builder is also responsible for paying all suppliers and subcontractors before the buyer is obligated to purchase the home.

Escrow of Purchase Price

A builder will usually require that the buyer obtain loan approval before starting construction. However, there are times when construction is not completely finished by the time the owner needs to take possession of the house. In this case, the buyer and the builder may agree to escrow the last 5 to 10 percent of the purchase price until the builder is able to complete the home. This ensures that these items will be completed before total payment is made.

For example, if the home is complete except for the laying of the sod in the yard due to adverse weather conditions, the buyer may close and take possession and escrow a portion of the purchase price until the builder lays the sod when the weather is more cooperative.

DISCRIMINATION IN HOUSING

Federal law requires that no discrimination occur in the sale or lease of real estate on the basis of race, color, religion, sex, national origin, handicap or families with children. Most states have similar types of laws.

Fair Housing Act of 1968

The Fair Housing Act of 1968 makes the following activities illegal:

1. Refusing to sell, rent or negotiate with any individual or otherwise make a dwelling unavailable to any individual based upon race, color, religion, national origin or sex.

2. Changing of terms, conditions or services offered for the purchase, sale or lease of a residence based upon the above classifications.

3. Discriminating through any statement or advertisement that restricts the sale or rental of residential property based on any of the above classifications.

4. Indicating to any individual of the above classifications that a particular dwelling is not available for sale or lease solely on the basis of that individual's classification.

5. Attempting to make a profit by persuading homeowners to sell or lease their homes because of the possible entry into their neighborhood of persons of a particular race, color, religion or national origin.

6. Changing or modifying the terms, conditions or requirements for a home loan to any individual who wishes to purchase the home, or otherwise denying such a loan on the basis of the above classifications.

7. Demoting or discharging of any employee or reduction of compensation of any employee who has otherwise complied with the nondiscrimination sections of this law.

8. Threatening, interfering, coercing or intimidating any individual who is otherwise exercising his rights as guaranteed under this law.

Please recognize that these fair housing laws do not apply to the sale or rental of commercial or industrial properties. Also recognize that a person may discriminate on the basis of any of the above classifications if he can meet the following tests:

1. He does not own any more than three homes at a time.

2. The seller is living in the home or is the last person to live in the home being sold (if this residency requirement is not met, the exception applies to only one sale every two years).

3. The seller cannot use a real estate agent to facilitate the sale.

4. The seller cannot use any type of discriminatory advertising in attempting to sell the property.

The Fair Housing Act also provides that a residence owned by a religious organization or sect does not have to be sold to an individual who is not a member of that organization, as long as the potential buyer is not prohibited from joining that religious organization. However, a religious organization owning the property involved cannot be based on one of the aforementioned suspect classifications. For example, a religious organization cannot be established and claim to accept only male members in an effort to exclude female buyers from purchasing a residence.

HOME LOANS

Most sales of residential real estate are contingent upon the buyer obtaining a loan to finance the purchase. When a bank, savings and loan, or mortgage loan company is used to obtain the purchase price for the home, the lender will always require security for the loan. In almost every case, the security for the loan will be the house being purchased. There are two ways for the lender to obtain security for the loan in the home.

Mortgages

One way is for the lender to obtain a mortgage on the property. A mortgage is a document that transfers a security interest in the home to the lender (from the buyer) until the loan is paid in full. Once the loan is paid, the mortgage is released by the lender.

Along with the mortgage, the borrower will also sign a promissory note stating the amount of money that is being borrowed, the interest rate that is being charged, and the period of loan payback time (usually ten to thirty years). The borrower is called the *mortgagor*, while the lender is called the *mortgagee*. The document reflecting the security the lender receives in exchange for the loan is called the mortgage. The lender will require that the mortgage be recorded in the appropriate public office to further protect its interest.

Deeds of Trust

A deed of trust is a security device lenders may use in making the loan to facilitate the purchase. A deed of trust consists of a situation where the deed to the home is transferred from the seller to the buyer. Immediately upon the loan being made, allowing the buyer to purchase the home, the buyer transfers a deed of trust to a third party, called the *trustee*. In the terms of the deed of trust, the trustee is required to hold the deed in trust until all the money is repaid from the buyer to the lender. The lender is called the *beneficiary*, while the buyer (borrower) is known as the *trustor*.

As with a mortgage, the deed of trust will be accompanied by a promissory note that specifically states the amount of money that is being borrowed, interest rate and term of repayment. Also, as with a mortgage, the deed of trust will be filed in the appropriate public office.

Default and Foreclosure

While both the deed of trust and the mortgage provide the lender with security for the loan, the main difference comes into play if a borrower defaults. In a mortgage situation, the lender must file a mortgage foreclosure lawsuit to remove the buyer from the home and eventually obtain title to the property and resell it in an attempt to recoup its loan.

In a deed of trust situation, however, no lawsuit is involved. Rather, the lender formally notifies the trustee that a default has occurred, usually nonpayment on the loan by the borrower, and the trustee conducts a sale of the property allowed by the *power of sale* clause in the deed of trust.

It has been the experience of lenders that mortgage foreclosure actions have allowed defaulting borrowers to delay the foreclosure process several months or more. In a deed of trust situation, however, it is much more difficult for the defaulting borrower to delay the house being sold by the trustee. Hence, many lenders prefer a deed of trust arrangement due to its speed of enforcement compared to a mortgage foreclosure.

Many states require that buyers who obtain a home loan and give a deed of trust as security also acknowledge the fact that they are signing a deed of trust as opposed to a mortgage. Usually this acknowledgement will specifically inform the buyer that enforcement provisions of the deed of trust are substantially different from a mortgage. This is designed to make the buyer aware of the consequences that are involved should a default occur under a deed of trust rather than a mortgage.

Deficiency Balance. If a default occurs and the home is eventually sold for less than the amount owed under the terms of the loan, the lender may proceed with a separate action against the borrower for what amounts to a *deficiency balance*.

That is, if the loan balance is $100,000, and the house is sold through the foreclosure or deed of trust process for $90,000, the lender will usually have the right to sue the homeowner for the $10,000 deficiency balance. Sometimes a lender will accept a deed from the defaulting homeowner in lieu of a foreclosure action or deed of trust enforcement in exchange for an agreement not to hold the borrower liable for any potential deficiency balance that may result. This way, the lender avoids any delay or costs involved in enforcing its deed of trust or mortgage.

RESTRICTION ON THE USE OF A HOME

One of the basic premises of home ownership in this country is that the homeowner can use his property as he so chooses.

However, certain restrictions, both public and private, do exist that place a limit on how the home can be used. The main types of restrictions of home use will be discussed below.

Zoning

Residential property *zoning* is defined as the power given to the local government to limit the extent of home use within certain boundaries. A zoning law provides that only certain types of activity may be allowed within a particular area. Most types of zoning are divided into four main groups: residential, commercial, industrial and agricultural.

As you might guess, only homes will be allowed within residential zones. Certain residential zoning laws specifically state what type of residences may be allowed. For instance, only single family dwellings (as opposed to duplexes or possibly apartment complexes) may be allowed within certain residential zoning areas.

Nonconforming Use. An exception to zoning laws is the theory of *nonconforming use*. This legal theory, which exists in most states, provides that an owner of a home may not be legally forced to discontinue his use of the property as a home due to zoning noncompliance, provided that the home existed prior to the implementation of the zoning law.

Variance. If the homeowner wants to build a home within an area that is not zoned for residential use, he may apply to the local zoning board or applicable governmental body for a *variance*. The homeowner asks for permission to deviate from the existing zoning law to build the home. Usually, a variance is allowed or considered when a minor or modest deviation from the zoning requirements is being sought.

Zone Change. If the property owner wants to use the property in a way substantially different from the existing zoning laws, he may ask for a *zone change*. Usually the owner of the property must show that the change in the zoning status will not have a detrimental effect on surrounding property values, or that the surrounding property owners have no reasonable grounds for objection to the requested zoning change. For example, a zoning variance often will be granted for a home-based business run from a single-family home if there is no danger of increased traffic or other detrimental effect on the surrounding community.

Restrictive Covenants

A *restrictive covenant* is a private agreement that restricts the use of a home, usually placed by real estate developers to maintain quality control over the homes in a particular area or subdivision.

Restrictive covenants, also known as protective covenants, usually contain very specific rules concerning the type of home that may be placed within the area affected. These rules typically involve minimum square footage and architectural design. Often restrictive covenants will specifically limit the type of activities that are permitted on the homeowner's property, such as prohibition of outdoor repair work on automobiles, front yard fences, satellite dishes, etc.

The purpose of restrictive covenants is the ensure that all the homeowners in a particular area are allowed to reap the benefit of maintaining quality control over their neighborhood by restricting certain activities regarding home usage and construction. Restrictive covenants are almost always on file or of public record and copies can be obtained easily. Whenever a homeowner is thinking of buying or building in a newer subdivision, restrictive covenants considerations may preclude an activity or type of home that the homeowner may be considering.

Easements

An easement is a nonpossessory interest in the homeowner's property that may limit the owner's use of the home. Easements in residential real estate are usually granted to local utility or telephone companies, and allow these companies to place, maintain, dig and repair any of their equipment that runs across, under or over the homeowner's property. Easements are also a matter of public record when the home is purchased, and the homeowner is obligated to see that these types of easements are not disrupted by any use the homeowner may have of his property.

Eminent Domain

The owner of the home should also be aware of the power of the government, including federal, state or local governments, to take private property (including a home) for public use. This governmental power is called the power of *eminent domain*.

If the government can demonstrate that all or part of the home needs to be taken and owned by the government to enhance the public good or benefit public use, the owner will have no legal option but to transfer the property to the government. The homeowner is entitled to "reasonable and just compensation" for his home or any part of it.

For example, if the homeowner is located along a street the city believes needs to be widened for the benefit of public transportation, the city will follow a set procedure, called a *condemnation proceeding*, to take the property and transfer title to its name. Other types of possible usages of the homeowner's property for the good of the community may involve the government taking the property for parks, schools, police or fire stations, governmentally owned buildings, etc. Again, if the government can demonstrate that the taking of the property is for the general good of the public, the homeowner will have no recourse. The homeowner needs to make sure that the compensation that is given is fair and reasonable. If the homeowner and the government cannot agree on a price, the homeowner does have the right to take his case to court and convince a judge or jury that he is entitled to more than the government is offering.

Construction Liens

Construction liens, also known as mechanics' liens, are sometimes used when the homeowner has a permanent improvement made on his property and has not paid the individual or company for the labor or material provided.

Creation and Enforcement. State laws for filing of construction liens will vary substantially. However, a construction lien is usually filed by an individual who has not been paid or believes that he will not be paid for work done or materials provided. Construction liens can usually be filed without the homeowner's consent.

As with other types of liens, to enforce a construction lien, the lienholder must begin a foreclosure action requiring the homeowner to either pay the lienholder or allow the lienholder to eventually take title to the home, subject to any other encumbrances against it, such as mortgages or deeds of trust.

Most jurisdictions require that the lien for material or work provided on a specific home must be filed within a certain period of time, usually just a few months after the work has been done. Some states allow the construction lien to be filed even before the work is done or material has been provided.

If the homeowner hires a general contractor who may be purchasing materials or using subcontractors, the homeowner should see that the general contractor is paid and in turn pays all suppliers and subcontractors. Lien releases from these people can be obtained, or the homeowner may wish to pay off the general contractor by a dual payee check in the name of the general contractor and all applicable suppliers or subcontractors.

OTHER TYPES OF RESIDENTIAL OWNERSHIP

This section will discuss the more nontypical methods of owning a home, including condominiums, cooperatives and time-share ownership.

Condominiums

A *condominium* is one particular unit in a multiple unit structure that is ownable by deed. The owner of a condominium also has an ownership interest in the land or *common use elements* within the building or structure. Condominiums are sometimes referred to as townhouses or townhomes.

When a condominium is purchased, the same types of documents and requirements involved in a typical home purchase are used, including a purchase agreement, financing, a title search and evidence of title, a closing, and a mortgage or trust deed used as security for the loan.

The common elements of a condominium are the ownership interest by all the condominium owners in the common usage areas of the structure. Examples would be areas of the condominium building used as hallways, elevators, stairwells or recreational facilities.

A condominium association will have a set of bylaws created by the association and complied with by owners of the condominium. The condominium association enforcing the bylaws is elected by all the condominium owners in their particular building or area. These bylaws will usually set forth how the condominium is to be run, including any fees or assessments the condominium owners must pay to keep the common elements in good condition.

Cooperatives

A cooperative (also known as a co-op) is a type of home owner-ship in which the land and the buildings are owned by a corpora-tion. The individual resident of the cooperative owns stock in the corporation.

These individual residents will have a lease to the specific unit they occupy, along with their stock ownership in the corporation. Since all the cooperative owners are the sole owners of the stock of the corporation, the cooperative is owned and managed by the individuals who have a lease to their respective units.

Since the cooperative homeowner is a part owner of the cor-poration's stock, the shareholders of the cooperation decide how the co-op is run. Thus, the homeowner in the cooperative is in effect acting as the tenant as well as a landlord.

The purchase of a cooperative is somewhat different from a typical home or condominium purchase. No deed to any type of real estate is transferred to the purchaser of a cooperative. The only financing necessary is for the cooperative owner to purchase the stock in the cooperative corporation and also enter into a lease agreement for the particular unit in which he will live.

As a general rule, many cooperative corporations are some-what strict and exclusive in who they allow to purchase the corpo-rate stock and enter into a lease. This way, cooperative owners maintain somewhat of an exclusive membership to their own residency environment.

Time-Share Ownership

Although not usually considered a method of home owner-ship, the interest in real estate obtained by a *time share* arrange-ment involves many individuals who own separate, undivided interests in a piece of residential property. Each one of these individuals will have the right to occupy the property for a specific predetermined period of time, usually a few weeks per year. Time shares are typically owned by people purchasing an interest in a vacation or second home to occupy the premises as their home for a short time, without the long-term commitment that goes with other types of home ownership.

A time share is purchased by written contract. Due to the vari-ous restrictions involved in the particular time that the property may be used, the transfer or resale of time-share property can sometimes be difficult.

LEASES AND LANDLORD-TENANT LAW

The focus of this section will be on the legal relationship between a residential tenant and landlord, and the terms and ramifications of a residential lease.

Residential Vs. Commercial Leases

Initially, recognize that the laws governing residential and commercial leases usually vary. Although both residential and commercial leases are created by contract, most states have landlord-tenant laws that give only the residential tenant certain rights that might not be contained within the lease itself. These laws are based on the premise that most residential lease terms are usually mandated by the landlord.

To ensure that a residential tenant is not unfairly taken advantage of, and in recognition of the public policy of keeping people from becoming homeless and/or evicted due to overly harsh lease terms, many tenant-oriented laws have been enacted. Although these laws vary from state to state, the general principles discussed in this section will reflect the landlord-tenant rights and obligations of most states.

Term Tenancy

Landlord-tenant relationships are differentiated based on the existence or absence of a formal written lease. If a formal written lease is agreed on and executed, the period of time that the tenant is entitled to possess the property will be precisely stated. This is known as *term tenancy*. For instance, if a lease is for six months, the lease will state the dates the tenancy period begins and ends. The lease will govern the period of time the tenant is allowed to remain on the premises legally.

Periodic Tenancy

A *periodic tenancy* is created when a tenant is occupying and renting the property without any specific agreement to the length of the leasehold term. Usually, if the rent is paid on a monthly basis, without any agreement to the contrary, a monthly periodic tenancy will exist. If the rent is paid on a weekly basis, a weekly periodic tenancy will exist.

The periodic tenancy exists until the tenant or the landlord advises the other that he wishes to terminate the lease. Generally, for such a termination to be effective, it must be given in advance for at least a period of time that was involved in the periodic tenancy. That is, if the tenant was paying the rent on a monthly basis, at least one month's notice must be given to the landlord for the tenant to have a legal right to terminate the lease at the end of one month. Many states have laws providing that if the periodic rent is paid on a weekly or biweekly basis, a tenant must give his landlord at least one month's notice of terminating the lease. A landlord must meet these same notice requirements in advising his tenant that the periodic tenancy is terminated.

Tenancy at Will

Tenancy at will is for an indefinite term and may be terminated by either the landlord or the tenant. As its name suggests, in a tenancy at will situation, the parties have agreed that either the landlord or the tenant can, by their choice or "at will," end the leasehold relationship. Most courts do not favor tenancy at will because the termination rights of either party are so easily enforced, with very little notice to the other party.

Tenancy at Sufferance

A *tenancy at sufferance* is created when a tenant who has previously and rightfully possessed the premises continues to occupy the property even after the expiration of the leasehold period. At this point, the tenant becomes a trespasser and may be legally removed at any time without further notice. Many times, at the end of a specific written lease term, the tenant remains on the property and is technically a tenant at sufferance. If the landlord continues to accept the rent on a periodic basis from the tenant, however, a periodic tenancy will generally be created.

Statute of Frauds

Mention was made early in this chapter about the *statute of frauds*, which requires that contracts for the sale of real estate must be in writing to be enforceable. The statute of frauds also comes into play in residential leases.

Generally, residential leases for periods longer than one year must be in writing to be enforceable. The law presumes that a lease for longer than one year is, by its nature, important enough to be put in writing so that there is little or no chance of a dispute regarding the terms or conditions of the lease.

Written Leases

As already mentioned, a lease is a legally binding contract between a landlord and a tenant where the landlord gives up a possessory interest in his property while the tenant agrees to compensate the landlord for transferring this interest to him. As long as the terms of the lease do not violate any local laws pertaining to residential landlord-tenant relationships, the terms of the lease will govern the conduct between the parties.

Written leases are usually for a specified length of time and set forth various conditions and requirements that the landlord and tenant are bound by during the term of the leasehold period. The next section will review the various provisions that should be contained in a residential lease.

Lease Requirements

A residential lease should always include the following:

- Name and address of the landlord and the tenant(s)
- Full names of all tenants
- Amount of rent and the date that the rent is due
- Any late charges if the rent is not paid on time, and when the late charges accrue
- Amount of any security deposit paid by the tenant at the beginning of the lease
- Term of the lease, preferably stating specific dates that the lease is to begin and end
- Whether the tenant is allowed to assign or sublet his interest in the lease
- Whether the tenant is allowed to have pets and, if so, what type and number of pets
- Who is to pay any utility charges on the premises, and whether the tenant is to have the utilities placed in his name
- What, if any, rights the landlord may have if the tenant abandons the property and leaves behind personal property

It is also best if the lease specifically states the care of the premises during the term of the lease. This is especially true if the property is a house rather than an apartment. The lease should specifically state whether the tenant or the landlord is responsible for maintaining the grounds and the home during the term of the lease. It should also make any noncompliance with this provision a material breach of the lease and cause for eviction.

Form Leases

Most residential leases are provided to the tenant by the landlord on some type of preprinted form. The tenant should not execute the lease without first reading and understanding all its terms and ramifications. If the tenant wishes to sign the lease immediately, and if the landlord does not object, the tenant may place a phrase on the lease after signing it as follows: "The tenant's obligations and rights under the terms of this lease are subject to tenant's attorney review and approval of the lease within seventy-two hours hereof." This at least allows the tenant an escape clause if there is some aspect of the lease that the tenant does not wish to abide by or does not believe is in his best interests. Of course, the tenant may always have an attorney look at the lease before signing it.

As with any contract, if the lease itself is clear on its face, any oral assertions, promises or statements made by either the landlord or the tenant, either prior to or at the time the lease is signed, do not become part of the leasehold agreement unless they are specifically provided for in the lease itself. On a related note, if the preprinted lease contains an illegal clause or provision, some state laws hold that the entire lease becomes null and void. A copy of a typical residential lease is found in the appendix.

Landlord Rights and Restrictions

A residential landlord has certain rights he may exercise within the terms of the lease, or that may be provided based on local law even if not stated within the lease itself. The landlord will usually have the right to receive and collect damages for any negligent or willful destruction of the leased premises, including any damages that may exceed the security deposit provided by the tenant at the commencement of the lease. The landlord may also charge whatever rent he chooses for the property, absent any local rent control laws.

The landlord may also specify various terms and conditions of the tenant's conduct. These include permissible use of the premises and upkeep and maintenance of the premises during the leasehold period. Generally, any rules or regulations that promote the appearance, convenience or safety of the premises or the welfare of any other tenants will be deemed reasonable and legally valid.

Recognize, however, that the landlord's inherent legal right to do as he pleases with the premises does not give him the right to discriminate against tenants or prospective tenants on the basis of the suspect classes mentioned previously that govern the sale of real estate. Also, the landlord may not discriminate against couples who may or may not have children if this is the sole reason for the granting or excluding these types of prospective tenants.

Many states have laws that prohibit certain provisions of the rental agreement. The inclusion of these agreements in the lease may not allow the landlord to enforce the lease if there is some alleged violation of the lease agreement by a tenant. For example, the landlord may not be able to disallow a tenant from enforcing his rights under the terms of the lease or provisions of the local landlord-tenant laws. Also, the landlord may be able to charge only a limited amount in security deposit, sometimes only an amount equivalent to one month's rent, or slightly more if pets are allowed.

Landlord Obligations

Even if the lease does not so provide, the landlord is usually required to provide certain basic services to the tenant under a residential lease. Most landlord-tenant laws require the landlord to deliver possession of the premises to the tenant at the commencement of the leasehold. That is, if a third party has possession of the premises it will be the landlord, not the tenant, who must see that the tenant is allowed to take possession.

Most state laws require that the landlord maintain the premises in a fit and habitable condition during the term of the lease. This generally means that all areas of the premises be kept in a clean and safe condition, including all electrical, plumbing, sanitary, heating, ventilating, air conditioning and other facilities, including elevators.

The landlord will almost always be required to provide running water (including reasonable amounts of hot water) during the leasehold period. Local minimum housing codes must also be met, even if the tenant should agree to the contrary in the lease.

Usually a landlord will not be given unlimited access to the premises without the tenant's permission. However, in the case of an emergency, the landlord may enter the dwelling unit without such consent. Most state laws will set forth the amount of time that the landlord must give a tenant notice with regard to his intent to enter. Twenty-four hours is fairly typical.

If a landlord deliberately or negligently fails to supply running water, hot water, heat or other essential services as provided by law, the tenant may be able to recover damages against the landlord. With some very limited exceptions, however, the tenant will not be permitted to stop making rent payments or otherwise break the lease without a court order. Most laws provide that the tenant will be able to recover more than the damages actually suffered, usually amounting to a certain portion of the rent and all applicable attorney fees. The rather severe penalty involved when the landlord fails to provide essential services is the law's way of trying to ensure that such services are provided to the tenant until such time that a formal eviction occurs.

Tenant Obligations

A tenant also has certain obligations to the leased premises. He must comply with all community housing codes and keep the rental property as clean and safe as conditions permit. Garbage is to be disposed of in a clean and safe manner. Further, the tenant must keep the plumbing sanitary and should only use the electrical, plumbing, heating and cooling facilities in a reasonable manner. A tenant may not deliberately or negligently destroy or damage any part of the premises. At the end of the lease, the premises must be left in as clean a condition as when the lease began, except for ordinary wear and tear.

If the tenant should make repairs or alterations on the premises (such as painting or minor carpentry work), he will generally have no legal claim to be reimbursed for his expenses or labor from the landlord, without a specific agreement to the contrary.

The tenant and his guests must always conduct themselves in a manner that will not disturb their neighbors. Any violation of these types of tenant obligations may result in the lease being breached and the landlord proceeding with an eviction action.

Security Deposit

If there has been damage to the premises during the leasehold period beyond ordinary wear and tear, the landlord may withhold all or part of the security deposit to reimburse himself for any such damage. Many disputes have arisen between landlords and tenants as to what constitutes ordinary wear and tear. As a safeguard to the tenant, at the time the premises are initially occupied, the tenant should walk through with the landlord and make a list that indicates any defects or existing damage to the premises at that time. The landlord should sign and acknowledge this list so that the tenant has some type of evidence to the condition of the premises when the occupancy began in the event the landlord attempts to retain the security deposit unjustly at the end of the rental period.

It should be understood that a security deposit is not designed and cannot legally be used to pay the final month's rent. This would negate the purpose of the security deposit, which is to protect the landlord in the event there is damage to the premises.

Insurance

Without a specific provision or agreement to the contrary, it will remain the landlord's obligation to keep the premises insured during the term of the lease. However, a tenant's personal property located on or within the premises needs to be insured separately, usually by purchasing a renter's insurance policy.

If a third party should be hurt on the premises due to the negligence of the landlord or the tenant, both could potentially be held legally liable. Accordingly, it is a good idea for both the landlord and the tenant to have insurance protection for such events.

Leases and Fixtures

Fixtures, as discussed earlier in this chapter, are items of personal property that, by being permanently attached to real estate, are considered legally part of that real estate. Once the real estate is sold, the fixture is transferred with the real estate unless specifically agreed to the contrary.

In residential leases, if a tenant should place a fixture on the property during the term of the lease, that fixture becomes part of the leasehold premises and is to remain with the premises and becomes the property of the landlord at the termination of the lease.

Accordingly, if a tenant believes that he will be involved in a fixture dispute, which often happens in lengthy residential leases, the item in question should be specifically provided for in the lease so that no dispute arises later whether the tenant is entitled to remove it when the lease expires.

Eviction

One of the words that a tenant hates to hear in a residential lease situation is *eviction*. An eviction is considered the legal canceling or forfeiture of a lease, usually through court action and procedure. The most typical reason for evicting a tenant is nonpayment of rent. If a tenant should fail to pay the rent during the leasehold period, most states require that the landlord give the tenant formal written notice of the fact that the rent has not been received. This is sometimes referred to as a *notice to quit*. If the rent has not been received within a very short period of time thereafter (usually within a few days), the landlord will not be obligated to accept any future rental payments and can immediately proceed with an eviction.

An eviction action is begun by filing a lawsuit against the tenant. The court will then require a hearing at which time the judge will determine whether the tenant has violated the lease. If the court so finds, it will enter an order of eviction allowing the sheriff or other local official to forcibly remove the tenant and his belongings from the premises. Local procedures and requirements regarding the eviction of a residential tenant can vary substantially, and must usually be strictly complied with before the court will allow a tenant to be evicted.

If a landlord attempts to evict a tenant for a reason besides nonpayment of rent, the law may require that he give the tenant more time to correct the situation before proceeding with an eviction lawsuit. Most landlord-tenant laws are designed to give the tenant as many chances as possible to maintain the leasehold relationship. The premise is not to terminate the lease unjustly thus creating a situation where the tenant (and possibly his family) do not have a place to live.

It should be noted that if a landlord is successful in evicting his tenant, or if the tenant prematurely leaves the premises, the landlord can hold the tenant responsible for any rent payments yet due under the balance of the lease. The landlord is obligated to make all reasonable attempts to re-rent the premises. However, if the premises are not re-rented, the landlord can file a lawsuit against the former tenant for any such back rent owed. Often local court procedure will allow the landlord to file an eviction lawsuit in conjunction with an action for rent owed.

Assignments and Subletting

Sometimes the question arises whether a tenant, without a lease prohibition to the contrary, is allowed to transfer his rights to the premises to a third party without the consent of the landlord. Many leases state that any assignment or subletting is illegal without the landlord's express or written permission. Many courts have ruled, and some state laws specifically provide, that a landlord may not withhold such permission unreasonably.

There is a difference between an *assignment* and a *subletting* of a leased residence. If the tenant transfers the entire term of the lease, it is an assignment. However, if the transfer allows the original tenant to retain part of his interest in the lease, no matter how small, a sublease situation is created.

For example, if a tenant enters into a lease for one year, and after three months assigns the remainder of the lease to a third party, an assignment has occurred. However, if a tenant has entered into a similar one year lease, lives on the premises for four months, and then subleases the premises to another for four months while retaining the right to occupy the premises for the final four months, a sublease situation exists.

The practical effect of this variance between a sublease and assignment is that in an assignment situation, the new tenant (person receiving the assignment) becomes directly liable to the original landlord for any rent due under the terms of the lease. However, in a subtenancy situation, the subtenant will be liable only to his sublandlord (the original tenant), who in turn remains liable to the landlord based upon the original lease.

Abandoned Property

Sometimes a tenant will leave behind various items of personal property when he abandons the premises. The question then arises regarding the landlord's disposal of such personal property, assuming it has any value whatsoever.

Many state laws provide that a landlord is obligated only to retain the apparently abandoned property for a specific period of time, holding the former tenant responsible for any storage costs. The landlord will usually be required to make all reasonable efforts to contact the former tenant and advise him to reclaim the property. If the former tenant is not located or does not reclaim the property, the landlord will be allowed to dispose of the property at his discretion. Any sale proceeds are to be applied against any money still owed the landlord under the terms of the lease.

Chapter Four

Criminal Law and Procedure

Laws and police regulations can be compared to a spider's web that lets the big mosquitos through and catches the small ones.
   —*Julius Wilhelm Cingref*

This chapter addresses the commission of crimes and the procedures and safeguards involved for those accused of a crime.

CRIMINAL ACTIVITY

In the United States, an act can only be prosecuted as a crime if a law has been enacted that defines the activity as a crime. In some instances, the failure to act will also constitute a crime. For example, the failure of a motorist involved in an accident to stop and render aid or the failure to file income tax returns are crimes.

Criminal Intent

In most crimes, not only must the accused have committed the act, but he also must have intended to commit a crime. There are some exceptions to this rule, however, such as when an individual is charged with criminally negligent driving or negligent homicide. These types of crimes require no *specific intent*, but only the *general intent* of placing the criminally accused in a situation where the act was an inevitable result of his prior actions. Proof of a motive, malice or specific intent must be given for the accused to be convicted of such a crime.

Corporations and partnerships may be charged criminally for certain violations. Examples include criminal negligence to its members or employees, violation of federal laws dealing with immigration or employment status, and so on.

Also regarding criminal intent, religious beliefs cannot generally be used as a justification for an act that would otherwise constitute a crime. For instance, if one's religion allows for multiple spouses, and the state has a law prohibiting polgamy, the fact that the accused's religion allows for or encourages multiple spouses cannot be used as a defense.

Similarly, voluntary intoxication or drunkenness is not a defense to most crimes. Most states will allow evidence of the intoxicated condition of the defendant. This evidence, however, is not a legal defense, but rather is permitted to allow the court to decide whether any type of deliberation or premeditation was involved in committing the crime.

Mental Capacity

Aside from the criminal act and the intent to commit it, the mental capacity of the accused must also be established. Without appropriate mental capacity, the accused may have a justifiable defense to the crime. Many states specify what types of incapacities determine whether the defendant has the necessary mental capacity to be convicted of a crime.

Usually, lack of intelligence, in and of itself, cannot be used as a defense unless the defendant can prove that his lack of mental ability rendered him incapable of knowing the nature or consequences of his actions.

Infants or under-age defendants may also have a defense to the lack of capacity to commit a crime. Most states have laws defining the age an individual must be to possess the necessary legal capacity to be charged with a crime as an adult rather than as a child.

For example, a state may provide that any person fifteen years of age or younger does not have the sufficient mental capacity to commit a crime. However, the prosecution may seek to convict such an individual as an adult. The burden will rest with the prosecution to show that the defendant completely understood and appreciated the nature and consequences of his actions.

Also, some areas have laws that provide that individuals between the ages of sixteen and seventeen may be criminally charged as adults or minors, depending on the type of crime involved and the discretion of the prosecution. The prosecution will usually bear the burden of establishing that because the defendant's criminal background and general character will suggest that he should be prosecuted as an adult and, if convicted, penalized accordingly.

Insanity

If a person is declared insane, he is considered to have insufficient mental capacity to commit a crime and cannot be held accountable for actions that would otherwise constitute a crime. Usually, if the defendant can establish that he was insane at the time the criminal act occurred, this constitutes a complete defense. States have different methods of determining whether a defendant was insane. Typically, medical experts will examine the defendant prior to trial and offer testimony to his mental state. It has been argued that if an accused was voluntarily intoxicated at the time the criminal act was committed, any alleged *temporary insanity* that stems from the intoxication will not be considered a legally viable defense.

Most states require the judge or the jury to decide whether the defendant is guilty or innocent, taking into consideration any evidence of insanity presented at the time of trial.

The presumption is always that a criminal defendant is sane. A defendant must overcome this presumption in establishing the fact that he was insane at the time the act was committed. However, in some states, once evidence of the defendant's insanity has been introduced to trial, the burden will shift to the prosecution to prove that the defendant was sane at the time of the offense. If insanity is used as the basis for finding the defendant not guilty, he usually will not be entitled to an immediate release. In all likelihood, he will be committed to a mental care institution, subject to periodic review and possible release at a later date.

As a corollary to the insanity defense, if the accused was sane at the time the act was committed, he still may not be tried and convicted if he does not have the mental capacity to comprehend the nature of the proceedings against him and assist in his defense at trial.

TYPES OF CRIMES

Misdemeanors and Felonies

Most crimes are divided into two categories: misdemeanors and felonies. A misdemeanor is legally a lesser or more minor crime than a felony. Misdemeanors and felonies are further divided into several categories or degrees of severity. Generally, a first-degree crime, whether it be a misdemeanor or a felony, is more severe in nature and has the potential for carrying a more extreme punishment. State laws vary greatly regarding classification and potential penalty of crimes.

Accessories, Aiders and Abettors

An individual who is held responsible for participating in the crime as an *accessory* is another type of criminal defendant. Although an accessory did not directly commit the crime, he participated in the crime.

An individual involved in a crime after the crime was committed is considered an *accessory after the fact*, and is often charged as one who knowingly assisted the criminal defendant in some manner, such as escape, comfort or other assistance. An accessory after the fact will be charged with a separate offense.

An *aider and abettor* to the crime is one who is considered responsible for the acts of the perpetrator of the offense. Aiding and abetting is a distinct offense, and the aider and abettor will be charged and tried separately. Although local statutes may vary, often the aider and abettor cannot be convicted unless the principal criminal actor is also convicted. That is, if no crime has been established, no one can be convicted as an aider and abettor.

It should be noted that many states have negated any distinction between an accessory and a principal to the crime. Usually, the principal must actually be present or participate in some way in the commission of the offense. Most criminal statutes now consider all individuals who are present at the commission of a crime as guilty as the principal. That is, any individual who aids and abets the criminal defendant, as well as those who helped perpetrate the act, will be considered principals to the crime.

STANDARD OF CONVICTION

In almost all criminal cases, the prosecution must show the defendant is guilty *beyond a reasonable doubt*. The judge or jury must not have any reasonable doubt of the guilt of the defendant before finding him guilty.

If the defendant can establish that the prosecution has not met this burden, the finder of fact will be instructed to enter a verdict of not guilty. This is different from civil cases, where the standard is the *preponderance of evidence*. Beyond a reasonable doubt is one of the safeguards to ensure that a criminal defendant is not convicted unless substantial evidence proves he committed the crime.

CRIMINAL DEFENSES

Once an individual is charged with a crime, many defenses may be used. Some defenses attempt to show that the defendant is not the person responsible for the crime, while others attempt to prove that there is a legal prohibition in bringing charges or convicting the defendant of the crime. The insanity plea discussed above is one such argument

Alibi

One of the most common defenses in a criminal trial is the *alibi*. An alibi attempts to prove that the defendant was not at the scene of the crime at the time it allegedly occurred, so, he could not have committed the crime.

In many states, the criminal defendant must plead an alibi defense prior to trial, while in other states the defendant may raise any evidence of an alibi under a general plea of not guilty. By requiring that the criminal defendant plead a defensive alibi, the prosecution is allowed to determine what evidence and/or witnesses the defendant may use to establish his alibi. This allows the prosecution pretrial maneuverability in determining the credibility of any witnesses.

Entrapment

Another defense in a criminal trial is *entrapment*. This is where the state, usually by and through its police authorities, induces a person to commit a crime that he would not otherwise have committed.

An entrapment defense must be proven by the defendant. The defendant's defense is that the crime did in fact occur, but would not have except for the overzealous acts of certain state authorities. The question will generally evolve around whether the situation created by the authorities would lead an otherwise noncriminal person to commit the act. In many states, the entrapment defense is recognized only on a limited basis in specific types of crimes.

The theory of entrapment is that the law will not allow the state to prosecute a criminal action against one who is induced to violate the law. Again, the issue will be whether the authorities involved, by their actions, created intent in the defendant, as opposed to the criminal intent originating in the mind of the accused.

Statute of Limitations

Many criminal laws have a statute of limitations: Unless prosecution is brought within a certain period of time after the alleged crime was committed, the prosecution may not be legally entitled to pursue its case.

For instance, a law may require that a first-degree misdemeanor charge of auto theft be brought within ten years from the date of the alleged theft. If charges are brought after that time, the defendant may use the statute of limitations to have the charges dismissed, with no chance of them being refiled at a later date based on the same set of facts.

The statute of limitations runs from the date the crime occurred, not from the date the crime was discovered. In most states, statute of limitation defenses are interpreted in favor of the accused.

Statute of limitations do not apply to most felonies. However, they do apply to many lower crimes such as misdemeanors. Local laws vary widely in this regard.

The rationale behind the statute of limitations is to prevent the prosecution from sitting on the evidence until a time when the defendant is unable to conduct his own investigation for a fact-oriented defense.

Double Jeopardy

Double jeopardy is the constitutional prohibition against prosecuting a defendant twice for the same offense. A trial must already have occurred on the particular charges involved. If the defendant entered a plea before trial but later withdrew it, the prosecution can still proceed with its case without being in violation of the double jeopardy rule. Also, if charges are filed and subsequently dropped based on various pretrial motions, a refiling of charges against the defendant will not constitute double jeopardy.

There are various other potential defenses that a criminally accused can invoke to have the charges dropped, or cause the exclusion of evidence that undermines the prosecution's case to such a degree that it would be impossible for the prosecution to win its case. Most of these potential defenses revolve around the constitutional rights of the accused and will be discussed shortly.

CRIMINAL PROCEDURE
The typical court procedure involved in an arrest and trial will usually progress as described in this section.

Arrest and Arraignment
If an individual is arrested and charged with a crime, the prosecuting attorney will file a formal charge against that individual as soon as possible. In the event that the defendant is being held in jail, an arraignment is the next step in the court process.

In an arraignment, the defendant is brought in front of a judge or judicial magistrate and informed of the charges against him. After the charge is read, including all potential penalties if he is found guilty, the court will ask the defendant to enter a plea of guilty, not guilty or no contest.

The purpose of the arraignment is to formally advise the defendant of the substance of the charges against him and call on him to respond to the charges by way of a plea. Usually, a copy of the indictment or criminal complaint is provided to the defendant or his attorney prior to the arraignment hearing. The arraignment is scheduled within several hours or days after the arrest if the defendant is being held in jail. If the defendant pleads guilty or no contest at the time of the arraignment, the court has the option of imposing sentence at that time or of delaying sentence until a presentence investigation is conducted.

Bail
Bail is the posting of a security, usually cash, to assure the defendant's presence in court at a later date, usually at an arraignment or trial. The amount of bail is set by the court and will depend on several factors, including: past criminal history, the severity and nature of the crime, and the likelihood the defendant

will flee to avoid prosecution. Courts are not obligated to set bail and may keep the defendant in jail until the trial, if convinced that the defendant will forfeit any amount of posted bail to avoid trial.

Once bail is set, most defendants will be released by depositing 10 percent of the total amount of bail with the clerk of the court. This is called a *regular bond.* A *cash bond* requires the entire amount of the bail money be posted before the defendant is released. When the case is concluded, either at conviction or acquittal, the bail money will be returned to the defendant, provided that all court appearances are made.

Preliminary Hearings and Motions

In some areas, a felony case requires a *preliminary hearing* to determine whether enough evidence exists to proceed to trial, usually in a higher court. The preliminary hearing is typically conducted by a court of lower jurisdiction and serves to determine whether reasonable grounds exist that the defendant committed the crime.

The defendant may file various motions prior to the trial date. The bulk of these motions will deal with the suppression of evidence based on what the defendant believes were illegal or improper methods of obtaining evidence or making the arrest. The basis of these types of pretrial motions will be discussed in the section regarding the individual rights of the criminally accused.

Trial

In most criminal cases, the defendant can request a jury trial. As previously mentioned, the jury, as the finder of fact and determiner of guilt, must conclude beyond a reasonable doubt that the defendant is guilty before it can enter such a verdict.

The judge will instruct the jury that, depending on how it interprets the evidence, it may enter different degrees of guilt. For instance, after listening to the facts of a particular case, the jury may be instructed to find the defendant guilty of either first-degree murder, second-degree murder, manslaughter or not guilty.

In some instances, the defendant may waive his right to a jury trial. Depending on the nature of the crime charged, the defendant must determine whether a trial only to a judge, as opposed to a jury, would be more beneficial to him.

Appeal

After a verdict is rendered against the defendant, he has a specific period of time to file an appeal. The appeal must outline particular legal reasons why the defense believes the guilty verdict was improperly rendered. Appellate courts will generally defer to the trial court judge or juries regarding interpretation of facts. The criminal defendant's right to appeal will be reviewed later in the chapter.

Postconviction Relief

Many states have different types of postconviction relief laws that allow convicted criminals serving prison time to formally request judicial relief of their situation. This request must be based either on some element of law not complied with at their trial or possibly some issue that has arisen since the trial. An example would be the discovery of new and pertinent evidence proving the defendant's innocence. A convicted defendant may bring an application for postconviction relief at any time after conviction. After receiving such a request, the court will determine whether it requires a formal hearing on the matter.

Grand Jury

A grand jury is composed of a specific number of citizens selected by the sheriff or other local authority to determine whether a crime has been committed. The grand jury is under oath and instructed by the court to proceed accordingly. This group will receive complaints, hear evidence presented on behalf of the state, and possibly file a criminal complaint or indictment in situations where they are convinced that certain criminal charges require a trial. If the grand jury determines there is no probable cause for the existence or commission of a crime, no indictments or complaints are issued.

SEARCH AND SEIZURE

The Fourth Amendment to the U.S. Constitution states that "the right of the people to be secure in their persons, houses, papers and effects, against unreasonable searches and seizures, shall not be violated, and no warrants shall issue, but upon cause, supported by oath or affirmation, and particularly describing the place to be searched, and the persons or things to be seized."

This means that every U.S. citizen has the right of privacy and security in his home, his person and personal property against any unwarranted searches or intrusions by government officials. The Fourth Amendment is applicable to all the states through the Fourteenth Amendment to the Constitution. Most state constitutions also contain prohibitions against unreasonable searches and seizures.

Even if the unlawful search should turn up incriminating evidence or illegal property, this does not validate the circumstances of an otherwise unlawful search. Any evidence obtained by an unlawful search is inadmissible in court.

Exclusionary Rule

Again, evidence obtained by unlawful search and seizure is not admissible against the accused in a criminal prosecution case. This is known as the *exclusionary rule*. The U.S. Supreme Court has ruled that any evidence obtained by a search and seizure in violation of the Fourth Amendment is inadmissible in state, as well as federal, courts.

If an otherwise unlawful search or seizure is made by a private citizen as opposed to a public official or employee, evidence obtained by the search or seizure is not necessarily inadmissible by application of the exclusionary rule. Also, if no state law is violated, any evidence obtained by letter interception, telephone or telegraph message interception, or by eavesdropping, is not necessarily inadmissible. The courts have ruled that the Fourth Amendment does not prohibit the unreasonable search and seizure of these types of communications and, accordingly, any evidence obtained in this manner may be used in prosecuting criminal cases.

It should be noted that the Federal Communications Act has been interpreted to require the exclusion of evidence intercepted by telephone or telegraph taps, but does not affect the admissibility of evidence obtained by eavesdropping through electronic or mechanical devices not involved in wiretapping. The exclusionary rule will not apply in circumstances where one of the parties in the communication has consented to the eavesdropping or wiretapping.

Search Warrant

In most cases, a search by a police officer will be considered unreasonable unless it has been authorized by a *search warrant*. A search warrant is a written order issued by a judge or judicial magistrate directing the sheriff or police officer to search and seize any property that may constitute evidence regarding the commission of a crime or the fruits of a crime. A search warrant is also used to take into custody any property designed for criminal use or for the commission of a crime. The warrant may be issued on affidavit or sworn oral testimony by a witness.

Warrantless Searches and Arrests

A search of an arrested person without a warrant is permitted if the search does not extend beyond the person of the accused and the area to which the accused might reach to grab a weapon or other potential evidentiary items. Generally, a police officer, following a lawful arrest, will have the right to search the defendant and his personal effects, including the defendant's automobile, if he is arrested while in it.

A police officer may arrest anyone if he has a warrant for their arrest or if he sees them violate the law. A police officer may also make an arrest without a warrant if he has sufficient reason to believe that he is arresting the same person who committed a crime, even if the arresting officer was not present when the original crime was committed. Thus, a search warrant is not required under the Fourteenth Amendment to the Constitution for a search or seizure following a valid arrest. Several court decisions have, however, limited this rule to an arrest for minor traffic violations. Further, a search that is consented to by the owner of the premises negates the necessity of a warrant.

Probable Cause

A warrant is also unnecessary in cases where the arresting officers have *probable cause* for the search and seizure or where certain "exigent" circumstances make it highly difficult or impossible to obtain a warrant.

Probable cause exists when the facts and circumstances give the arresting officer reason to believe that a crime is being committed or has just been committed.

The implementation of the probable cause exception to obtaining a warrant prior to a valid search and seizure is couched in factual considerations depending on the day-to-day situations of the arresting officers and potential criminals.

Reasonable Arresting Force

If the criminally accused resists a lawful arrest, the police can use all reasonable force necessary to make the arrest. Once the accused has been physically restrained, however, no further force is allowed to subdue the defendant.

Due Process Rights

The due process clauses of the Constitution protect the fundamental rights of a defendant in a criminal case. *Due process* means that all criminal prosecutions will be within the realm of fundamental principals of liberty and justice inherent in American law.

Generally speaking, the base requirements of due process are as follows:

- Reasonable and timely notification of the criminal charges against the accused
- Adequate and fair opportunity to defend against criminal charges
- Fair and impartial tribunal to decide the issues of fact in the case
- Opportunity for the defendant to present his side of the case within the confines of a fair hearing or trial
- Adequate protection against any coerced confession or testimony of the defendant
- Right to examine and confront all adverse witnesses
- Right to be represented by an attorney

Understand that these basic due process requirements do not mean that all criminal prosecutions must be without fault, or that the trial be procedurally perfect. Rather, if these fundamental rights are protected in a fair and adequate manner, due process considerations will be satisfied.

Rights and Appeal. When a convicted criminal contends or believes he was convicted by fundamentally unfair methods, due process requires that the right of appeal be made available for the defendant to obtain a remedy.

False or Suppressed Evidence. Other violations of due process include the use of false or perjured testimony by the prosecution, or a suppression or withholding of material evidence by the prosecution that could prove the defendant innocent.

Jury Consideration. In many states, the defendant in a criminal case has the right to have the jury *polled*. This means that the defendant (or his attorney) may ask each juror his individual finding. This procedure is designed to assure that a unanimous verdict has, in fact, been reached and that no one juror has been coerced or threatened to agree to a guilty verdict.

One of the cornerstones of the American criminal justice system is that every person accused of a crime is entitled to the benefit of the doubt; he will be presumed innocent until proven guilty beyond a reasonable doubt. Most jury instructions in a criminal case will provide that if the jury has a reasonable doubt of the defendant's guilt, no verdict of guilty shall be rendered.

Confession. As a general rule, any confession obtained under the influence of fear (whether of bodily harm, torture, personal violence or abuse of a family member) or by promising a reward or hope of immunity from the charges involved, will constitute a confession obtained by involuntary means and the confession will be excluded as evidence. If a defendant's confession is not obtained from a rational mind or a free will, it will be inadmissible and deemed coerced, regardless of whether the coercion consists of physical intimidation or psychological tactics.

Recognize, however, that if an otherwise admissible confession is made while the defendant is under arrest, and the arrest is illegal, this does not necessarily make the confession inadmissible. The circumstances of the custody or arrest may be taken into consideration by the court in determining whether or not the confession was given voluntarily. Although prolonged questioning in and of itself does not make a confession involuntary, a prolonged and unremitting interrogation process combined with any type of deprivation of rest, food or other physical comforts, may reach the level of coercion and cause the confession to be ruled inadmissible.

Miranda Rights

In the case of *Miranda v. the State of Arizona*, the U.S. Supreme Court ruled that arrested individuals must be advised of their constitutional rights when arrested. Without the "feeding of the rights" to the arrested party, any evidence or information obtained after the arrest may not be admissible in court.

The Miranda ruling provides that, prior to any questioning of a person in custody or under arrest, the person must be advised that he has the following rights:

- To remain silent
- That any statement that he makes may be used against him
- That he has the right to the presence of an attorney, and if he cannot afford one, one may be appointed for him
- That the opportunities to exercise these rights are afforded him throughout the interrogation process

The arrested person must be asked if he understands these rights. These rights may be waived and the defendant may proceed with answering any questions or making a statement to the authorities as he so chooses. However, the prosecution bears the burden of showing that the Miranda rights were effectively delivered to the defendant, and that the defendant indicated that he understood these rights prior to the introduction of any evidence obtained after arrest.

The rules of Miranda come into play only with the interrogation of criminal suspects. It does not affect the admissibility of any statement that may be volunteered by another person, or information that is furnished without formal questioning or requests by authorities.

Motion to Suppress

If the defendant believes that evidence was obtained due to an unlawful search or seizure, or rendered by the defendant prior to the effective communication of his Miranda rights, a *motion to suppress* the evidence will be made. It will then become the duty of the court to conduct an evidentiary hearing and rule on this motion prior to proceeding to trial. A copy of a typical motion to suppress is located in the appendix. Often, if the motion to suppress is sustained (upheld), the prosecution will not proceed with its case because the necessary evidence to prove its case has been ruled inadmissible.

Fair Trial

As previously stated, one of the fundamental rights of criminal due process is that every individual charged with a crime has a right to a fair and impartial trial. In essence, a fair trial involves an impartial judge and an honest jury, without the presence of a hostile crowd that may improperly pressure prospective witnesses or the jurors themselves. Also, adverse pretrial publicity has sometimes been held as sufficient to cause denial of a fair trial. Also involved in the right to a fair trial is the right of the defendant to have a reasonable amount of time to prepare his defense, produce witnesses, and so on.

Speedy Trial

A criminal defendant's right to a *speedy trial* is secured by the Sixth Amendment to the Constitution and is also provided for in most state constitutions. A speedy trial is generally defined as one free of oppressive or unreasonable delays that might keep the defendant incarcerated or may prejudice the defendant by not allowing him to use evidence that is sensitive to the passage of time. The defendant does not have the right to demand a trial immediately upon arrest, as the prosecution is also allowed a reasonable amount of time to prepare its case for trial. Of course, if the defendant continues to move for delays in the trial date, he cannot later complain that his right to a speedy trial was violated.

Generally, to invoke the right to a speedy trial, the defendant will have to motion the court for a trial date. Otherwise, he is implying acquiescence to the trial date that is eventually set by the prosecution. Unless the defendant makes some effort to secure a speedier trial than the state will otherwise provide him, he cannot later complain that he was denied his right to a speedy trial.

Public Trial

Along with a speedy trial, the criminal defendant is also entitled to a public trial. Under certain circumstances, the denial of a public trial may violate the requirement of due process of law governing criminal procedure.

What is and is not a public trial is open to interpretation, depending on the jurisdiction. Some courts have held that a public trial is a trial the public is free to attend. Other courts have held that a public trial means only that it is not secret. Generally, if a reasonable proportion of the public is allowed to attend the trial, without particular favoritism or screening, the right to a public trial is upheld. This does not mean that an unlimited number of spectators need to be present throughout the trial. Rather, the limitation of spectators to the trial will be within the trial court's discretion.

Presence at Trial

A criminal defendant has a right to be present at his trial. When this right is denied, the defendant does not necessarily have to show any actual injury or prejudice to have his conviction overturned.

The right of a defendant to be present at all stages of his trial, including any substantive preliminary hearings, applies in all felony cases. The courts have ruled differently in misdemeanor cases to the necessity of the presence of the defendant throughout the trial process. Also, court decisions have been inconsistent in determining whether a defendant can waive his right to be present throughout the trial procedure.

Right to an Attorney

A criminally accused defendant is also guaranteed, by the Sixteenth Amendment, the right to be heard and assisted by an attorney in defense of the charges against him.

The criminal defendant is always allowed to represent himself; however, if he cannot afford an attorney and he desires to have legal representation, the court will appoint him an attorney at no cost. The court must be satisfied that the defendant cannot afford an attorney before such an appointment is made.

Generally, the defendant is entitled to the assistance of his attorney at all preliminary stages and hearings, from arraignment through trial and appeal. He also has the right to have an attorney present at any police lineup, where the victim or a witness identifies the defendant.

The accused can waive his right to an attorney. This waiver must be made intelligently, understandingly and competently, without pressure or coercion. There has to be some type of affirmative statement or action on behalf of the defendant to waive his right to an attorney. The mere failure to request an attorney does not constitute a valid and effective waiver.

The court is not responsible for appointing the specific attorney requested by the defendant. The court must only be satisfied that the attorney assigned to the defendant has the ability and experience to represent him effectively. If the defendant's court-appointed attorney is so incompetent that the trial, as a whole, has not effectively protected the defendant's rights, the conviction may be declared invalid as an invasion of the defendant's constitutional right to have legal representation.

In an appeal, an indigent defendant will be entitled, upon request, to have an attorney appointed to him to allow for an appeal of his conviction.

Nature of the Charge

An individual accused of a crime is constitutionally entitled to be informed of the nature of the crime with which he is charged. Most states require the prosecution to provide the defendant with a written copy of the indictment or complaint filed against him, indicating the factual basis for the particular crime and the specific law that was violated. In some states, the defendant is entitled to see a list of witnesses the prosecution intends to produce against him at trial or preliminary hearing.

Access to Evidence

A criminal defendant also has the constitutional right to speak with any persons having knowledge of the matters bearing on the case and to interview prospective witnesses who may assist him in his defense.

The defendant is not constitutionally entitled to inspect, before trial, any evidence that may be in the possession of the prosecution. Understand, however, that these rules have been liberalized in many states and the courts will often grant the defendant the right to inspect certain aspects of the evidence prior to trial.

Cross Examination

The constitution also guarantees the criminal defendant the right to be confronted by his accusers. This right is termed as the right of *cross examination*, which allows the defendant, usually through his attorney, to ask questions of any witnesses the prosecution may use to prove its case.

Generally, the right to be confronted by witnesses used against the defendant only pertains to the actual trial and not to any preliminary hearing to determine evidence admissibility. The defendant is ordinarily allowed to inspect any documents a witness may rely on during his testimony.

Self-Incrimination

The Fifth Amendment to the U.S. Constitution states that no person shall be compelled in any criminal case to be a witness against himself. Similarly, a criminally accused defendant cannot be forced to produce private papers or documents that may contain incriminating evidence. However, once the defendant has testified in his own defense, the prosecution can cross examine him on any matter he previously testified to. The prosecution may also question the defendant about any document that could have been produced at the time the defendant testified. Most states have similar provisions in their constitutions.

As a corollary to the right against self-incrimination, the prosecution cannot make any statement or comment to the jury about why the defendant is not testifying to prevent an inference that the defendant is guilty.

Most courts have ruled that it is not a violation of the defendant's right against self-incrimination to allow a third party, such as a scientist or physician, to testify to the results of a physical examination of the defendant, even if the examination is made without his consent. Thus, most courts do not consider it improper to require the defendant to submit to various scientific tests such as a blood analysis, urinalysis or breath test.

It is not a violation of the defendant's right against self-incrimination to require him to perform an act outside the court and have a third party witness testify to that act. A crimiinal suspect or defendant can be made to put on certain clothes, appear in a police lineup or even submit to a physical examination, including fingerprints or footprints, to allow third parties to determine whether the accused was, in fact, the party involved in a crime.

Trial Venue

One of the offshoots of a criminal defendant being afforded the right to a fair and impartial trial is the *venue* (location) of the trial. Most states have statutes that provide for the change of the location of the trial if there are local prejudices or publicity that may deny the accused a fair trial. Such a change would then be required to meet the ends of justice.

The prosecution may consent to a change of venue, or the defendant may motion the court for a change of venue based on his alleged inability to obtain a fair trial locally. The federal rules of criminal procedure also authorize the transfer of criminal cases from one district to another, with the consent of or at the defendant's request, within the discretion of the trial court based on the grounds previously mentioned.

PLEAS

A criminal defendant pleas to the court to the charges made against him. The court must afford the defendant an opportunity to plead, and if the defendant says nothing or indicates in no manner how he wishes to plead, the court will enter a plea of not guilty and direct the prosecution to proceed toward trial.

Not Guilty

When a defendant in a criminal case pleads *not guilty*, he is in essence denying every essential fact of the prosecution's case necessary to establish guilt. The issue of the defendant's guilt, and the necessary elements to establish guilt, must be proven beyond a reasonable doubt by the prosecution after a not guilty plea is made.

Guilty

When a defendant pleads *guilty* to the criminal charges against him, the court must be convinced that his guilty plea is made intelligently, knowingly and voluntarily. The guilty plea must not be made if it was induced by fear, promises or fraud.

Before accepting the plea of guilty, the court must determine that the defendant understands the consequences of the plea, including facts such as the maximum potential punishment involved. The court must also advise the defendant who pleads guilty of his specific constitutional rights, including the right to a jury trial, the right to a speedy and fair trial, the right to an attorney, the right to confront and cross examine witnesses, the right to call witnesses on his own behalf and the right to remain silent throughout the trial. In essence, an accepted plea of guilty by the court is a confession of guilt by the defendant and waives any potential defenses that the defendant may have.

No Contest

Sometimes a defendant will plead *nolo contendre*, which means *no contest* or that "I do not wish to contend the charges against me." It has the equivalent effect of a plea of guilty.

The main difference between a guilty plea and a no contest plea is that a plea of no contest to criminal charges cannot be used later as an admission of guilt in any other civil or criminal action. This is not true of a guilty plea. The potential sentence does not differ between a plea of no contest and a plea of guilty.

Withdrawal of a Plea

Unless a specific law or particular court rule indicates to the contrary, the trial court may allow a defendant to withdraw his plea in a criminal case. The trial court enjoys broad discretion in allowing the defendant to withdraw his plea. However, the criminal defendant is not constitutionally guaranteed a right to withdraw his plea, assuming that the plea was made within the confines of the aforementioned procedural rules.

Plea Bargain

When the defendant and the prosecution work out a mutually satisfactory disposition of the case, it is called a *plea bargain*. This will usually entail the defendant pleading guilty or no contest to a less severe offense than was originally charged. Plea bargains often become a necessity in dealing with a high volume of criminal cases.

PUNISHMENT AND SENTENCING

Generally, the parameters of the specific sentence or punishment for the conviction of a crime will rest with a state legislature or Congress. For most crimes, the applicable sentencing provision allows discretion by the court. It is generally the function of the jury to determine guilt or innocence, and the function of the trial judge to determine an appropriate sentence.

The Eighth Amendment to the U.S. Constitution prohibits the infliction of cruel and unusual punishment on a criminally convicted defendant. Many cases have dealt with the exactness and extent of these limitations, and these cases continue to unfold. Currently, the death penalty is not considered cruel and unusual punishment within federal constitutional law.

It should be noted that if a court imposes a particular sentence that is determined on appeal to be excessive or does not fall within the confines of applicable sentencing parameters, the sentencing can be modified, but the conviction itself will be upheld.

PROBATION, PAROLE AND PARDON

Probation

When a court sentences the defendant to *probation* after he is convicted of a crime, he is released into the community under the supervision of a probation officer. Generally, the person on probation is allowed a degree of freedom after his conviction, as opposed to jail time, subject to certain conditions prescribed by the court and monitored by the probation officer.

The defendant is usually required to report to his probation officer on a periodic basis to allow the probation officer to determine whether the terms of the probation are being met. If these terms and conditions are not met, the defendant will be required to surrender himself to the probation officer for further proceedings in court, usually a stricter or harsher sentence.

The court may require that the defendant attend various types of meetings (such as Alcoholics Anonymous) and refrain from specific types of activity or avoid certain establishments to abide by his probation.

Pardon

A *pardon* is a declaration that a defendant is relieved from any legal consequences of his alleged crime or conviction. It will also restore any lost rights to the convicted defendant, such as the right to vote, serve on a jury, or citizenship. State governors and the President have the power to grant pardons.

Parole

Parole is when a criminally convicted defendant is released from prison and placed under strict conditions that must be met during his term of parole. Parole does not vacate the conviction against the defendant or excuse the crime whatsoever. It only suspends the execution of the penalty involved and, at least temporarily, allows the defendant to avoid any imprisonment that the sentence mandated.

Similar to probation, parole involves supervising the defendant by an officer of the court — in this case a parole officer. The parole board or state correctional board will determine which prisoners are entitled to parole. Typically, the paroled criminal defendant must periodically report to his parole officer to allow him to determine if the terms of the parole are being complied with.

HABEAS CORPUS

Mention should also be made of the concept of *habeas corpus*, which covers a variety of procedures employed to attempt the release of a criminal defendant from allegedly unlawful imprisonment. In essence, the use of habeas corpus is not to determine a defendant's guilt or innocence, but to determine whether the conviction is invalid due to a violation of the defendant's constitutional rights, such as the coercion of a confession, the denial of a right to counsel, etc.

RIGHTS ON APPEAL

As already mentioned, the criminal right to appeal is not guaranteed under the due process laws of the U.S. Constitution. Generally, an appeal from the trial court must allege that certain irregularities or errors were committed by the court during or prior to the time of trial that denied the criminal defendant his constitutional rights. These errors or irregularities can include any procedural violations that affected the final verdict of guilty against him.

Due process laws provide that, in criminal cases, an appeal cannot be denied because of the defendant's inability to pay the expenses involved, including the cost of an attorney and various filing fees and court costs.

For a criminal conviction to be reversed on appeal, the alleged errors at the trial court level must have been prejudicial to the defendant. The defendant must prove that the verdict would, in all likelihood, have been different if not for the particular error. In essence, the defendant is entitled to a fair, but not perfect, trial and mere technical errors that do not deny substantial rights of the defendant will not constitute grounds for an overturn of a conviction.

The types of errors alleged by a criminal defendant on appeal generally involve the wrongful admission of evidence or the erroneous instruction of the jury to the applicable law.

It should be noted that in murder cases the appellate court will generally review the trial court record with meticulous prudence for the possibility of prejudicial error, as opposed to technical error. Only when prejudicial error is found, however, will there be a potential basis to overturn a conviction.

Chapter Five

Consumer Contracts, Credit and Bankruptcy

Let all the learned say what they can, 'tis ready money makes the man.
— *William Somerville*

It is one thing to have a right to the possession of money, and another to have a right to use money as one pleases.
— *Pope Leo XIII*

This chapter will review the various types of contracts most typically entered into between consumers and merchants. The different types and effects of these contracts and the warranties and liabilities that apply will be discussed. Also included is a review of the laws governing credit billing and credit reporting, as well as equal credit opportunity laws. Finally, debt collection laws and bankruptcy will be discussed.

CONSUMER CONTRACTS

A consumer contract is a legally binding agreement in which property, goods or services are provided in exchange for money or something else of value. A consumer purchase is considered a contract even though a formal written agreement may not be executed. When a consumer purchases an item, an implied contract is created. The merchant is agreeing to provide the consumer with the product being sold, and the consumer is providing the merchant with the purchase price or a promise to pay. By selling the product, the merchant is making either an express or implied warranty regarding the condition of the product.

Credit Purchases and Conditional Sales Contracts

In certain instances, the consumer will not have enough cash to make a purchase or will prefer to make periodic payments toward the total purchase price. If a major item of personal property is purchased on a time payment plan, the consumer is entering into what is called a *conditional sales agreement* or *contract*.

A conditional sales contract, also known as a *retail installment sales contract*, occurs when the merchant retains a security interest in the item being purchased. The buyer will take possession of the merchandise and promise to make periodic payments until the purchase price, including any interest and finance charges, is paid in full. While the buyer has possession of the merchandise, and the seller is still owed money, the seller retains a security interest in the merchandise. Hence, during the time of the contract, the buyer has a possessory interest and the merchant has a security interest in the merchandise.

In most states, the execution of this type of conditional or retail installment sales contract in consumer goods will automatically create a security interest between the merchant and the buyer. If the merchandise is not considered consumer goods, the contract must be recorded in a local public office to create a security interest. The effect of a security interest if the buyer defaults will be discussed in the section concerning collection procedures and remedies.

Most conditional sales contracts outline what the buyer will be paying in interest over the life of the contract. Local laws dictate the maximum allowable interest and finance charges. Interest rates in these types of contracts are fairly high due to the inherent risk the merchant takes in parting with the merchandise prior to payment of the total purchase price.

Uniform Commercial Code

The Uniform Commercial Code is a body of law currently adopted in forty-nine of the fifty states. Its purpose is to clarify and simplify the laws governing commercial sales transactions. Many transactions between merchants and consumers are governed by section two of the Uniform Commercial Code regarding written contracts for the sale of merchandise for $500 or more. The Uniform Commercial Code also applies to any sales transaction intended to create a security interest in personal property, including goods, documents, contract rights, etc.

CO-SIGNING AND PERSONAL GUARANTEES

There are other ways to become liable for a debt without being the actual purchaser. Co-signing a note or purchase agreement, whether a conditional sales contract or otherwise, is one way of becoming liable for the debt involved.

Co-Signer

A *co-signer* is an individual who obliges himself legally to make payments and other requirements of a purchase contract. The co-signer is just as responsible as the individual who makes the purchase and receives the merchandise. Not receiving the merchandise makes the co-signer no less liable for the underlying debt.

Any co-signer on a promissory note or purchase agreement needs to be aware of these inherent risks and potential liabilities. The decision to co-sign for an obligation should be based on his personal knowledge and confidence of the other co-signer's financial responsibility and ability to pay off the obligation.

Guarantees

A person who guarantees an obligation of another is called a *guarantor*. A guarantor is not the same thing as a co-signer. Generally, the guarantee must be in writing to be enforceable. Some states have exceptions to this rule.

Types of Guarantees. The liability of a guarantor on a consumer purchase agreement will depend on the terms of the guarantee. The guarantee may be limited, contingent or total. A *guarantee of payment* on a consumer purchase contract creates an absolute liability on the guarantor to pay the debt of the individual who originally signed the agreement. The original signer is known as the *principal*.

A *guarantee of collection* provides that the creditor must exhaust all remedies against the principal debtor before looking to the guarantor for payment, unless it is possible for the creditor to show that such efforts would be futile because the primary debtor is insolvent.

Defenses to Guarantee Liability. A guarantor to a consumer purchase agreement may have certain legal defenses. If the merchant has expressly or implicitly released the principal debtor from his obligation to make payments under the contract, the guarantor will also be released from any further liability.

A merchant will usually have the duty to disclose to a guarantor all facts that may materially increase the risk the creditor intends to assume. This would include any secret arrangements between the merchant and the principal debtor or any information on the financial condition of the principal debtor unknown to the guarantor.

A guarantor may terminate the effect of his guarantee by written notification to the merchant. This notice will only relieve him of any liability for future debts incurred by the principal debtor, as opposed to existing debts covered by the guarantee.

THIRD PARTY LIABILITY

This next section will cover situations when an individual can become liable for the debts of another, despite the lack of a formal agreement to do so.

Spousal Liability

Most states make one spouse liable for consumer debt purchases made by the other that constitute *necessaries of life*, even though one spouse was unaware that the purchases were made. This may prove true even if the spouse or other members of the family did not receive any direct benefit from the purchases.

Necessaries of Life. Often the particular issue involved regarding spousal liability is what constitutes *necessaries of life*. In general, necessaries of life will include food, board, lodging, clothing, utility articles, medical services, the children's educational requirements, and so on. In most situations, unless the spouses are formally separated or legally divorced, the obligation and liability of one spouse for the other spouse's purchases for necessaries of life will continue.

Spousal Agency Liability. Another theory of liability between spouses involves the concept of *agency* — a legal theory where one person acts for and on behalf of another. The law of agency for spousal purchases of consumer goods assumes that one spouse is always acting as an agent for the other. Consequently, any purchases made by the agent spouse for the principal spouse can potentially bind both to the liability involved.

Dependent Minor Liability

The question sometimes arises whether a minor can be held liable under consumer contracts for purchases made. Unless a statute indicates differently, any consumer contract entered into by a minor is avoidable and cannot be enforced as long as the minor remains under age. However, if a minor enters into a contract to purchase consumer goods when he is seventeen years old, retains possession of the goods until age eighteen (at which time he becomes an adult), and makes payments under the contract but later defaults, in all likelihood that contract can be upheld in court because the former minor *ratified the contract* after he became an adult. If that same individual had stopped making payments at the time he became an adult, and the creditor tried to enforce the contract, the minor would probably not be held liable for the debt.

Parental Liability

The issue also arises of when a parent can be held liable for the debts of his minor child. As a general rule, if the minor makes purchases for necessaries of life that are not otherwise being provided for by his parents, the parents may be held responsible for these purchases. This is based on a law that requires parents to provide their children with the necessaries of life.

So, if the parents fail to provide their children with the necessaries of life, and a merchant enters into a contract with a minor to sell such goods or services, and the minor defaults, the parents may be held responsible. The merchant must prove that the parents have refused or neglected to provide for the minor child before the parents can be held liable.

If a minor signs a purchase agreement for merchandise and does not make the required payments, the merchant may still repossess the merchandise. The minor could not, however, be held liable for any money owed under the terms of the contract.

UNSOLICITED SALES

Often a purchase will be made by a consumer as a result of door-to-door or telephone sales. There is nothing inherently illegal about these types of sales techniques; however, many laws recognize that certain companies use high-pressure sales tactics and grandiose statements of discounts and bargains to convince customers to purchase things that they may not truly desire or be able to afford.

Three-Day Cancellation Period

Certain federal regulations give the consumer protection from unsolicited sales. Most consumers will have three calendar days to cancel a contract for the purchase of consumer goods that is signed through a door-to-door sale. This is true even if the sale involves a service as opposed to a product. However, the sale must be for at least $25 and may not take place on the merchant's premises. The sale must also be in *interstate commerce* — the sale or merchandise affects more than one state's commercial or economic activity.

The salesperson in an unsolicited sale must give the consumer a written explanation of his three-day cancellation right. If the consumer cancels the transaction within three days, the merchant is required to return any money that was given at the time of the sale.

If a consumer agrees to a sale during an unsolicited telephone call, the facts of the sale may dictate whether the transaction can later be canceled. Usually it will depend on the type of sale involved, the technique used and the merchandise sold. Often, the salesman will record the conversation to provide that an agreement was entered into. The salesman must tell the buyer the conversation is being recorded.

The Federal Trade Commission, an administrative branch of the federal government, adopted the law that makes it illegal for merchants to deny a consumer three days to cancel a home-solicited sale. It is presumed that a sale conducted in the buyer's home is particularly susceptible to high-pressure sales techniques. Two requirements for a three-day right of cancellation exists: There must be a personal solicitation at the buyer's residence, and the buyer must agree to the purchase at his residence.

CREDIT CARDS

A credit card provides another method of buying goods or services without paying the entire purchase price at the time of sale.

A credit card may be issued by a bank, department store or other merchant to allow the merchant to loan money to make purchases. The interest rates charged for such a loan, including any annual service charges or fees, are often regulated by law. The issuer of the credit card must inform the consumer in writing of the conditions of the credit arrangement, including the annual interest rate billing error procedures.

If a consumer's credit card is lost or stolen, he may be liable for a portion of any unauthorized purchases. Once the credit card company or creditor is notified of the theft or loss of the card, any unauthorized purchases will not be the liability of the credit card holder.

Under most circumstances, the maximum amount a consumer will be responsible for on any unauthorized charges on a credit card is $50. This limitation is provided for by the Federal Truth in Lending Laws, which will be discussed later in this chapter.

If a credit card is used by a third party without the permission of the credit card holder, and the credit card holder does not wish to pay for these purchases, the credit card issuer will request that the card holder sign a document indicating that the purchases were made without his permission. Once this document is signed, the credit card issuer can collect the debt from the individual who actually made the purchases.

If an individual receives a credit card he did not request, he is not liable for any use of that card unless the card is expressly accepted by him or if he proceeds to use it. If the consumer who receives an unsolicited credit card fails to destroy or return it, he will not automatically be responsible for any charges made by other individuals.

It is illegal for credit card issuers to send a consumer a credit card unless he requested it or otherwise agreed to receive one. However, a credit card issuer may send, without request, a new card to replace an existing one.

If a consumer loses his debit bank card (used to make automatic cash withdrawals), he may be able to limit subsequent losses stemming from an unauthorized withdrawal. If the consumer contacts the bank within two business days from the date the card was lost or stolen, he is liable for a maximum of $50. If the consumer notifies the bank after two days, but before sixty

·days, the maximum liability increases to $500. After sixty days there is no liability cap, and the card holder is responsible for all money withdrawn from the account.

WARRANTIES

A *warranty* for merchandise is a promise by the seller to be responsible for any damages caused by false assurances made about the condition of the property sold. A warranty is usually considered part of the contract for sale and may be either express or implied, written or oral.

Express or Implied Warranties

When a seller guarantees or specifically promises the condition of the product sold, or assures the buyer of the product's performance, an *express warranty* is created.

An express warranty may exist even without the seller using the term warranty, depending on the facts and conditions of the sale. An *implied warranty* generally is created by operation of law, even though the seller did not intend to create a warranty. For most situations concerning consumer contracts, the existence of a warranty is more important than whether the warranty is implied or expressed.

Magnuson-Moss Act

The Magnuson-Moss Act created an entire body of federal law covering consumer warranties. This act applies only to consumer products that cost $15 or more for which a written warranty is supplied by the seller.

Under Magnuson-Moss, the seller is not required to give the buyer any type of written warranty. However, if the seller does provide a written warranty for the merchandise, the following information must be included:

- Who is entitled to the protection of the warranty
- Identification of all the parts covered by the warranty
- Statement of remedies for correcting defects or failures, including the financial responsibilities of the seller and the consumer
- Effective date of the warranty (unless it is the date of purchase)

- Steps the consumer must follow to obtain performance under the warranty

As previously stated, the Magnuson-Moss Act will apply only to consumer products. Generally, this is defined as any type of personal property typically used by a family or household. Commercial or industrial products are not governed by Magnuson-Moss.

Uniform Commercial Code Warranties

As already mentioned, the Uniform Commercial Code is a body of law enacted by most states in various forms to provide rights and remedies between sellers and buyers. The Uniform Commercial Code also contains certain warranty provisions.

Any time a sale is transacted for $500 or more, the merchant is providing the buyer, by law, a *warranty of merchantability*. This, in essence, means that the merchandise must be acceptable for the purpose for which it was designed. The seller can conspicuously exclude this implied warranty of merchantability in writing at the time of sale.

The *warranty of fitness for a particular purpose* is another type of implied warranty provided for by the Uniform Commercial Code. Under this type of warranty, if the merchant knows of any particular purpose for which the merchandise is going to be used, and if the buyer is relying on the merchant's judgment or skills when he purchases the product, the seller legally warrants that the merchandise will be fit for the intended purpose.

As with the warranty of merchantability, a warranty of fitness for a particular purpose may be avoided by conspicuous language excluding all implied warranties. A statement such as the following will suffice: "No warranties exist that extend beyond the description of the product itself."

Generally, no warranty is offered when certain language is placed on the product. If the purchase agreement indicates or the product itself states that it is being sold, *as is*, or *with all faults*, no warranty would exist. A statement in the purchase agreement indicating that the buyer has examined the product or has had ample opportunity to do so will further disclaim any warranty.

AUTOMOBILE LEMON LAWS

For most consumers, an automobile is one of the largest purchases they will make. Furthermore, the automobile is usually not considered a luxury but a necessity in today's society. With this in mind, almost all states have passed *lemon laws* that are enforced when an automobile owner repeatedly experiences substantial defects in his vehicle.

Lemon laws were created to provide protection to consumers who purchase or lease new and/or demonstrator automobiles from an authorized motor vehicle dealer. Most lemon laws will define consumer as the owner of a vehicle who uses it primarily for personal use.

Most lemon law provisions require that the alleged defects occur within a certain period of time from the date of purchase, usually between ten and fifteen thousand miles, or twelve months, whichever comes first. Also, the manufacturer and *not* the local dealer is always potentially liable for defects covered by lemon laws.

Generally speaking, lemon laws are applied when the vehicle suffers a substantial defect subjected to four or more unsuccessful repair attempts, or if the vehicle is out of service for a total of thirty or more days during the protection period.

A substantial defect greatly impairs the use, safety or value of the vehicle. To determine if the defect involved is substantial, the following factors are considered:

- Repair costs
- Number of attempts to repair the vehicle (including the amount of time taken to repair the vehicle)
- Consumer's loss of confidence in the vehicle
- Type of defect involved (The more serious or vital the defect, the greater chance the lemon law will apply.)

Some lemon laws require that the consumer give formal notice of the invocation of the lemon laws to allow one additional opportunity for the dealer or manufacturer to correct the defect. Procedurally, once a lemon law action is started, the owner of the vehicle and the manufacturer present their respective cases to an impartial third party who makes a decision based on the evidence. Many states have their own arbitration process, while others use arbitration programs comprised of private citizens. If the consumer loses his case at the arbitration level, he may file a lawsuit against the manufacturer for lemon law violations.

Available defenses by the manufacturer to a lemon law claim include any abuse, neglect or unauthorized modification of the vehicle. It is not a defense for the dealer to claim he had to wait for a particular part and the delay caused the vehicle to be out of service for more than the prerequisite thirty days. If the consumer received a loaner vehicle at no cost during the time of repair, the calculation period is not affected.

Almost all state lemon laws provide for either a new or comparable vehicle replacement for the defective one or a refund of the purchase price if the consumer wins. Some states allow the manufacturer to choose compensation; others require the consumer choose replacement or refund. If a lawsuit is required, some lemon laws allow recovery of attorney fees and court costs, and may even award double or triple damages against the manufacturer if the consumer should prevail.

Aside from a lemon law violation, other legal actions may be brought against the vehicle manufacturer, including a claim under the Magnuson-Moss Warranty Act, or a claim under the Uniform Commercial Code for breach of express or implied warranty. Neither the Magnuson-Moss Warranty Act nor Uniform Commercial Code provisions contain clear-cut guidelines for determining warranty violations. In contrast, the lemon laws provide a precise determination for when a violation by the manufacturer has occurred and, accordingly, may be the preferred remedy for a consumer who believes that he did not get what he bargained for.

INTEREST RATES AND USURY LAWS

When a consumer borrows money or is extended credit by a merchant, the merchant will charge interest on the unpaid balance. Most states have laws governing the maximum amount of interest that may be charged.

Usury Laws

Usury laws regulate interest rate charges. A usurious loan's interest rates are determined to be in excess of those permitted by law.

Most states will have several different types of interest rates that may be charged, depending on the type of sale and whether it is consumer oriented. For example, the law places a ceiling on the interest rate a consumer and a merchant agree may be charged for any unpaid balance. Some states, however, have no limit on an agreed upon contractual rate of interest. Obviously, local provisions will govern in this regard.

Violation of Usury Laws

Generally, the penalty for charging usurious interest is the forfeiture of all interest paid to date, or the forfeiture of the right to collect any interest on the remaining principal balance. Other states legally cancel the contract that contains interest rates beyond the maximum rate allowed.

Some state laws mandate that if the consumer has paid interest at a rate beyond the maximum allowed, he may recover double the amount of all interest paid, including any attorney fees or costs involved. Also, criminal penalties may be brought for charging usurious interest. If a consumer believes he is being charged interest above the legal rate, he may consult with an attorney or contact the consumer affairs division of his attorney general's office to learn if the interest rate complies with local usury laws.

TRUTH IN LENDING LAWS

Truth in lending laws are a body of federal regulations that covers credit transactions, advertising, billing and consumer leases. Also included in the truth in lending laws is *Regulation Z*, which covers the determination of finance charges, annual percentage rates when granting credit, and general requirements regarding disclosure to a potential borrower. Regulation Z emphasizes that the issuer of credit must disclose to the potential borrower certain ramifications of the loan before the contract is signed.

Generally, truth in lending laws will cover all consumer-related installment sales that involve four or more payments. As mentioned, the cornerstone of the truth in lending laws, and specifically Regulation Z, is disclosure. Before the extension of credit can occur, the consumer must be made aware of all finance charges, and the annual percentage rate of any interest charged. Once disclosure has occurred, theoretically the consumer is in a position to intelligently decide whether to enter into the contract.

Truth in lending laws also apply to any advertising for consumer credit. All published advertisements, including radio and television commercials, must include applicable finance charges and interest rates.

If truth in lending laws are violated, civil damages may be awarded against the creditor or merchant involved. Recognize, however, that the creditor may have a defense to a truth in lending law violation if he can show that the violation was unintentional and the result of honest error.

Certain transactions are not covered by truth in lending laws: transactions extending credit for business, commercial or agricultural purposes. The truth in lending laws apply to banks, savings and loans, retail and department stores, credit card issuers, automobile dealers, credit unions, consumer finance companies, mortgage bankers, and individuals who may perform services (doctors, plumbers or dentists) if these service-oriented providers extend credit as part of their billing system.

In sum, the primary function of the truth in lending laws is to act as a disclosure mechanism so consumers shopping for credit can effectively compare terms and conditions. Finance charges and annual percentage rates must be made in a clear and conspicuous fashion to give the consumer notice of the consequences of the credit being extended.

EQUAL CREDIT OPPORTUNITY ACT

In 1975 the federal government created and passed the Equal Credit Opportunity Act prohibiting discrimination against credit applicants based on certain illegal criteria.

The purpose of the Equal Credit Opportunity Act is to require that lenders extend credit and make credit available to all credit worthy customers, and not make credit available on a discriminatory basis. The act prohibits discrimination in extending credit on the basis of race, color, religion, national origin, sex or marital status. Also, the act prohibits credit discrimination based on an applicant receiving public income (such as veteran benefits, welfare or social security).

The Equal Credit Opportunity Act further provides that any of the abovementioned discriminatory classes or reasons cannot be used to discourage an individual from applying for a loan.

The Equal Credit Opportunity Act applies to all creditors who regularly provide or arrange for extending credit. This would include banks, finance companies, department stores, credit card issuers, loan brokers, and so on.

The creditor cannot use age as a basis for a credit decision. As provided for in the Equal Credit Opportunity Act, a creditor may ask the age of the applicant to determine whether he is old enough to enter into a binding contract. But the creditor cannot refuse credit solely on the basis of age nor ignore any type of retirement income in determining the applicant's financial ability to repay the loan or credit extended.

The general rule under the Equal Credit Opportunity Act is that an individual may not be denied credit because of their sex, or because they are married, single, widowed, divorced or legally separated. In most situations, the creditor may not ask the sex of the applicant applying for credit. Moreover, the creditor may not inquire about any type of birth control devices or whether the applicant plans to have children.

The creditor must take into consideration all sources of income, including part-time employment. Alimony and child support are primary sources of income for some applicants, but these do not have to be disclosed unless the applicant wants them considered as part of the credit application. A creditor may not inquire of a female applicant information regarding her husband or ex-husband when she is applying for credit based solely on her own income. Of course, if one or all of the source of income is alimony or child support or separate maintenance payments from an ex-spouse, this type of information may be allowed.

The Equal Credit Opportunity Act also requires creditors to inform applicants of the decision made on the application within thirty days after the creditor has received the completed application. If credit has been denied, the creditor must notify the applicant in writing of the denial and advise the applicant that he has a right to know why the application was denied. An exception to this rule exists if the creditor receives less than 150 credit applications in the previous calendar year.

A creditor who violates any provisions of the Equal Credit Opportunity Act may be subject to a penalty of up to $10,000, plus any actual damages that the applicant is able to prove. If a class action is brought against creditors who are in violation of the Equal Credit Opportunity Act, the liability may not exceed

$500,000 or one percent of the creditor's net worth (whichever is less), in addition to the aggrieved applicant's court costs and attorney fees.

FAIR CREDIT REPORTING ACT

Another of the truth in lending laws is the Fair Credit Reporting Act, which provides that a consumer who is turned down for credit is entitled to receive the name and address of the appropriate consumer reporting agency at the time of the denial. This allows the consumer access to credit information kept on him so that any misinformation in his file may be corrected. If credit is denied based on any information from a source other than a consumer reporting agency, the creditor must inform the consumer of his right to request the nature of the information within sixty days from the date of denial.

Regardless of whether adverse action was taken against the consumer, he will nevertheless have the right to learn the nature and substance of any information contained in his consumer reporting agency file. Understand, however, that under rulings made by the Federal Trade Commission, only the nature and substance of credit information must be provided to the consumer — the consumer is not necessarily entitled to receive a copy of the file.

The Fair Credit Reporting Act also requires that credit reporting agencies maintain reasonable procedures to assure that reports do not contain obsolete information and that only specified and qualified recipients, such as merchants or credit extenders, receive the information contained in their files.

FAIR CREDIT BILLING ACT

Also somewhat related to the law of lending is the Fair Credit Billing Act. This is a body of law that sets up various procedures and safeguards requiring creditors to promptly correct any billing mistakes in consumer transactions. Other aspects of the Fair Credit Billing Act allow a consumer to withhold credit card payments on defective goods or inadequate services purchased through the credit card procedure. The act also requires creditors to promptly credit all payments made under the credit card agreement.

If the credit card agreement allows that no finance or other interest charges accrue before a particular due date, the creditors must mail their statements at least fourteen days before the date payment is due. Further, the payments must be credited on the day they are actually received, as long as the payment instructions are followed and payment is made to the correct address. As mentioned previously, a consumer does not have to pay for any unauthorized charges after the credit card issuer is notified that the card has been lost or stolen.

DEBT COLLECTION AND COLLECTION LAWSUITS

If a consumer fails to make payments to a particular creditor, he will have several legal options, depending on the type of debt involved. The option chosen by the creditor will also depend on whether the debt is secured or unsecured.

Types of Debts

A *secured debt* uses some type of property as collateral to secure payments. If a large item of personal property is purchased on payments, such as a refrigerator or stove, the item itself will usually serve as collateral. The contract that gives the creditor security in the property will also give him the option of repossessing the property if the debt is not paid as agreed. Sometimes a creditor making a money loan to a consumer will require collateral as security for the loan. Again, if payments are not made as agreed, the creditor may be able to repossess the property and sell it to satisfy, in whole or in part, the debt.

An *unsecured* debt is owed to a creditor without any type of collateral as security. Examples of unsecured debts include utility bills, medical bills and credit card debts in which the merchant has not obtained a security interest in any item that has been purchased.

Breach of Peace

Generally, a creditor cannot *breach the peace* in taking possession of any collateral in pursuit of the collection of a secured debt. However, if the creditor has notified the consumer that he is in default, and that the creditor wishes to repossess the collateral given as security for the debt, the creditor can take possession of the collateral if the consumer does not object. This is called a *self-help* remedy. If the consumer objects, the creditor must pursue collection through the judicial system.

Sale of Collateral

As mentioned, if the creditor repossesses the collateral without a breach of the peace, he must use the collateral in an attempt to satisfy the debt. This means that the creditor must give notification, to the debtor and the public at large, before proceeding with a public or private auction or sale of the property taken. If the property sells for less than is owed on the debt, the remainder of the debt is considered unsecured, and the creditor may be able to proceed with a separate action for the balance owed.

Notice to the Debtor

Before taking any action to repossess collateral or collect on a debt, a creditor will most likely be required to send the debtor one final notice that he is in default and must make up all delinquent payments by a certain date or risk applicable legal consequences. If the consumer defaults on a loan, the contract will almost always provide that the entire remaining balance becomes due. It is not illegal for the creditor to proceed with formal legal action against a consumer who continues to make periodic payments on the debt if such payments are not in accord with the original agreement or otherwise agreed to by the creditor.

FAIR DEBT COLLECTION PRACTICES ACT

Consumer debts are sometimes turned over to *collection agencies*, which are usually compensated by retaining a percentage of any money they collect on behalf of the creditor. Collection agencies are subject to a specific body of federal laws called the Fair Debt Collection Practices Act. This act regulates the collection activities and tactics used by individuals and companies attempting to collect money owed to others.

Applicability

The Fair Debt Collection Practices Act is only applicable when the debtor is a consumer, as opposed to a commercial debtor (such as a partnership, business or corporation). To constitute a consumer debt, the obligation must stem from personal, family or household transactions.

Only a person or company attempting to collect a debt on behalf of another is subject to the provisions of the Fair Debt Collection Practices Act. Also, the collector must be in the business of collecting debts. The collector or his agents are not subject to the provisions of the Fair Debt Collection Practices Act if that is not their primary business. Although attorneys were initially excepted from the Fair Debt Collection Practices Act, this exception has recently been omitted. Now any attorney who collects debts for a client is subject to the provisions of the Fair Debt Collection Practices Act.

Prohibited Activities

The primary focus of the Fair Debt Collection Practices Act is to define the conduct a collector may use in attempting to collect a debt. Generally, a collector may not contact the consumer debtor at any unusual place or time, such as before 8:00 A.M. or after 9:00 P.M., or at the debtor's place of employment, if the debtor or his employer has requested that no such contact be made. Further, if the collector knows that the debtor is represented by an attorney, all communication must go through that attorney.

If the consumer gives the debt collector written notice of his refusal to pay the debt and wants the collector to cease further communication, that request must be honored. Without the consent of the debtor, a collector cannot communicate with any third party regarding the debt other than his attorney or a consumer reporting agency.

Illegal Collection Tactics

Under the Fair Debt Collection Practices Act, the following will constitute harassment or abuse and, accordingly, collectors may not resort to these types of activities in trying to collect a debt:

- Use or threat of violence
- Use of obscene or abusive language
- Publication of a list of consumers who do not pay their debts
- Anonymous telephone calls to the debtor
- Continuous or repeated telephone calls to the debtor

Also, the Fair Debt Collection Practices Act prohibits false or misleading statements from the collector to the debtor concerning the legal status of the debt. Examples of this would be:

- Threat of legal action that may not actually be available

- Threat that the failure to pay a debt is a crime
- Communication of credit information that is known to be false by the collector

Several other types of conduct constitute violations of the Fair Debt Collection Practices Act. These include:

- Accepting a post-dated check of more than five days, unless the collector gives written notification to the debtor that he intends to deposit it within three to ten days.
- Soliciting a post-dated check for the intention of using bad check laws to create possible criminal prosecution.
- Threatening nonjudicial action against the debtor's property in which there is no security interest, including the intent to repossess the property if no legal right to repossess actually exists.
- Using any type of verbiage or symbol other than the collector's address on any mail to a debtor, except for the collector's name or business name if it does not reveal the nature of the collection business.

One final note about the Fair Debt Collection Practices Act. Whenever a third party acting on behalf of a creditor initially contacts a consumer debtor in writing concerning payment of a debt, the following notice must be made at that time:

The following notice is required pursuant to 15 U.S.C.A., 1601, et seq: Unless you notify this office within thirty days after receipt of this correspondence that the validity of this debt or any portion thereof is disputed, it will be assumed that this debt is valid. If you do notify this office of a dispute, verification of the debt will be forwarded to you. However, suit may be filed against you without waiting said thirty days. This correspondence is an attempt to collect a debt, and any information obtained will be used for that purpose.

After this initial notification to the debtor, any further written correspondences or communications with the debtor must contain the following notice, in clear and conspicuous language: "This correspondence is an attempt to collect a debt, and any information obtained will be used for that purpose."

COLLECTION LAWSUITS

If a lawsuit is filed by a creditor against a consumer for money owed, whether the debt is secured or unsecured will determine which route the lawsuit may take.

Replevin

If the debt involved is secured by personal property or collateral, the creditor may wish to file a *replevin*. This is a special type of legal action designed to obtain a court order to take the collateral from the debtor. If the court order is obtained and the collateral is removed by the creditor (usually with help from the sheriff), a separate legal action must be brought for any balance still owed if the collateral itself does not satisfy the debt.

Unsecured Debts

If the debt is unsecured, a creditor will usually file a *money owed* lawsuit. The creditor will have to prove to the court that an agreement (either express or implied) for payment was entered into, subsequently breached, and that the balance remains due and owing.

Execution on a Judgment

Once a judgment is entered by the court for the amount owed, plus interest, court costs and sometimes attorney fees, the creditor has different methods of *executing* on the judgment in the attempt to collect the debt. Execution means the legal process to enforce a judgment—that is, collect the money owed. The creditor, not the court, is obligated to see that the judgment is collected.

Garnishment

The most common way of executing on a judgment is a *garnishment*, where a third party, such as an employer or a bank, is obligated to notify the court of money owed to the judgment debtor. In most cases, any money held by a bank in the debtor's name will be subject to a garnishment, and these funds must be forwarded to the court, which in turn sends the money to the creditor.

When a garnishment is filed against a judgment debtor's employer, that employer must advise the court if the judgment debtor is employed, how much he earns, and how often he is paid. Generally, the court will then enter some type of garnishment order directing the employer to forward a certain percentage (usually between 10 and 30 percent) of the judgment debtor's wages to the court.

Attachments

Beyond the garnishment process, the judgment creditor can execute (take possession and sell) on property that the judgment debtor may own. This may include any real estate in the debtor's name. Most states refer to this type of execution option as *attachment* while others call it a *levy*.

Exemptions

Most states have exemptions to personal property that may not be sold to satisfy a judgment. These usually entail all the debtor's immediate personal possessions, including clothing, kitchen utensils and furniture up to a certain amount in value. Also, the tools and equipment of the judgment debtor, again not to exceed a specified value, will be exempt.

Many states have other exemptions, such as a certain amount of cash or a certain amount of equity in the debtor's home. The purpose of these exemptions is to keep judgment creditors from taking every last nickel from a judgment debtor, thus making the debtor a burden on the state, which is considered contrary to public policy.

Other Collection Options

If the creditor is unable to locate any property of the debtor to execute on a judgment, or if the debtor has no bank account or place of employment, the creditor can require the debtor to appear in court and answer any questions the creditor may put to him about his financial condition or sources of income. This procedure is designed to allow the creditor to determine if a judgment is collectible, or to uncover any assets the creditor can use to collect the judgment. This procedure is sometimes referred to as a *debtor's exam*.

Credit Counseling Services

Some consumer debtors will go to a credit counseling service. These counseling services are often provided for free or at a minimal charge and are designed to assist consumers who have trouble handling their debts. The counselor will usually contact individual creditors and explain the debtor's situation in an attempt to work out a mutually acceptable payment plan. Sometimes the creditor agrees to compensate the credit counseling service by having a small portion of the debt go to the counseling service.

Soldiers' and Sailors' Civil Relief Act

The Soldiers' and Sailors' Civil Relief Act is a federal law providing protection for active duty military personnel regarding civil matters and lawsuits. It does not apply to any type of criminal action.

A consumer on active military duty may have a civil trial postponed if he can show that his military service will deter his ability to defend himself. The act also provides some protection to military personnel on contracts made prior to their entry into the service. Military personnel can seek a court order to reduce or cease payments due under a consumer contract, but must show that their military service has materially affected the ability to pay. There will be no termination of the ultimate liability, only a postponement of any payments required under the contract. The Soldiers' and Sailors' Civil Relief Act also provides protection against repossession of personal property that may have been purchased prior to entry into the military.

Many state laws require an affidavit from a creditor submitted at the time a judgment is entered indicating that, to the best of the creditor's knowledge, the debtor is not an active member of the United States military service. This is required to show that no violations of the Soldiers' and Sailors' Civil Relief Act have occurred in filing the lawsuit or obtaining a judgment.

TAX COLLECTION

This next section reviews the authority of the Internal Revenue Service to collect unpaid taxes from a consumer. If the full amount owed in federal income tax is not paid when due, the I.R.S. collection process will begin.

If a consumer is contacted by the I.R.S. regarding unpaid taxes and no acceptable arrangement for repayment is reached, the I.R.S. may take any of the following actions:

1. file a Notice of Federal Tax lien;
2. serve a Notice of Levy; or
3. seize and sell the consumer's property (including personal or business property or real estate).

Tax Liens

A *tax lien* notifies the public that the federal government has a legal claim on all the consumer's property. This includes any property acquired after the lien was filed. These types of liens are only released when the owed taxes are paid in full, including any interest or penalties.

Tax Levies

A *levy* is a method the I.R.S. uses to collect unpaid taxes. Levies can be made on a consumer's property, wages or bank accounts. A levy is different from a tax lien. While a tax lien is a claim used as security for the tax debt, a levy is used to take property to satisfy the debt. In most cases, the I.R.S. does not need court permission to take levy action, unless it is entering the consumer's residence to seize property.

Exemptions. Certain types of property are exempt from an I.R.S. levy. These include clothes, personal effects and furniture up to $1,650, tools used in the debtor's business or trade up to $1,100, disability payments, child support money, unemployment benefits and other types of public assistance funds.

BANKRUPTCY

Bankruptcy laws are a body of federal laws that provides for the specific remedies, procedures and elements involved in filing a bankruptcy. The bankruptcy court is a division of the federal court system, and the bankruptcy laws are referred to as the bankruptcy code.

There are several different types of bankruptcies that can be filed, usually referred to by the different chapters of the bankruptcy code from which they arise. Included are Chapter Seven Bankruptcy, also known as a straight bankruptcy; Chapter Eleven or business reorganization bankruptcy; Chapter Twelve bankruptcy that involves family farm reorganization; and Chapter Thirteen bankruptcy that applies to individual debt adjustment and repayment.

In the last several years, approximately one out of every 120 consumer households filed some form of bankruptcy, with about forty involving both husbands and wives. Approximately 70 percent of all bankruptcies filed are Chapter Seven.

Automatic Stay

When bankruptcy is filed, regardless of the chapter, the first thing that happens is the issuance of the *automatic stay*. Once the bankruptcy is filed, it operates as an immediate order to cease any collection activity by any creditor against the debtor. This includes any act to improve the creditor's position, such as filing a security interest against the debtor, or enforce any type of interest that the creditor may have after the bankruptcy has been filed.

The automatic stay also stops any further activity on lawsuits currently filed against the debtor. If a creditor takes any action against the debtor after the bankruptcy is filed, the creditor may be held in contempt of court and in violation of the automatic stay. The creditor will also have to return any money collected in violation of the automatic stay.

The purpose of the automatic stay is to provide immediate debt relief to the debtor who has filed bankruptcy. In essence, it declares that all collection activity must stop until the bankruptcy procedures have run their course. Any action by a creditor against the debtor subsequent to the bankruptcy being filed must be done with the bankruptcy court or trustee's approval.

Chapter Seven

In the Chapter Seven bankruptcy, the debtor surrenders much of his property so that any nonexempt assets can be sold and the proceeds go to creditors. When the bankruptcy is filed, a trustee is appointed to take control over the debtor's property and determine which property is exempt from sale. Most creditors will receive an equal share of any net proceeds from the sale. For example, if the debtor had nonexempt property worth $5,000 and an unsecured debt of $50,000, the trustee would allow the debtor's unsecured creditors to receive ten cents of every dollar that is owed.

Reaffirmation Agreement. As mentioned, a person who files a Chapter Seven bankruptcy will be allowed a number of exemptions under the bankruptcy code. Often the exemptions will apply only to property in which the creditor is not secured; that is, the creditor has no lien. If the debtor wishes to retain possession of the property upon which a creditor has an enforceable lien, he may be able to enter into a *reaffirmation agreement* with the creditor to continue making payments outside the scope of the bankruptcy liquidation procedure. Generally, the court must approve any reaffirmation agreement between a creditor and a debtor covering secured property the debtor wants to retain.

Exempt Property. The Bankruptcy Code provides exemptions from sale for certain property in a Chapter Seven bankruptcy. If an individual is filing a Chapter Seven bankruptcy, a homestead exemption in the debtor's residence of up to $7,500 of equity (the value minus any mortgage or security interest) is allowed. If a husband and wife jointly file bankruptcy, this exemption may total $15,000. A debtor may be able to claim up to $1,200 in exempt equity for a motor vehicle.

Other types of exemptions under the Bankruptcy Code are certain household furnishings, goods, clothes, household appliances and books. If the debtor can show that these items are held primarily for personal or family use, up to $200 for each item (or $400 if joint) may be declared exempt, up to a maximum of $4,000 ($8,000 if joint). Also allowed is a $500 jewelry exemption. The debtor can further use a "wild card" exemption of $400 for any type of property, plus up to $3,750 of any unused homestead exemption. This amount would double in a joint filing of bankruptcy by spouses.

Also exempt under the Federal Bankruptcy Code in a Chapter Seven bankruptcy are tools of the trade, or trade implements owned by the debtor. Up to $750 of these items may be exempt. A maximum of $4,000 of life insurance loan value in an unmatured life insurance contract can be declared exempt.

Other exemptions under the Federal Bankruptcy Code include any money that may be received in the future from Social Security benefits, unemployment benefits, local public assistance, veterans' benefits, disability or insurance benefits, or unemployment benefits. Also, to the extent necessary for the support of the debtor and his family, the debtor may declare exempt alimony, child support and pension or profit sharing payments.

The Bankruptcy Code has a provision that allows the debtor to "opt out" of the federal exemptions and claim whatever exemptions state law may allow. Some states have exemption laws more liberal than the federal bankruptcy code. These state exemptions will be similar to the federal ones but may allow for greater dollar amounts making it more desirable for the debtor to take state exemptions.

Discharge. Once the debtor has declared which property is exempt and reaffirms any debts with secured creditors, if so desired, the balance of the debtor's debts are *discharged*. This means that, for all practical purposes, the debt no longer exists and the creditor can take no action against the debtor for these previous debts. There are situations where a secured creditor requests court relief from the automatic stay to protect the collateral used as security for the debt. Typically, mortgage holders and lienholders on motor vehicles will be allowed to foreclose or enforce their lien unless the debtor reaffirms these debts. While these secured creditors can proceed with taking back their secured property, any remaining debt will be discharged.

Nondischargeable Debts. Certain types of debts are not subject to discharge in the bankruptcy code. Generally, any type of money owed by the debtor stemming from owed taxes, child support or alimony payments, and student loans not more than five years old will not be discharged in bankruptcy.

There are other types of debts that a creditor may challenge in bankruptcy court to have them declared nondischarged. If a creditor believes that a debtor fraudulently obtained credit, money or property in anticipation of filing bankruptcy, the creditor may file an application to have that particular debt declared nondischargable. For instance, if a debtor goes on a spending spree with a credit card immediately prior to filing bankruptcy (knowing that under normal circumstances the debt will be discharged) the creditor may file an application with the court to have the court determine that the debtor took advantage of the bankruptcy discharge laws.

Also, a creditor may request that the court declare certain

types of prebankruptcy transfers by the debtor void. For example, if the debtor transfers the bulk of his property to another person within a certain period of time prior to filing bankruptcy, the creditor may be able to have this prebankruptcy transfer voided and, accordingly, have the property sold and the funds made available to creditors. Each case will hinge on its own particular facts as to whether a prebankruptcy transfer was fraudulent in nature.

Chapter Thirteen

In a Chapter Thirteen bankruptcy, the debtor must have a regular source of income. A Chapter Thirteen bankruptcy requires that the debtor pay all or part of his debts on a monthly basis over a period of at least three years, and possibly up to five years. The debtor needs to submit a repayment plan to the court and his creditors for approval. However, the court may approve the Chapter Thirteen plan even though the creditors, both secured and unsecured, may object.

As mentioned, a Chapter Thirteen bankruptcy can be filed by an individual with regular income. However, the individual, on the date of filing, must have unsecured debts of less than $100,000 and secured debts less than $350,000. At the time of this writing, however, legislation is pending to change the debt limits to remove the distinction between secured and unsecured debts and also raise the limits to $1 million.

The trustee appointed by the bankruptcy court will administer the Chapter Thirteen repayment plan.

The Repayment Plan. The trustee is obligated to recommend approval or disapproval of the plan to the court based on its feasibility. The Chapter Thirteen trustee also acts as the agent through which all payments are made and distributed under the plan.

The Chapter Thirteen debtor is required to repay secured debtors 100 percent of the fair market value of the property used as collateral for the debt, plus any interest. Unsecured creditors, however, are entitled to receive, at the minimum, an amount of money that they would have received under a Chapter Seven proceeding. If a debtor in a Chapter Seven bankruptcy had property worth $20,000 after all the exemptions were subtracted from the debtor's property, and an unsecured debt of $200,000 remained, the unsecured creditors would receive approximately ten cents on the dollar. If this same debtor filed a Chapter Thirteen plan, the unsecured creditors would be entitled to at least that same ten cents on the dollar payment.

If the debtor's Chapter Thirteen plan pays less than 100 percent of his unsecured debt, the Bankruptcy Code requires that all of the debtor's disposable income go toward the debtor's debt load. *Disposable income* is the amount of money left after various necessaries of life payments are subtracted from it.

A debtor is allowed to pay in full any debt that may have been co-signed or guaranteed by another, even if other similarly classified creditors receive less than 100 percent repayment. This is allowed to protect the co-signer from any separate action taken by the creditor.

If the debtor cannot continue to make payments approved under the Chapter Thirteen plan, the court will sometimes grant an extension on the schedule of payments. However, if the debtor's income should dramatically decrease, a Chapter Thirteen bankruptcy can be converted to a Chapter Seven bankruptcy so all applicable debts can be discharged.

The advantage of a Chapter Thirteen bankruptcy as opposed to a Chapter Seven bankruptcy is that, generally, a Chapter Thirteen bankruptcy will be less harmful to the consumer's credit rating. This is because a Chapter Thirteen bankruptcy indicates a willingness by the debtor to pay his debts, at least on a partial basis. A Chapter Seven bankruptcy can be filed once every six years, while a Chapter Thirteen may, with some restrictions, be filed more often.

Chapter Eleven

Chapter Eleven bankruptcy is a section of the Bankruptcy Code that is known as a business reorganization. It is most often used by corporations or business partnerships, but can also be used by individuals who may wish to pay a portion of their debts over a period of time but whose debt load is more than what would qualify for a Chapter Thirteen wage earner repayment plan.

A Chapter Eleven plan, as with Chapter Thirteen, proposes a payment of secured and unsecured creditors over a period of time. There are several procedural variations in the Chapter Eleven bankruptcy that may become quite complex depending on the debtor's situation and business concerns.

Chapter Twelve

A Chapter Twelve bankruptcy entails the reorganization of the debts of a family farm. Although the specifics of a Chapter Twelve bankruptcy are beyond the scope of this book, a few are as follows: The farmer involved cannot have more than $1.5 million in debt and 80 percent of the debt must be related to the farming operation itself. Also, at least 50 percent of the debtor's income must come from a farming operation.

The reorganization plan under Chapter Twelve must be filed within ninety days from the date of filing, and creditors are not allowed to vote on the plan, but may object to it. It will be up to the court to determine whether or not the proposed Chapter Twelve reorganization plan is viable. Typically, the approval standards for a Chapter Twelve reorganization plan are less severe than a Chapter Eleven plan.

Effect of Bankruptcy

As you might expect, the filing of a bankruptcy by a consumer is probably the single most detrimental act that can affect his credit rating. A bankruptcy filing will generally remain on an individual's credit record for up to ten years.

Reestablishment of credit after the filing of a bankruptcy may take several years. It is not illegal for an individual or company to ask whether the applicant has ever filed bankruptcy on any type of credit application, including rental agreements. A bankruptcy should not be considered a short-term financial solution due to its potential long-term negative consequences.

Chapter Six

Personal Injury Law

"Lawsuit Mania" . . . *a continual craving to go to law against others, while considering themselves the injured party.*
— *Cesare Lombroso*

This chapter will discuss the different types of liabilities that arise when an individual is injured through the fault of another. These types of legal actions are commonly known as *torts*. A legal tort is a recognized cause of action by one party against another, usually stemming from a wrongful act or omission by the wrongdoer, known as the *tort-feasor*.

The three general elements involved in every type of tort action include a legal duty from the wrongdoer to the injured party; the breach of that duty; and damages that result from the breach.

NEGLIGENCE

Negligence is involved in many torts cases. Negligence is the failure to exercise the care that an ordinary prudent person would use under similar circumstances in dealing with other people. That is, if an individual should fail to do what a reasonable person would otherwise do, the failure to act constitutes negligence, provided that an injury resulted from it. Similarly, if a person engages in conduct that an ordinary reasonable person would not, negligence may also result and allow the injured person to recover damages.

For example, if an individual leaves a loaded gun in a neighborhood park, and a child finds the gun, fires it and injures himself, the person who left the gun in the park could be held liable. The person who left the loaded gun in the park never meant to harm anyone — and that doesn't have to be proven. Rather, the careless act of leaving such an item in such a place would constitute, in all likelihood, negligence.

Types of Negligence

Some states have laws pertaining to different degrees of negligence. However, the more recent trend in the law has been to disregard liability on the basis of different degrees of negligence, whether it be *slight, ordinary* or *gross*. In some types of torts, however, gross negligence must be proven before the injured party is entitled to recover. For instance, many states require a showing of gross negligence before recovery is granted under certain automobile liability rulings. This will be discussed in the section under motor vehicle liability.

Contributory Negligence

Contributory negligence is where the injured party did something, or failed to do something, that an ordinary reasonable person would have done. It is this action (or inaction) on behalf of the injured party, coupled with the wrongdoer's conduct, which causes the injury. Without the additional contributory negligence of the injured party, the negligence of the wrongdoer would not have caused the injury. A finding of contributory negligence bars recovery on behalf of the injured party.

Comparative Negligence

In some states the doctrine of *comparative negligence* measures the degree of negligence each person contributed. If the court is convinced that the wrongdoer was 70 percent responsible for the injury, and the injured party was 30 percent responsible, only 70 percent of the damages will be the legal responsibility of the wrongdoer. The injured party will receive damages if his percentage of fault is less than the wrongdoer's.

Some areas of the country employ the *more than slight* rule. If the injured party contributed more than slight negligence to the injuries suffered, such contribution by the injured party will prevent any recovery.

Violations of the Law

In most states, a violation of a law or statute by the wrongdoer does not automatically mean he is negligent. Usually, any violation of the law will be allowed as evidence, but other facts must establish negligence. For example, if it was proven that the wrongdoer was speeding and illegally intoxicated at the time of his negligence, a cause and effect between his conduct and the resulting injury must be established.

Proximate Cause

As already mentioned, no liability will exist unless it can be proven that the wrongdoer's conduct was the *proximate cause* of the injured party's damages. The cause of the injury does not necessarily have to be the immediate or direct result of the action of the wrongdoer. Put another way, for a proximate cause to exist, the injury must be proven to be the likely consequence or outcome of the negligence of the wrongdoer.

Any intervening facts between the negligence of the wrongdoer and the resulting injury is weighed and interpreted by the court to determine the necessary proximate cause to establish liability. The issue is whether the negligent action (or inaction) by the wrongdoer could have foreseeably led to the injuries involved.

Imputed Negligence

Imputed negligence is the legal theory that allows one person to be liable for the acts or failure to act on behalf of another. For example, the general rule is that the negligence of one spouse will not be attributed to the other spouse. Conversely, if an employee negligently causes injury to another, the negligence of the employee could be passed on to his employer, provided certain other conditions are met, such as the negligent act being committed during the course of employment.

A parent may be liable for the negligence of his child if the parent entrusts a dangerous instrument, such as a knife, gun, etc., to the child, or fails to adequately restrain or supervise the child who he knows has dangerous tendencies. Parental liability may also be established if the parent consents to the child's conduct, which brings about a lawsuit.

These types of imputed negligence situations generally revolve around the law of agency, which makes one party the legal agent or representative of another for certain types of actions or inactions.

DEFENSES TO NEGLIGENCE

Even though there may have been negligence on behalf of the wrongdoer, the wrongdoer has defenses to negate his liability.

Assumption of Risk

If the wrongdoer can establish that the injured party *assumed the risk* of any injury suffered, the assumption of risk defense may negate the wrongdoer's negligence. To establish an assumption of risk defense, the wrongdoer must prove that the injured party knew and understood the specific danger involved. The wrongdoer must also show that the injured party voluntarily exposed himself to danger and, as a result, suffered an injury.

The assumption of risk defense is used when an injured party deliberately makes a choice to subject himself to a known potential risk. Even if the risk is negligently created by the wrongdoer, he will not be considered proximate cause of any resulting injury. Accordingly, when an assumption of risk defense is established, the injured party may not recover damages.

There is a difference between assumption of risk and contributory negligence. Generally, an assumption of risk defense relates to the mental state or willingness of the injured party to partake in the conduct that resulted in his injury. Contributory negligence is a concept that relates to the relative conduct of the injured party. For example, suppose a person walked into a grocery store, saw that the floor was slick, read the warning sign, and walked on it anyway. He could be barred from any type of recovery by the assumption of risk defense. If that same person ran into the store, could not avoid the slippery floor, even though he wanted to, and fell, his conduct (running haphazardly into the store) may amount to contributory negligence and bar recovery stemming from the negligence of the store in having a slick floor.

Last Clear Chance Doctrine

Some states have a type of defense to a negligence action known as the *Last Clear Chance Doctrine*. In essence, this doctrine provides that recovery from a negligent third party is blocked if the injured party through reasonable care and diligence could have avoided injury. That is, if the injured party had the last reasonable opportunity to avoid the accident (despite the fact that the negligence of the wrongdoer created the injurious circumstances in the first place) the injured party will be considered totally responsible for any injury he may suffer.

For example, a person leaves his unattended stalled car in the middle of a highway at night, with no warning devices indicating that the automobile was in the lane of traffic, and another automobile crashes into it, the person who had abandoned the stalled car would be negligent and legally responsible for any injuries sustained. However, if it could be established that the individual who ran into the stalled car was traveling at a very high rate of speed, was intoxicated, and was in the wrong lane of traffic at the time of the accident, the Doctrine of Last Clear Chance may come into play. The court may determine that the injured party could have avoided the accident entirely if he had not been drunk and speeding, despite the fact that the stalled automobile should not have been left in the highway.

GOVERNMENTAL LIABILITY

Before a reform in the law, no government or governmental agency could be held liable for the torts of their officers, agents or employees. However, this doctrine has been rejected in large part. The United States government has specifically waived a major portion of this immunity by enacting of the Federal Tort Claims Act. State and local governments can also be held liable, usually through some form of state tort claims law provisions.

Federal Tort Claims Act

The Federal Tort Claims Act allows an injured party to file suit against the United States for alleged negligence by its officers and employees. To hold the government liable, however, the negligence involved must be within the scope of the office or employment of the person who committed the negligence.

State Liability

Most state laws covering liability for negligent acts of its employees or agents require, as a prerequisite to a lawsuit, an administrative determination whether the case can be resolved without court action. Other states have statutes that require the injured party to make a formal demand on the state within a certain period of time before filing a lawsuit against the state or other local governmental entity.

Also, many states have laws that require a judge to hear the tort action against the state rather than a jury. The public policy reason behind this law is that a jury may be apprehensive about granting a large judgment against the government in fear that it may increase taxes to pay for such a judgment. It is presumed that a judge would be immune from such considerations.

STANDARDS OF NEGLIGENT CONDUCT

There are different standards of negligent conduct that pertain to certain classes of individuals.

Negligence of a Minor

A person who has not yet reached the age of majority can be held responsible and liable for his negligent actions or inactions. However, although this person can be held liable, the standard applied will be that of a person of similar age and experience.

For instance, to determine if a twelve-year-old who leaves a loaded gun at a playground was negligent, consider whether a person of similar age and experience (an ordinarily reasonable twelve-year-old) would have committed such an act. The issue is whether leaving a loaded gun at a playground is reasonable and prudent conduct for a twelve-year-old, taking into consideration the maturity and experience of a typical twelve-year-old. Obviously, the accepted conduct of a four-year-old will be different from a twelve-year-old, which will differ from an adult.

Depending on the facts of the particular case involved, the court will determine whether the conduct of the minor constitutes negligence. The jury will be instructed that negligence in the case of a child is the failure to use the care that would be used by a reasonably careful child of the same age, intelligence and experience under similar circumstances. As with an adult, the standard is the same, only the application of the standard is changed to meet the maturity of the wrongdoer.

Malpractice

The negligent standard applied to professionals, such as physicians and attorneys, is that the professional is under a duty to use reasonable care and skill for the well-being of his patient and/ or client. An injury stemming from an inability or lack of care involved will ordinarily cause that professional to be liable for *malpractice*.

The general principle used in determining malpractice will be what constitutes reasonable care, skill and diligence in the community where the professional practices. If that community standard has not been met, and other defenses do not apply, the professional is liable for negligence and malpractice is established. Of course, damages or injuries must proximately result before any recovery can be had.

RES IPSA LOQUITUR

Another type of tort that needs to be mentioned in connection with the law of negligence is *res ipsa loquitur*, an evidentiary recognition of a type of negligence that cannot be specifically proven to be the fault of another. The classic case of *res ipsa loquitur* is when a person purchases a sealed bottle of soda pop, opens the bottle, and consumes the beverage. At the bottom of the bottle is a dead mouse. The individual who consumes the soda pop suffers related intestinal sickness and incurs medical damages. To recover under *res ipsa loquitur*, the injured party must show only that the bottle and its contents were in the exclusive control of its manufacturer and that under normal circumstances a dead mouse is not found in bottles of soda pop distributed for public consumption.

The law of *res ipsa loquitur* does not provide that the injured party specifically prove a negligent act by the manufacturer, but only that if due care had been used by the alleged wrongdoer, the negligent act could not have occurred. If *res ipsa loquitur* is established, negligence will be inferred, and the injured party will be able to recover for any injuries suffered.

STRICT LIABILITY

Another offshoot of negligence is the concept of *strict liability*, which will hold an individual liable, without any evidence of fault, for any injury that results from an activity determined to be inherently dangerous. If the wrongdoer engaged in conduct that is unusually dangerous to others, any injuries suffered by others as a result of this activity will cause the wrongdoer to be held strictly liable.

Generally, the types of activities that fall under the strict liability umbrella include storing or transporting hazardous explosives or toxic chemicals, or keeping dangerous animals on one's premises. Any injuries that arise from maintaining or using these items can, under some circumstances, cause the party involved to be held strictly liable without any evidence of negligence. The underlying theory of strict liability is that the activity of maintaining these devices or engaging in this type of activity is sufficiently dangerous to warrant complete liability.

INTENTIONAL TORTS

Aside from strict liability and negligent torts, there are *intentional torts*. These typically include slander and libel to reputation, assault and battery, false imprisonment, or intentionally inflicting mental distress. The common thread among these types of torts is that the wrongdoer intentionally causes the injury to the aggrieved party.

While certain types of intentional torts, such as assault and battery, may also constitute criminal activity, the law of torts is based on compensation. As a result, an injured party who files suit in civil court based on an intentional tort is attempting to recover for injuries sustained. The types of damages recoverable will be covered later in the chapter.

MOTOR VEHICLE LIABILITY

Negligence in operating a motor vehicle is the failure to exercise ordinary or reasonable care to avoid injuring others or their property.

Standard of Care

Generally speaking, an operator of a motor vehicle must use the degree of care that an ordinarily careful and prudent person would use under the same circumstances. The circumstances involved in the accident, road and weather conditions, will always contribute to negligence. The care that an operator of a motor vehicle must exercise includes the duty to maintain a diligent lookout for others in light of the circumstances present.

The motor vehicle operator does have the right to expect

other drivers and pedestrians to obey all applicable laws to keep themselves out of harm's way. A motor vehicle operator is not responsible for any harm to another person if the injured party has not taken all reasonable steps necessary to protect himself. The motor vehicle operator does not have to anticipate any negligent conduct on behalf of another.

Sudden Emergency Doctrine

There is a theory in motor vehicle negligence called a *Sudden Emergency Doctrine*. Generally, this theory involves a situation where the motor vehicle operator is suddenly confronted with an emergency situation he did not create. This emergency situation compels the motor vehicle operator to act instantaneously to avoid any injury to himself or his passengers. In such a case, if an injury or damage occurs to a third party, the motor vehicle operator will not be considered negligent.

Violations of the Law

As with other types of negligence, the violation of a traffic law does not necessarily mean that the driver is negligent. However, the violation of traffic laws can be used as evidence against the driver to determine whether his negligent conduct caused injury to another.

Proximate Cause

Also, as with other types of negligence, it must be shown that the driver, by his actions, proximately caused the resulting injury. If the injured party was contributorily negligent, or other intervening causes came into play that caused the accident, the driver cannot be held liabel.

Emergency Vehicles

Negligence laws do not hold emergency vehicles to the same standard of care as are other motor vehicles. Police cars, fire department vehicles and ambulances are measured by the due care used by other operators of emergency vehicles. Also, there will usually be specific laws that govern the type of conduct permissible by operators of emergency motor vehicles.

Pedestrians

The operator of a motor vehicle is obliged to extend his duty of care to all pedestrians who lawfully use the roadway. The driver must always anticipate the reasonable presence of pedestrians along the road and must exercise all reasonable care in avoiding injury to them. Pedestrians also have a duty to protect their own interests by doing whatever is reasonably necessary to avoid anticipated traffic and motor vehicles.

Similarly, if a driver knows there are children in the area, he is required to be especially alert and operate his motor vehicle accordingly. Usually a higher degree of care is required of a motorist approaching a school or other area in which children might be present.

Motor Vehicle Passengers

Many states have laws pertaining to injuries suffered by passengers in a motor vehicle. With certain variances and exceptions, these laws provide that if the injured party is a guest in the vehicle involved, the driver must be shown to be either under the influence of alcohol or his operation of the motor vehicle was grossly negligent. As with other negligence actions, the injuries suffered must be the proximate cause of the grossly negligent operation of the motor vehicle.

A guest is defined as one who is invited, directly or indirectly, to enjoy the hospitality of the driver. There can be no payment or benefit received by the driver beyond the mere pleasure or acquiescence of having the passenger travel with him. An individual who is paying for a ride in a taxicab is not a guest.

Gross Negligence

If it is established that the passenger is a guest in the motor vehicle, he must show that the driver was more than merely negligent, but was *grossly negligent*, in the operation of the vehicle. Gross negligence can be defined as excessive or to a very high degree. It is the reckless disregard for the potential consequences of one's conduct.

Gross negligence will usually entail more than one particular act. For instance, if the driver was in violation of the speed limit, intoxicated, and disregarded all rules of the road while driving, gross negligence could be established. Whether gross negligence exists will be a factual determination, depending on the circumstances of the accident.

Imputed Liability

If the owner entrusts his motor vehicle to another person he knows is incompetent or careless, negligence by the driver can be passed on to the owner. Also, an employer will usually be held liable for the negligent operation of a motor vehicle by an employee, provided that driving is in the course of employment.

Family Purpose Doctrine

Many states have what is known as the *family purpose doctrine*. If the owner of a motor vehicle kept and maintained it for family use, a family member caused an injury while driving and the driver was using the vehicle for its intended purpose, any negligence liability of the driver may be passed to the owner. Although this theory has been rejected in some states, it allows the injured party to hold the owner of the motor vehicle liable, as opposed to only the driver.

Last Clear Chance

As discussed earlier, the doctrine of *Last Clear Chance* allows an injured party to recover for damages despite his own contributory negligence. If the driver had the last opportunity to avoid the accident and did not do so even though a person of reasonable prudence would have, the driver will be held liable despite contributory negligence by the injured party.

A typical petition in a lawsuit alleging negligence on behalf of a motor vehicle operator is located in the appendix.

LIABILITY OF PROPERTY OWNERS

Sometimes the use or ownership of real estate can cause the owner to be liable for the injuries of another. The liability must be shown to stem from negligence on the part of the owner or operator of the property. To a large degree, the status of the injured person will dictate what is owed that individual. There are three classifications of individuals who enter the property of another: a trespasser, a licensee and a business invitee.

Trespasser

A *trespasser* is an individual who enters or remains on someone else's property without the express or implied consent of the owner or his agent. To establish negligent liability, a trespasser must prove that the owner acted willfully in causing the injury. The property owner may also be negligent if he knew or had reason to know that trespassers constantly used the property, and he did not inform them of any hidden danger or peril.

For instance, if the owner of several acres of land knew that individuals crossed over it without permission and that quicksand existed on the property, he would have a duty to warn the trespassers of the quicksand. The owner could also avoid liability by erecting barriers around the quicksand to warn trespassers of the existence of the dangerous condition on his land.

Licensee

A *licensee* is allowed to enter or remain on the property with the express or implied consent of the owner. A social guest is generally considered a licensee. Also, a police officer or fire fighter entering the premises on business would be considered a licensee.

If a licensee is injured while on another's property, he must show that the owner failed to warn him of a hidden danger or peril, which was known to the owner but unknown and unobservable by the injured party by the exercise of his reasonable care. The duty owed to a licensee by the property owner is considered somewhat greater than the duty owed to a trespasser.

For example, if someone attended a social function at another's house, and his foot accidentally went through the floorboards, in all likelihood, the homeowner would be held liable for any injuries sustained. However, if the injured person saw that the front porch to the house was coated in ice, yet ran onto the porch, slipped and fell, causing injury to himself, it is doubtful that he could recover since the condition that caused the injury was observable. The theory of contributory negligence by running on an observable dangerous condition would also in all likelihood preclude recovery. An example of a lawsuit involving premises liability is found in the appendix.

Business Invitee

A *business invitee*, also known as a business visitor, is invited to enter and/or remain on another's property to conduct business with the property owner. An individual who enters the business premises of another for the purpose of shopping or conducting business would be considered a business invitee. However, a police officer who enters a store on the basis of an emergency call would be considered a licensee.

If it is determined that the injured party was a business invitee, then he must show that the property owner created or knew of the condition that caused the injury or could have discovered the condition by the exercise of reasonable care. The injured party must also prove that the property owner should have realized that the condition causing the injury was an unreasonable risk to business visitors and that they would not have been able to discover the danger or would not be able to protect themselves against the danger. It must also be established that the property owner failed to use reasonable care to protect the injured business visitor against the danger that caused the injury. As with other types of negligence, the injury suffered must be proximately caused by the condition created or allowed to exist by the owner.

The standard of care owed to a business invitee is higher than that owed a licensee and substantially higher than that owed a trespasser. Since the business invitee enters the property for the potential benefit of the owner, the law has created a higher standard of care. As with a licensee, however, if it can be established that the business invitee knew or should have known of the danger involved, and either assumed the risk or acted to substantially contribute to owner negligence, recovery against the business property owner could be precluded.

Strict Liability

Under a theory of strict liability, a property owner who is using ultra-hazardous products or devices on his property may be held strictly liable. An individual who is storing dynamite or other highly explosive items on his property, which become the proximate cause of another's injuries, usually result in strict liability being applied. Explosives and fireworks are considered activities or products that, if proximately causing an injury to another, will mandate that the property owner be held legally responsible under the theory of strict liability.

Attractive Nuisance

The theory of *attractive nuisance* maintains that an individual who keeps on his property an object or a condition that children would have a tendency to be attracted to, but that is inherently dangerous and that the property owner fails to exercise reasonable care to protect children from, can be held liable for any resulting injuries. It has been held that the existence of a cave, an open mine, a construction site, or even a swimming pool can be considered an attractive nuisance.

If the owner of the property does not take proper measures to ensure the safety of children from an attractive activity, and a child suffers an injury because of these conditions, the property owner may be held liable due to his negligence. It must be shown, however, that the property owner knew that the condition was alluring to children and could potentially endanger them. It must also be established that the property owner should have reasonably anticipated the presence of children on his property. The theory of attractive nuisance is designed to protect children who are peculiarly susceptible to being attracted to certain conditions and are not capable of appreciating or understanding the inherent danger it creates.

PRODUCTS LIABILITY

Sometimes a person can establish liability against a manufacturer or distributor for a faulty product that causes him injury, based on the manufacturer's negligently designed or manufactured product. In product liability situations, the manufacturer, distributor or processor will be held responsible for the product's ordinary or reasonable care.

Understand that under a theory of negligence regarding products liability, the manufacturer is not a guarantor of absolute safety of the product. However, if the injured party uses the product in the manner for which it was designed, and an injury is proximately caused by the manufacturer's failure to warn of any inherent dangerous condition of the product or if the product is negligently designed, recovery can be had.

Negligent liability for injuries sustained by the use of a product are often based on its negligent design. The manufacturer must use reasonable care in the design and testing of a product before making it available to the public. Also, the manufacturer must usually have an adequate inspection procedure for any products placed on the market for the general public, such as food or pharmaceutical items.

As with other types of negligent actions, the theories of contributory negligence and assumption of risk are also applicable in product liability cases based on negligence. If the product is misused or instructions for its use are not followed, it is unlikely the manufacturer will be liable.

Negligent product liability may also stem from the manufacturer failing to place a suitable warning on the product. If the manufacturer knows of a specific danger connected with the product, especially if the danger is not ordinarily discoverable by a user, a warning label must appear. It will be a question of fact as to whether the product that caused the injury is innately dangerous or has dangerous characteristics the average consumer cannot appreciate.

DAMAGES

In most tort cases, the injured party is entitled to recover any injuries suffered or damages incurred due to the negligence or liability of the wrongdoer. Only if damages or injuries are the proximate result of negligence or the legally imposed liability of another, does the law provide a remedy.

Types of Damage

When an injured party is successful in court against a personal injury wrongdoer, the court will award a judgment for the amount that the jury or judge has determined will compensate the injured party for the harm or damages suffered. Generally speaking, the primary types of damages in a personal injury tort case that are recoverable are as follows:

- Medical expenses incurred and any that will be incurred by the injured party
- Any lost wages or income, or loss of future earning capacity
- Any physical and/or mental pain and suffering
- Any physical disability, both temporary and permanent

- Any loss of value stemming from damage to property of the injured party, or the amount of money necessary to repair the damaged property
- Any other types of provable, reasonable expenses stemming from the injury

Establishment of Amount

It will be the burden of the injured party to prove the actual amount of money expended in treating his injury or repairing his property. Opinions of the value of lost property are also used in establishing the amount of damages.

Future Economic Loss

Future economic loss (lost wages or future medical expenses) determines how much money the injured party will, in all likelihood, spend in treating his injury. This usually takes into consideration his life expectancy coupled with the costs of treating the injury or resulting disability.

Lost or future lost wages are considered *special damages*, because they can be calculated with a certain degree of preciseness. Another type, *general damages*, such as pain, suffering and mental distress, cannot be calculated.

Physical pain and suffering will usually compensate the injured party for not only past pain and suffering but also for future pain and suffering, as can be reasonably certain or probable to occur as a consequence of the injury. This will usually include physical and mental pain, including mental anguish. Many jurisdictions require some type of physical manifestation to award an injured party for mental pain and anguish, and without some type of physical injury, no award for this type of general damage will be allowed.

Loss of Consortium

Loss of consortium can be awarded to a spouse of an injured party. Loss of consortium refers to the things to which a person is entitled in a marriage relationship: love, affection, companionship, comfort, assistance, services and moral support. The spouse of the injured party will normally have to file a separate lawsuit for the recovery of loss of consortium, although often the lawsuits are later combined for the sake of judicial economy.

Punitive Damages

Punitive damages are available in some states. Punitive damages are considered to be a penalty against a wrongdoer. Unlike damages that compensate the injured party, punitive damages are based on the public policy that when a negligent party is held liable for more money than it would take to compensate the injured party, it will serve as a warning or additional deterrent to other such negligent wrongdoers. Usually, it must be shown that the negligent wrongdoer acted willfully, maliciously or outrageously before punitive damages are allowed.

Determination of Damages

It is difficult to come up with a precise rule or standard by which damages, especially general damages, can be determined in personal injury. It will generally be up to the factfinder, usually a jury, to determine the amount of compensation the injured party should receive. The jury, however, is not given a blank check to compensate the injured party; rather, any judgment against the wrongdoer must be based on the evidence presented at trial, and not on any sympathies the jury may have for the injured party that do not relate to the damages proven at trial.

Wrongful Death Damages

Special mention should be made of damages awarded in wrongful death cases. There are two types of wrongful death cases. One, a party is severely injured due to the negligence of another, and the injured party lives for a period of time and eventually dies as a result of his injuries. In this case, the survivor of the deceased would be entitled to compensation for any medical costs or expenses that were incurred prior to death, plus pain and suffering and reasonable burial expenses.

Two, the injured party dies almost immediately, incurring very few postinjury medical costs. In such a situation, the survivor of the deceased, whether a spouse, child or parents, looks to the wrongdoer for compensation. The amount of damages will stem from any future loss of economic support the deceased would have provided.

Loss of consortium is also an element of damages that can be recovered in a wrongful death case brought by a surviving spouse. The jury is usually instructed that any life insurance money or inheritance that would go to the surviving spouse or deceased family members is not to be considered in determining the amount of damages recoverable in a wrongful death case.

Fee Arrangements

Most individuals who are involved in a personal injury suit will hire an attorney on a contingency fee basis. As discussed in chapter one, in a contingency fee agreement, the attorney agrees to represent the injured party in exchange for a percentage of any money collected.

Contingency Fee. The attorney representing a personal injury client will usually take a lower percentage of the money collected if the case is settled through pretrial negotiation. The percentage of compensation will sometimes increase if a lawsuit is required. The client will be responsible for all court costs and other agreed on costs the attorney must incur in representing his client. These usually include filing fees, court reporter fees, and possibly mileage, postage and other related administrative charges.

In many personal injury lawsuits, the attorney for the plaintiff (injured party) negotiates with the attorney for the defendant (wrongdoer) before the trial. Any settlement offer made by the defendant will always have to be weighed against the potential recovery in court, including the possibility of losing. Although the attorney can advise the personal injury client whether any settlement is worth taking, the client will decide to accept or reject any offers.

INSURANCE COVERAGE

In many situations, the wrongdoer will have insurance to provide coverage for damages resulting from his negligent conduct. Most insurance policies also provide an attorney if the insurance company believes the claim against its insured is without merit, or if the amount of money requested is unreasonable based on the type of injury involved.

Sometimes the injured party will have automobile liability insurance to compensate him for any injuries suffered that are not compensatable by the wrongdoer. This is usually termed *underinsured* or *uninsured coverage*. Such coverage will compensate the injured party if the insurer is satisfied that the wrongdoer or the wrongdoer's insurance company provides insufficient coverage to compensate the injured party.

Subrogation

Sometimes an insurance company will have the legal right to file suit against the individual who the compensated party could have sued due to the negligence of the wrongdoer. Most underinsured and uninsured policies will have a specific clause that allows the insurance company to file these direct suits.

Subrogation is an attempt by the insurance company to reimburse itself for the money it previously paid to its insured. The insurance company must be able to prove that the wrongdoer was negligent in causing the injury to its insured.

Chapter Seven

Wills, Trusts and Protective Proceedings

Let's talk of graves, of worms, and epitaphs; make dust our paper, and with rainy eyes write sorrow on the bosom of the earth; let's choose executors and talk of wills.
   —*William Shakespeare*

Will you still need me, will you still feed me, when I'm 64?
   —*Lennon and McCartney*

This chapter reviews the basic legal provisions concerning wills, the probate process, trusts and other related devices concerning the disposition or protection of a person's property or interests.

WILLS

A *will* is a written document that provides for the disposition of an individual's property at the time of his death. It is sometimes referred to as a *Last Will and Testament*. The individual who makes the will is called the *testator* (or in the case of a female, the *testatrix*). An individual who dies with a valid will is said to have died *testate*. An individual who dies with no will, or with a will that is not valid, is said to have died *intestate*. The laws of intestacy will be discussed later in this chapter.

   A will may also contain requests regarding the testator's children, including their care, well-being and economic support.

Requirements of a Will

   Each state has specific laws that set minimum requirements for the creation of a valid will. When a will meets these requirements, its terms are required to be carried out.

Generally speaking, an individual who creates a will must not be a minor. If the testator is married, however, generally no minimum age is required. The individual making the will must also be of sound mind. A sound mind is determined by whether the testator knew that the document involved is considered a will; that he knew the extent of his property; that he understood the terms of the will with regard to the disposition of his property; and that he understood that the terms of the will direct the property to certain individuals or entities.

Generally, the mental capacity involved in determining whether a testator has a sound mind is not as stringent in other types of legal mental conditions, such as the capacity to commit a crime or enter into a legally binding contract.

Most states will uphold a will even if it is shown that the testator suffered from a failing memory or periodic bouts of senility or eccentricities. All that needs to be proven is that he was cognizant of the effect of the will at the time he signed it. Evidence concerning the testator's general mental condition is admissible, however, to help determine whether the testator was of sound mind when the will was executed.

Witnesses. Some states have laws that require a valid will be in writing, signed by the testator and witnessed by at least two disinterested individuals. Witnesses to the signing will attest to the fact that the testator affirmed to them, in their presence, that he is aware that the document is his last will and testament, and that he is signing it freely and voluntarily and is aware of its consequences. Although it is always best to have a disinterested party as a witness to avoid any possible conflict of interest, many states do allow an interested party to act as a witness. An interested party is defined as an individual who may receive property under the terms of the will.

Self-Proved Wills. A *self-proved will* is where the testator and the witnesses state in writing that the will is valid. This declaration is notarized and becomes part of the will itself. The provisions add an element of validity to the will, creating a legal presumption that the will was entered into voluntarily and that the requirements of a will were met. This makes it very difficult for the will to be declared void at a later date.

Guardianship Provisions

Aside from the disposition of the testator's property, if the testator has minor children at the time of his death, the will usually states who the testator wants to act as legal guardian for his children until they reach adulthood. In most circumstances, if only one parent should die, the surviving parent will remain as legal guardian despite any provisions to the contrary in the deceased parent's will.

The terms of the will that choose the guardian will not be binding on the court, but they will give it direction and information as to who the parents would like to have as guardian. The court must still determine if the testator's choice for guardian is acceptable, keeping in mind the children's best interests.

Specific Requests

Aside from general statements in the will disposing of property, specific bequests of particular items of personal property can also be made. For instance, a family heirloom may be directed to go to a specific relative, or a different proportion of the testator's estate could go to one child as opposed to another.

Sometimes a will contains a specific reference to a separate document, which, by such a reference, is included in the will. This type of document makes bequests to particular individuals. The specific bequest document can be changed or modified by the testator, without an attorney, provided that it specifically refers to the will and defines the particular items of property and who is to receive what at the time of the testator's death. This separate specific request document adds flexibility to the will as it allows a periodic modification of his will. A copy of a typical will is located in the appendix.

Executor

A will also provides who the testator wants to be his *executor*, also known as the personal representative. An executor is the individual or entity with the legal responsibility of seeing that the terms of the will are carried out. Generally, spouses name one another as executors, although this is not a legal requirement. Most states allow the executor to be reimbursed for his time and expense. The executor usually hires an attorney to see that the will is probated correctly.

If he so chooses, the testator can will anybody to be co-executors. Usually a will provides for a second or even a third choice for executor, if the prior choices are not available or are unwilling to serve. If local law requires a bond for the executor, most testators will waive such a requirement in their will.

The executor does not have to be a resident of the state in which the will was probated, but he must be otherwise qualified and have the sufficient capacity to carry out responsibilities to the estate. Usually a minimum age requirement is all that is necessary in this regard. It will be incumbent upon the executor to compile, after his appointment by the court, an inventory of the deceased's property and notify all interested individuals of the death of the testator and the terms of the will. The executor will be required to pay all valid debts, claims and expenses of the estate, and distribute the balance of the estate following the terms of the will.

Joint Wills

Sometimes a husband and wife will enter into a *joint will*, which contains the wills of both people and is executed jointly by them. Joint wills are sometimes known as mutual wills. A joint will disposes of all property owned jointly, in common or individually. Joint wills usually provide for the distribution of property upon the death of one of the testators and also provide for how the property will be subsequently distributed upon the death of the other testator. A joint will is usually executed between spouses.

In states that allow joint wills, a separate document that waives each spouse's right to change the will during the term of the marriage must also be signed. Obviously, this reduces the flexibility if one spouse changes his will.

When a joint will is executed, it can be revoked at any time by either testator unless a separate agreement to the contrary exists.

Holographic Will

A *holographic will* is written by the hand of the testator. Any essential part of the will typed or printed, even by the testator himself, invalidates a holographic will. Usually, legal requirements such as attestation and signatures will not be necessary if a will is holographic. Even an informally executed document, such as a letter, may be considered a valid holographic will if the document was clearly intended to be a will.

Accordingly, a holographic will is considered valid and legally binding even if the laws pertaining to the requirements of will are not met. Most holographic wills must be in the testator's own handwriting, contain his signature, and be dated.

Payment of Debts

Any bequests under the terms of a will are initially subject to all debts of the testator and also to certain exempt property and allowances that may go to a surviving spouse and children. These laws typically provide that the spouse and/or children of the testator are guaranteed a certain minimum amount of property, which is exempt from certain creditor claims, and will pass prior to any other bequests the will may make.

Exempt Property

Most surviving spouses will be guaranteed a *homestead allowance*, usually in the neighborhood of $5,000 to $15,000. Also, a surviving spouse or his children will usually receive a certain exempt amount in personal property, including household furniture, appliances, automobiles and personal effects. Many states also have a family allowance provision that grants the surviving spouse and/or his children a certain amount of money for their reasonable support for a certain length of time. These allowances are made in addition to any share that may pass to the surviving spouse or children by the terms of the will, unless the will specifically provides otherwise. In many situations, secured creditors such as a lienholder on a car or mortgage are not subject to these allowances or exempt property. The aforementioned types of exempt property and allowances will usually apply only to unsecured creditors or other designated beneficiaries.

Elective Share

If an individual is married at the time of his death, most states do not require him to provide for his surviving spouse in the will. However, the majority of states have laws that protect a surviving spouse against the possibility of total disinheritance by the testator.

The surviving spouse who takes nothing by the terms of a

spouse's will usually will be entitled to receive an *elective share*. This means that a certain portion of the estate will go to the surviving spouse, regardless of the terms of the will. Various states have complicated formulas that determine what exactly is the surviving spouse's elective share. These laws usually take into consideration certain gifts or any transfer of property that are made before the death, which are considered part of the estate.

Omitted Spouse

Somewhat different, but nevertheless related, is the situation where a married testator neglects or fails to provide for a surviving spouse. If it can be shown that the will was executed without a cognizant act by the testator to specifically omit his spouse (such as the situation where a will was written before a marriage), the surviving spouse may be able to take whatever is due her under the laws of intestate in the state in which the will is probated. If this is the case, all of the provisions of the will remain in effect, but only after the surviving omitted spouse has been provided. If a prenuptial agreement has been entered into, which specifically waived the surviving spouse's right to take any property of the estate, local laws will vary as to whether such a prenuptial agreement is binding.

Omitted Children

As with a forgotten spouse, any children of the testator who are not provided for in the will are entitled to receive their intestate share of the parent's estate. However, if it is determined that such an omission was intentional, and not accidental, or that the testator had made provisions for his child outside the scope of the will, the child may not be allowed to take his intestate share. Also, if it is shown that the testator, at the time the will was signed, had a child and left substantially all of his estate to the parent of the omitted child, the child may be prohibited from taking his intestate share.

Children and Grandchildren

It is not necessary that the will name the specific children of the testator. If the will refers to "all my children, including all children that may be born subsequent to the date of this will," all such children will be provided for by terms of the will. Most parents' wills provide for a distribution of assets to their children in equal shares. It usually will also provide that if their child should predecease them and the child has children, these grandchildren are to receive a portion of the grandparents' estate that would have otherwise gone to their child. For example, if one of the testator's children was to have received 50 percent of the testator's estate, and that child had two children but then died before the testator, each one of his two children (grandchildren of the testator) would receive one-fourth of the testator's estate. This is considered taking *per stirpes*, which means to take *by the root*.

Alternate Beneficiaries

If a named beneficiary under the terms of a will predeceases the testator, the will should specifically state where that particular share should go. If the will fails to provide for an alternative beneficiary, generally the next of kin of the beneficiary will receive his share or, if no such alternate beneficiary exists, his share will *escheat* to the government — the state will be entitled to claim the property.

Codicils

Sometimes a valid will is entered into, but the testator wants to add to or change some of its terms. The testator may then use a *codicil*. A codicil is a document that supplements or adds to a will. It may explain, modify or even subtract from the will's original terms. Usually, a codicil must meet the same requirements that a will must meet to create a legally binding document. That is, the testator must sign, date and have witnessed (or possibly notarized) before the codicil will have any effect on the terms or conditions of the will.

Joint Property

Property that is owned in joint tenancy will not be controlled by the terms of a will. When the last survivor of the joint tenancy dies, however, the property will be disposed of by the terms of his will.

Typically, spouses hold the bulk of their property in joint tenancy. When a spouse dies, the surviving spouse will own the property outright as the surviving joint tenant. When the second spouse dies, that property will then become subject to the terms of his will, absent any change in ownership before that time.

Recognize, however, that half the value of any asset owned jointly with a spouse will be included in that spouse's estate for calculating federal estate taxes. Whether this same property will be computed in determining any state death or inheritance tax will depend on the particular state involved. Also, if the property is owned with someone other than the testator's spouse, such as a child, the entire value of the property will be taxable as part of the testator's estate, unless the child can prove that he paid a fair price for his interest in the property.

Life Insurance

Life insurance proceeds that are paid on the death of a testator are considered nonprobate property if they name a specific beneficiary. However, if the named beneficiary is the estate of the testator, it will be considered part of the estate, distributed by the terms of the will. Life insurance proceeds generally are considered part of the estate and subject to federal estate taxes, if the testator has the right to change beneficiaries or borrow against the cash value of the policy before his death.

Community Property

Several states provide that any property acquired during the term of a marriage by either spouse (with some exceptions) will be owned and held in equal shares by the spouses as *community property*. If one of the spouses should die, any community property will be subject to the terms of the testator's will. The remaining half of the property will belong to the surviving spouse, regardless of the provisions of the will. The rules that define what is and is not community property will be different from state to state and should be specifically reviewed in determining what property will be subject to the testator's will.

Change or Revocation

Unless a specific contract exists to the contrary, a will may be changed at any time. As mentioned, the parties of a joint will have executed a contract agreeing not to change the terms of the will without mutual consent or after the death of one of the joint testators and may not change or modify the will. Any time a will is entered into, a statement will usually be contained within it stating that the current will, by its terms, expressly and unequivocally revokes any prior wills. Even absent such a specific declaration, the law will presume that the most recent will is to have effect and be considered the expressed intent of the testator, despite any changes or inconsistencies to a prior will. Of course, a codicil can always modify or change the terms of an original will.

A will can be revoked by other methods. If the testator should intentionally destroy the will, it will likely be considered an effective revocation. Most states have specific legal methods regarding how a will may be revoked, or when it is presumed that the testator intended to revoke his will. The prime focus will be what the intention of the testator was, compared to his acts, to determine if he intended to revoke the terms of a previous will. If the will is accidentally destroyed or severely mutilated, that act in and of itself will not necessarily negate the terms of the will, without the intent of the testator to do so. In such a case, if the original is destroyed, a copy of the will, although unsigned or unwitnessed, may suffice.

Generally, the testator cannot change the terms of his will by strike throughs, erasures or other changes made to the face of the document, which would give new meaning to the altered part, unless these changes are executed and witnessed in the manner provided by law for the making of a will. However, any changes by a testator of a specific word, name, clause or new independent bequest, after the will has been executed, will not necessarily revoke the will.

Certain changes to the personal circumstances of a testator may constitute an implied or legal revocation of the will. For instance, certain changes in the family or domestic situation of the testator (such as a marriage or divorce) may be consequential enough to allow the law to infer that the testator did not intend for the terms of his will to apply due to these subsequent major changes.

Many states also have specific laws for children born after the execution of a will. Most of these laws provide that where the testator has a child after the will has been made, such a birth operates as a revocation of the will and allows the child to share in the testator's estate, usually under the laws of intestate.

However, if it was clearly the intention of the testator, as stated in his will, to disinherit such a child, even though yet unborn, such an intention will usually be honored. Any child adopted after the execution of a will is considered the testator's child by birth. Also, unless a specific law exists to the contrary, the issue of whether a will should be revoked by a subsequent birth of an illegitimate child of the testator will depend greatly on whether the illegitimate child would otherwise share in the testator's estate as an heir if no will existed.

Relocation of the Testator

Although the general rule is that if a will is executed and meets the requirements of the testator's resident state, and the testator then moves to another state, the new state of residence will honor the terms of the will even though it may not meet its requirements for a valid will. Nevertheless, any time a change of residency is made by an individual who has made a will, the laws pertaining to wills should be consulted in the new state to make sure the existing will is valid.

Undue Influence

As mentioned, for a will to be valid, it must be shown that the testator was of sound mind and under no undue influence at the time the will was executed. *Undue influence* is considered any type of mental or physical coercion or pressure that affects the way the testator disposes of his property or provides for others in the will.

Although the particulars will vary from state to state, it generally must be shown that the following occurred before a finding of undue influence will be made:

- The testator was susceptible to undue influence (this usually means that he was in a weakened state, either mental or physical).
- An opportunity existed for a third party to exercise undue influence over the testator.
- The individual or individuals accused of undue influence over the testator benefited from the exercise of the influence.
- The will was the result of undue influence.

When it is established or proven that undue influence occurred, the court may either declare the entire will invalid or void any bequests made to those who benefited by the undue influence. The issue of undue influence is usually going to be a question of fact, which will depend on the particular circumstance of the testator and the individuals who had contact with him.

The fact that an individual may have given the testator advice or rendered an opinion to the disposition of his property will not necessarily constitute undue influence. The existence of a confidential relationship between the testator and the beneficiary will also, in and of itself, not amount to undue influence. For instance, if an individual bequeaths his entire estate to his physician in lieu of his family, the confidential relationship between the physician and the patient does not imply that undue influence of the testator. Such a relationship, however, could establish that an opportunity existed for undue influence to occur. The mental condition of the testator is an important factor. The weaker or more infirmed (mentally or physically) the testator is at the time of the will's execution, the more susceptible he would probably be to undue influence.

Fraud

Closely related to the element of undue influence and the validity of a will is *fraud*. Fraud is usually used by a third party in informing or convincing the testator of a certain act or condition that leads the testator to modify or change his will.

For example, if a third party fraudulently convinced a testator that his spouse was having an affair, causing the testator to intentionally omit his spouse from his will, the will could be declared void. The third party, if named as a beneficiary, would take nothing under the terms of the will. It must be established that the third party intentionally attempted to deceive to his benefit the testator. Fraud is generally considered a deception, while undue influence is considered coercion. The result of both, however, is an invalidating of all or part of the will.

Location of the Will

Only the original will has any legal effect. A copy is not sufficient under most circumstances, even if it contains the signatures of the testator and any witnesses. Accordingly, the original will should be kept in a safe and secure place. A safety-deposit box is often used, although if the testator is the only person allowed access, it may prove difficult to retrieve the will at his death.

Another option is to have the original will held by the attorney who drafted it. The testator retains a copy for his reference and indicates on it where the original can be located. Some states allow the probate court to keep an original will on file until the death of the testator. At his death and proper application, the will is then admitted to probate. Until such time, the will is not accessible to the public.

INTESTACY

The distribution of property of someone who dies without a will, or dies with a will that is later declared invalid, will be determined by the laws of *intestacy*. These laws prescribe which persons, the order and the proportion they will take from the deceased's estate. As a general maxim, spouses and children of the deceased are usually preferred as designated beneficiaries under most laws of intestacy.

Some states have intestacy laws that do not give the surviving spouse the entire estate. If the intestacy laws of the state in which the deceased died gives the entire estate to both the surviving spouse and their children, the surviving spouse may usually use the minor child's inheritance for the child's support, but this must often be done under court supervision until the child reaches the age of majority.

Other laws provide that the surviving spouse receives the first set amount of the estate (for example the first $50,000), and one-half of the balance. The children of the deceased, if any, would take the remainder of the estate. If the children of the deceased have predeceased him and have left grandchildren, these grandchildren would normally receive the deceased child's share.

Other examples include situations where the deceased is survived by his parents and has no surviving spouse or children. In that case, the deceased's parents would typically receive 100 percent of the estate. Another more remote situation would be where the deceased is only survived by maternal and paternal grandparents. In this case, the deceased's estate would probably be divided equally between the maternal and paternal grandparents, or their brothers and sisters if the grandparents have predeceased the decedent.

The laws of intestate succession can vary greatly from state to state and will always depend on the particular circumstances and family situation. Intestacy laws make no provision for any friends or charities of the deceased. The laws of intestacy succession will not have any specific provision as to who would presumably be the most fit guardian for any minor children. Furthermore, if an individual dies with no will, or with a will that is declared invalid, and has no surviving relatives whatsoever, the deceased's estate will *escheat* totally to the state.

PROBATE

Probate is the court procedure that establishes the legal transfer of a deceased's property and carries out the terms of his will, if any. Most states have different types of procedures used in probate depending on the value of the estate. These different types of probate will be used to effectively close the deceased's formal affairs and distribute his property either according to his will or in compliance with the laws of intestate succession. Each state has its own procedural requirements and notification laws in probating an estate.

In most probate proceedings, the will is filed in the applicable court in the county where the deceased lived. Usually, one of the initial steps is to file an application to have the executor appointed. A complete inventory of the deceased's property is prepared and filed with the court, usually accompanied with a statement of value. The executor of the estate then proceeds to pay all debts he believes are justly owed and eventually sells and distributes any remaining property to the deceased's heirs, family members or others as provided in the will or by the laws of intestacy.

Although the executor has the responsibility of seeing that the terms of the will are carried out and that the deceased's estate is opened, managed and closed according to state law, most executors will hire an attorney to assist with the probate process.

There is sometimes a misconception that the will of the deceased needs to be formally read to all family members or interested parties before or as part of the probate proceedings. Most state laws do not require such a formal reading; rather, the will is filed as a matter of public record in the court of appropriate jurisdiction when the probate process commences.

LIVING WILLS

A *living will* is a document that states that the person signing it does not wish to continue with life due to any type of terminal illness or medical vegetative state. The individual who executes a living will is requesting that family or friends instruct appropriate medical personnel not to take any extraordinary measures in prolonging or continuing their life in the event of a terminal illness or physical condition that, without the implementation of the living will, would serve merely to prolong a hopeless medical situation.

Most states now have laws that allow for living wills. These laws usually permit the withdrawal of life support systems when a patient is determined to be terminally ill or in a persistent vegetative state. Living will laws require that they are carefully drafted according to the law, then witnessed and notarized. Of course, as with a will, the living will can always be revoked or modified. A sample living will is contained in the appendix.

POWER OF ATTORNEY

A *power of attorney* is a document authorizing another person or entity to act as one's agent. It usually needs to be executed only by the person transferring the power. A power of attorney can be either a general power of attorney or a limited power of attorney.

General Power of Attorney

A *general power of attorney* allows another to act in all matters as one's agent. That is, the person receiving the power of attorney can literally "step into the shoes" of the person giving the authority and, accordingly, do whatever that person may have been able to do with his property or assets. A person who has received a general power of attorney can sign legally binding documents on behalf of another. He may also sell, transfer or purchase any property that the person may have without any further authority.

Limited Power of Attorney

A *limited power of attorney* will allow a person to act as another's agent in certain situations only. Depending on how the limited power of attorney is drafted, the person receiving the power of attorney may have the power to, for instance, handle only matters regarding real estate or money held in a particular bank account. A limited power of attorney is also known as a *special power of attorney* in some parts of the country.

The creation of a power of attorney is through a legal document usually prepared by a lawyer or provided by a legal stationery store. The person receiving the power of attorney does not have to be an attorney. If a limited power of attorney is desired, it is best to obtain legal assistance to make sure that the intended power is, in fact, the only power.

Powers of attorney are only valid during the life of the individual who is transferring the power. Once the person receiving the power of attorney is aware of the death of the other, he is obligated by law to cease implementing the power given him. Thus, powers of attorney are not adequate substitutes for a will.

Termination

There are specific methods that can be used to terminate a power of attorney. Destroying the power of attorney document and notifying the individual who has received the power of attorney will typically suffice.

Legal Effect

Powers of attorney are usually only used when one person wants to give another person the power to manage or control all or part of his affairs. It should only be given to individuals who the party trusts and believes that whatever type of action is taken under the power of attorney is in the best interests of the individual who is granting the power. Powers of attorneys are often granted between spouses, and between parents and their adult children.

Durability Provision

If the power of attorney has a *durable power* provision contained within it, it will state that the power of attorney will survive any future disability of the individual granting the power. That is, if a spouse grants his spouse the power of attorney, and the grantor falls into some type of vegetative or senile state, the power of attorney will survive as long as it has the aforementioned type of language as to any future disability. In fact, this is one of the main reasons why a power of attorney is granted. If an individual cannot conduct his own affairs due to mental incapacity or extreme physical infirmness, the person who has received the power of attorney can step in and continue with the day-to-day management of the grantor's affairs without obtaining a court-ordered guardianship or conservatorship, as discussed below.

Remember, however, that a power of attorney will only survive as long as the grantor survives. Once the grantor dies, and the grantee is aware of the death, the power of attorney has no further legal affect. The will of the deceased or the laws of intestate succession will dispose of the estate and final affairs. The appendix includes a durable general power of attorney form.

GUARDIANSHIP-CONSERVATORSHIP

If a person becomes incapacitated to the point that he can no longer care for himself or maintain his financial affairs, a *guardian* and/or a *conservator* is appointed to act on the incapacitated individual's behalf. As mentioned, however, if a general durable power of attorney has been previously executed by the incapacitated person, this may supersede the necessity of the appointment of such a guardian or conservator.

Appointment Procedure

When an application is made to the court to have someone appointed as a guardian for another, it must be shown to the court that the individual involved (known as the *ward*) can no longer provide for his own care, education, support and maintenance and cannot amply or satisfactorily care for himself. Usually a family member or friend files the application with the court and a formal hearing is then scheduled.

At the hearing, evidence is presented regarding the condition of the potential ward and may include medical reports and relevant facts to both the mental and physical condition of the person involved. If it is established that the person can no longer care for himself or his financial affairs, the court must next determine who is an adequate and responsible person to be named as guardian or conservator. Usually a family member will request to be appointed. However, the court can appoint a third party or institution if it believes such an appointment is in the best interest of the ward. Many states have procedures that appoint a third party (usually an attorney) to conduct an independent investigation and report to the court on whether a guardian or conservator is necessary.

Duty of Guardian or Conservator

If an individual is appointed a guardian or conservator, he will have the legal duty to see that the ward's health, care and well-being is adequately protected. A conservatorship, which is usually invoked to supervise only the monetary affairs of the ward, must observe the standard of care in dealing with the protected person's assets that would be observed by any prudent person in dealing with the property belonging to another.

Periodic accountings and financial statements must be presented to the court on any money spent on behalf of the ward by a guardian to ensure that he is meeting his obligations to the health, care, well-being and financial affairs of the ward.

Other Procedural Considerations

The procedure of applying for and appointing a guardian or conservator can sometimes be expensive and, in the case of a contested situation, may involve strained emotions and mental anguish. To avoid this, a wise person will create a general durable power of attorney relationship with a competent friend or relative. A living trust arrangement is another viable option and is discussed below. In a guardianship or conservatorship, the court will almost always require a bond in the event there is any abuse in power by the guardian or conservator to the detriment of the ward. It will usually be the ward's expense to provide for this bond, since theoretically it is for his benefit that the guardianship or conservatorship exists.

TRUSTS

A *trust* is a legal relationship between two or more people where one person, usually known as the *trustee*, holds or manages property for the benefit of the beneficiary. In some trust situations, an individual may be both the trustee and the beneficiary. If a trust is created during the lifetime of the property owner, the person creating the trust is known as the *settlor*. The agreement that creates the trust is known as the *trust agreement* or *trust declaration*.

There are several different types of trusts, including trusts created by courts or by operation of law. However, for purposes of this book, the focus will be on trusts that are created on a voluntary basis.

Creation of a Trust

Usually, a trust must be created or evidenced by a written document. Most states will have laws on this point, but generally speaking, a trust involving real estate will have to be in writing to satisfy the statute of frauds. Also, for a valid trust to exist, any legal title to all property placed into the trust will need to be held by the trustee and not by any beneficiary. As with other written legal documents, the intent of the trust's creator needs to be ascertained in case any questions arise concerning the terms, conditions or effect of the trust arrangement.

Purpose of a Trust

The purpose of the trust arrangement is to transfer property from one individual to a trustee for management, tax or simplification advantages, to include the avoidance of probate at the death of the individual who creates the trust. A trust may also be used to place property beyond the reach of creditors and others who may be entitled to the property of the trust or have unlimited access to the trust property. Another advantage of a trust arrangement is to place the trust property under the control of a trustee, who is given broad discretion in managing it, with investment techniques or abilities used to increase the trust property. Along these lines, a trust can be set up to allow the trust property to be used or managed for the benefit of beneficiaries for many years.

The creation of a trust is usually private and not subject to public inspection or recording, as a will would be at the time of an individual's death. Accordingly, a trust may be used to maintain privacy and save probate expenses that would otherwise be incurred by a deceased property owner who would, in the absence of a trust, transfer his property as provided for in his will.

There are usually ongoing expenses involved in any type of trust arrangement, including annual fees to the trustee or maintenance costs to the trust itself.

Duty of Trustee

The trustee is usually given specific authority as to the amount of power he may have concerning the disposition or maintenance of the trust property. Many types of trusts allow the beneficiary to also be the trustee. A trustee must exercise reasonable care and skill when handling or administering property of the trust. Annual or periodic accounting of the trust property is usually required by the trust's terms. The trustee also has a fiduciary responsibility to any beneficiary of the trust—he must put the interests of the beneficiary, and the trust itself, above his own. A violation of this fiduciary duty may cause the trustee to be personally liable for any lost assets subject to the trust.

Living Trusts

One of the more common types of trust arrangements is a *living trust*, also known as an *intervivos* trust. A living trust can be either *revocable* or *irrevocable*. A revocable living trust is always subject to change or cancellation by the settlor of the trust prior to his death. However, an irrevocable trust cannot have its terms changed or modified.

Revocable Living Trust. A *revocable living trust* allows a trustee to manage the settlor's assets during his life. Currently, revocable trusts contain no inherent tax advantages because the settlor of the trust retains the power to decide how the trust assets are used or dispersed. Even if another individual or beneficiary receives income from the trust, the Internal Revenue Service will still consider the settlor the owner, since he retains the right to receive any income or take back the assets of the trust, if he should so choose.

Revocable living trusts can be used to avoid probate. The trustee will continue to administer the trust assets even after death. The trust, however, can be drafted to allow the trustee to make final distribution of the trust assets at the death of the settlor. A revocable trust can also give a trustee a greater amount of discretion than an executor under a will would have.

Certain conditions and prerequisites can exist in the trust before any disbursements of assets take place, even several years after the settlor's death. For instance, if the settlor does not want his child to receive otherwise inherited property until he reaches age twenty-five, these instructions can be specifically given to the trustee. Without the creation of such condition in a trust, the deceased's child would receive his inheritance or bequest at the time he reaches the age of majority.

Life insurance proceeds can also be directed to go to a trust rather than a named individual. The assets of a revocable trust will likely be subject to any creditors' claims, judgments or levies. Some states, however, do have laws that protect the assets of a revocable living trust against creditor claims.

As mentioned, the individual whose property goes into the trust will be taxed as earned income as long he has the right to receive income, to revoke, or to name or change any beneficiaries of the trust.

Irrevocable Living Trust. Another type of living trust is known as an *irrevocable trust*. When an irrevocable trust is created, the settlor parts forever with whatever assets are being transferred. These trusts are generally created for certain tax benefits and require precise drafting to ensure their validity.

The settlor of an irrevocable trust is transferring, without recourse, his assets to the trust, but the conditions of the trust will allow him to retain some control over its use or disposition.

In addition to being able to specifically state who the beneficiaries of the trust will be, usually the settlor of the irrevocable trust can also provide for which purposes the income from the trust can be used, including the rate at which it will be disbursed, when it will be disbursed, and any other condition the settlor may desire.

The creation of an irrevocable living trust will generally transfer the obligation to pay income taxes from the settlor to the trust itself, or to the beneficiaries of the income derived from the trust. Depending on the amount of money involved, and the tax situation of the settlor, an irrevocable living trust can be used as a significant tax advantage.

Effect of Living Trusts. A prime difference between an irrevocable and a revocable living trust is that, with very few exceptions, the settlor of an irrevocable trust cannot be the trustee.

With both revocable and irrevocable trusts, any property that is not transferred will be subject to probate. If the purpose of creating the trust is to avoid probate, careful monitoring must be made to ensure that any asset in the name of the settlor is immediately and effectively transferred to the trust. However, property held in joint tenancy or previously designated to have a specific beneficiary (such as a life insurance policy) will be subject to probate. However, if the settlor of the trust holds the property in joint tenancy with himself and his trust, or designates the trust as the beneficiary of a life insurance policy, the probate process can be potentially eliminated.

Another point to make regarding irrevocable trusts is that they also may protect the trust property from a state's medicaid program. This fact alone has caused many individuals to create an irrevocable trust to avoid the depletion of their estate by medical bills or nursing home maintenance costs. Unlike revocable trusts, however, an irrevocable trust is very difficult to destroy or negate once it is put into place. For this reason, careful consideration should be made before entering into an irrevocable trust situation.

Testamentary Trust

Another type of trust used is a *testamentary trust*, which is created under the terms of an individual's will, and, like a will, its terms can always be modified during the life of the person who creates it. However, no one can change the terms or provisions of a testamentary trust, including the will executor, after the person who created the trust has died.

Testamentary trusts are often used to minimize income or estate taxes. An example of a testamentary trust is a *qualified terminal interest property* trust, also known as a *Q-tip trust*. All the income from this type of trust is paid to a spouse, and the estate's executor makes sure that the trust is eligible for the marital deduction, thus exempting it from gift or estate taxes. Any assets in a Q-tip trust are taxed through the surviving spouse's estate.

Another type of testamentary trust is a *qualifying domestic trust*, also known as a *Q-dot trust*. This trust is used when the spouse of the deceased is not a U.S. citizen. It preserves the marital deduction of the surviving spouse. Without a Q-dot trust, a portion of the deceased's estate would be subject to federal estate taxes. A Q-dot trust is similar to a Q-tip trust in that the surviving spouse must receive all the income during her lifetime and the executor of the estate must decide how to qualify the trust for this marital deduction. The use of this type of trust results in a tax deferral until the surviving spouse receives certain principal payments or dies. Both a Q-dot and a Q-tip trust need to be specifically drafted to meet these requirements and conditions.

Another type of testamentary trust that is directly contained in a will advises a trustee to hold and maintain property that would otherwise go to the deceased's heirs. For instance, if an individual dies with minor children, his will may provide that a trustee be appointed and hold the property in trust for the children until they reach the age of majority or other designated age.

The trustee is usually given the power to use any money or property being held in trust for the deceased's children for their health, care and well-being until they reach the age of majority.

Trust Limitations

As can be seen from the above discussion, a properly drafted trust can sometimes negate the need for a will. However, I believe it is important to understand the things that a trust cannot do.

If an individual dies with minor children, a trust cannot state the desired person the deceased wants appointed as guardian. Without a will stating who the deceased desires to have as guardian, the court will be in essence "flying blind" on this issue.

If the trust settlor should die without placing all of his property in the trust, the deceased's will controls the disposition of any property that is not subject to the trust. If no will exists, the laws of intestacy in the state in which the deceased resided will be controlling.

The interplay of a trust (whether revocable, irrevocable or testamentary) and a will is often a complex issue that needs to be addressed on a situation-by-situation basis. It is difficult to know precisely if a trust or a will, or some combination thereof, is the best choice without objective professional advice.

Chapter Eight

Law and
the Work Place

A fair day's wages for a fair day's work: It is as just a demand as governed men ever made of governing. It is the everlasting right of man.

— *Thomas Carlyle*

T his chapter will discuss the different issues and topics involved in employment law. Although many of the laws discussed are federal in nature, regulations affecting workers' compensation law and employment contractual law will vary from state to state.

EMPLOYEE AND INDEPENDENT CONTRACTOR

Before a person is covered by the various laws affecting employment, it must first be determined whether he is an *employee* or an *independent contractor*. If an individual is an independent contractor, generally the person who has hired him will not be responsible for any tax withholding consequences, workers' compensation laws or other national labor relation laws or standards. Individuals or companies who hire independent contractors are usually not liable for any acts or wrongdoings of the independent contractor. This is not typically the case when an employee is involved.

Factors to Consider

Although the factors will vary from state to state, generally the most important test in determining whether an individual is an employee or independent contractor is the right to control the performance of the work. That is, if the person is able to exercise complete control and discretion over his work and work product, and his only obligation is to accomplish the desired result or goal, he will in all likelihood be considered an independent contractor.

For instance, if a homeowner hires an individual to install a fence around his yard, the fence-builder is not an employee but an independent contractor hired to accomplish a certain result (build a fence). Conversely, if the person who hires the individual maintains control over the work and can suggest, advise and sometimes dictate how the work is to be accomplished, then chances are the person doing the work will be considered an employee.

Also considered is how the individual doing the work is to be paid. If the compensation is based on payment of a particular sum for the completion of a specific work task, an independent contractor presumption will usually arise. If payment is made on an hourly or weekly basis, without regard to how much work is actually completed, an employee relationship may be involved. Another factor to consider is whether the person doing the job furnishes his own materials, tools or additional employees to accomplish the desired result. Examples of individuals who are considered independent contractors are electricians, plumbers, doctors, attorneys and architects.

Remember that, even if the person doing the work and the person who hires him formally agree to an independent contractor status, the I.R.S. or State Department of Labor may disagree with that assessment.

EMPLOYMENT CONTRACTS AND AT-WILL EMPLOYEES

When an employment relationship is not guaranteed for any definite period of time and no legal prohibition (such as discrimination) exists for the employer to discharge the employee, an employer may terminate the employee whenever and for whatever cause he chooses, without incurring any liability. This is known as *at-will* employment.

The employment-at-will doctrine has been the generally accepted rule in terminating employees for the better part of this century. Through the enactment of both state and federal legislation, and the implementation of union agreements, this doctrine is now being eroded and challenged, based on several theories and concepts.

The social theory often employed to circumvent the employment-at-will rule is that employees should not be terminated without a just reason as a matter of public policy. The argument is that it is in society's best interests to allow an employee to continue employment, unless the employer can demonstrate a good reason (either for business reasons or job performance) why the employee should not continue to work.

Employment Contracts

Aside from this social policy theory regarding the right to continual employment, the primary argument used by an employee against termination is contractual in nature. The employee tries to show that a contract, either express or implied by the nature of the relationship, existed, which was not violated or breached by the employee and, thus, does not give the employer a legal right to terminate the employee's job.

The employee is usually required to show two things to prevail in a breach of contract case for wrongful termination. First, the employee must show the existence of a contract between himself and the employer. The employee must also show that the employer did not abide by the terms of the contract or breached its terms. This is most often accomplished by showing that the employer either failed to follow required procedures in the termination process or fired the employee for no justifiable reason.

Implied Employment Contracts

In other situations, if an employee can demonstrate that the employer consistently and constantly followed certain practices or procedures in terminating employees only for cause over a long period of time, and terminates an employee for no justifiable reason, a court may rule that the termination was invalid due to the creation of an implied contract to terminate employees only for cause. This is true even without the existence of an employee handbook or other type of employment manual. By establishing a pattern of conduct over a long period of time, some courts have held that certain justifiable employment expectations have been created to discharge employees for just cause or serious misconduct only.

Also, if the employee can show that various verbal promises or assertions were made by his employer over a period of time, with these promises stating that job security or long-term employment would be guaranteed or provided as long as satisfactory job performance was maintained, termination of employment without just cause may not be legal.

Whether or not a contract for employment exists, express or implied, will depend on the nature of the job, the facts surrounding job performance, the actual terminology and specifics contained in any employee handbook, and any promises made (whether written or oral) by the employer.

Employee Manuals

In recent cases, employee manuals have been used and interpreted as written evidence of a contract between an employee and an employer. Although originally considered merely statements of employment policy and guidelines for employee conduct, courts have been willing to interpret the language of certain employee manuals as having created a contract between the employer and the employee, outlining acceptable job performance and procedures that need to be followed before any type of termination of an employee can occur.

Many courts have considered employee manuals as contractual in nature containing terms that, either expressed or implied, create standards or procedures that must be met before an employee can be legally discharged. That is, the existence of an employee manual can potentially remove an employer from an employment-at-will situation and place him in a contractual relationship with his employees. This would limit to a certain degree the latitude that he would otherwise have in terminating his employees.

If an employment manual contains a procedure that is to be followed before termination for cause can occur, this procedure must be adhered to before the employer can legally terminate the employee for cause. Generally, the employment manual will outline a step-by-step process before a termination can occur. These steps will usually involve a verbal warning, followed by a written warning or memo to the employee listing the type of conduct considered detrimental or unacceptable to the employer, after which time, if the conduct does not cease, a probationary period may follow. If the unacceptable conduct or performance still does not cease, a short-term suspension or total termination will occur. All these procedures, if required by the employment manual, will often be documented by the employer to avoid any future potential claims for wrongful termination by an employee who, in the employer's opinion, was fired for just cause or for reasons that were outlined in the manual. If these procedures are not followed by the employer, a court may rule that the termination of an employee is not legal. Of course, even if these procedures or standards are in place as stated in the employee manual, if the employer can show that the necessary procedures were followed or just cause existed for the termination of an employee, the employer may still be able to legally terminate the employee.

If an employer is attempting to terminate someone for poor job performance, and the employment manual provides for a periodic employee evaluation process, this process is usually used to document or evidence the employer's past disappointment with the job performance. This also may serve as future evidence for termination of an employee who would otherwise have a contractual right to continue employment.

Employment Manual Disclaimer. Many employers have in their manuals language that makes it clear that the procedures and guidelines contained are not considered or interpreted as a legally binding employment contract. Typically, the following type of language will be conspicuously contained: "The employment relationship between employee and employer will at all times remain an 'at-will relationship' and may be terminated by either party at any time for any reason."

Many employment manuals also contain statements that the employer reserves the right to modify, delete or add to any employment policy in the employment manual. Many employers also have each employee sign a letter of understanding indicating that he appreciates and understands the "at-will" nature of his employment.

The more sophisticated employment manuals also typically contain disclaimers stating that no one in the company, or on behalf of the employer, has the authority or right to enter into any type of agreement for employment for any specific period of time or to make any agreement contrary to the specific terms, disclaimers or conditions of the employment manual. This type of language is used to negate any oral statements or promises made by an immediate supervisor, which might be relied on by the employee as some type of guarantee of future employment.

Effect of Employment Contract

If a precise and express contract is entered between an employee and employer that gives the employee the express right to work for the employer for either a specified period of time, or in perpetuity, an employment contract will exist. Usually these contracts will also contain specific reasons that the employer may terminate an employee. The employer may also retain the right to terminate the employee for no cause, provided that a certain amount of notice is given. If the employee agrees to the terms of the contract at the time he begins employment, and no further promises, assertions or guarantees are made by the employer, the employment contract will govern the relationship between the parties and be the determining factor to whether any subsequent wrongful termination did occur.

Just Cause Termination

As previously referred to, many employment contracts allow the employer to terminate an employee for *just cause*. Just cause is usually considered to be the failure of the employee to perform his work in a diligent and reasonably skillful manner. Most employment contracts require that the employee exert all his skill, knowledge and power for the benefit of the employer.

Just cause for termination of a contractual employee also means that the employee must remain competent. However, incompetence does not mean an occasional omission of duty but, rather, the incompetent actions by the employee must be consistently against the interests of the employer and must prejudice his valid business interests.

It has also been held that when an employee becomes disabled to a degree that greatly affects his job performance, just cause for termination may exist. However, the recent enactment of the Americans With Disabilities Act may modify this right to terminate for just cause to a certain degree. The Americans With Disabilities Act will be discussed later in this chapter.

Termination for just cause also means that an employee must remain loyal to his employer. An employee who uses information, knowledge or his position to the detriment of his employer, usually by providing this type of information to a competitor, will undoubtedly create just cause for his discharge.

DISCRIMINATION IN THE WORK PLACE
There are several federal bodies of law that make it illegal for most employers to discriminate in the hiring, firing and/or promotion of individuals when those acts are based on certain discriminatory classes. The majority of states will also have nondiscriminatory laws that will either mirror or enhance these federal nondiscrimination laws in the work place.

Title VII
Title VII of the Civil Rights Act of 1964 prohibits discrimination in hiring, promoting, firing, paying, providing fringe benefits or other aspects of employment on the basis of race, color, religion, sex or national origin. With some exceptions, all employers who have fifteen or more employees and are engaged in business affecting interstate commerce will be subject to Title VII requirements. An amendment to this law broadens the definition of employer to include state and local governments.

To show that an illegal discriminatory discharge or action occurred against an employee, the employee must first establish inclusion in a *protected category*, such as African American, female, or member of a particular religion. The employee must then prove that he was treated differently, to his detriment, than other employees. It must also be demonstrated that a connection exists between the employee's *protected category* status and the discriminatory act. For instance, if the protected category employee can show that, with all other facts being equal, he was discharged for poor work performance, while other employees with the same or lesser work performance are not, an establishment of cause will have been made.

Age Discrimination
The Age Discrimination in Employment Act prohibits age discrimination of employees and protects job applicants and employees forty years of age or older from discrimination on account of age in hiring, promotion, termination, compensation, terms, conditions or privileges of employment. The Age Discrimination

in Employment Act is applicable to employers that employ twenty or more employees for at least twenty or more calendar weeks in the current year, or in a preceding calendar year, and are engaged in business affecting interstate commerce. The act also includes employees of state and local governments.

A 1986 amendment to the Age Discrimination in Employment Act removed the upper age limit of seventy from the protected category of discrimination for private sector workers who were covered under the act. This amendment had the effect of eliminating a mandatory retirement age of seventy and, further, mandates that employers keep equal group health insurance coverage in place to all employees over age seventy.

Sex Discrimination

Although sex discrimination is prohibited by Title VII of the Civil Rights Act of 1964, the Equal Pay Act protects employees of either sex from pay discrimination on the basis of their gender. The Equal Pay Act does not prohibit variances in pay between men and women if the differences are due to a seniority or merit system, or a system that measures earnings by quantity or quality of production, or any other differential based on factors other than employee's sex.

Federal Contracts

Employers under contract with the federal government, or a subcontractor on a federal government project, will be affected by other federal laws concerning discrimination and employment acts. By executive order, these types of employers are not only prohibited from job discrimination on the basis of race, color, religion, sex or national origin, but must also invoke affirmative action policies to ensure equality of opportunity in all aspects of employment.

Employers under federal contracts or subcontracts are also prohibited from job discrimination because of an employee's handicap. These employers must take action to employ a qualified handicapped individual who, with reasonable accommodation, can perform the functions of a particular job. Further, the Vietnam Era Veterans' Readjustment Act specifically prohibits job discrimination against and requires affirmative action to employ and advance qualified Vietnam veterans.

Damages

An employee who was discriminated against during his employment will usually be compensated by receiving pay retroactive to his discharge. The courts will always try to "make the victim whole," which usually means by trying to place the employee in a place that he would have been in but for the illegal discriminatory act.

The court will, however, sometimes reinstate an employee in the position that he was wrongfully terminated from. The court may also specifically mandate that the employer grant a promotion that was illegally refused to the employee, or possibly grant tenure to the employee, if applicable, and negate any harmful or derogatory information from the employee's file.

Generally speaking, no damages will be awarded under Title VII discrimination acts for pain and suffering that an employee may have experienced due to the illegal discriminatory acts. Punitive damages against the employer are also not made. Attorney fees, however, are usually awarded to the employee if he is successful in establishing his claim under a Title VII, Age Discrimination, or Equal Pay Act violation. It is also possible for an employer to recover his attorney's fees if he can satisfy the court that the employee's case was frivolous or without a reasonable basis in fact.

Some states have laws that allow for the employee to recover damages beyond the recovery of attorney fees and lost wages. These laws vary substantially from state to state, and depending on the type of discrimination involved, an employee may be better served by proceeding with a discriminatory action under state law as opposed to the various aforementioned federal laws.

Sexual Harassment

Claims of sexual harassment in the work place have become more commonplace in recent years. In previous times, unlawful discrimination based on sex or sexual harassment fell under Title VII actions. That is, sexual discrimination was usually couched in a situation where an employee's refusal to accept requests or demands for sex resulted in the demotion or lack of promotion in employment.

However, the Equal Employment Opportunity Commission has established certain criteria in determining whether sexual harassment has in fact occurred, which could lead to a violation of Title VII of the Civil Rights Act. These guidelines usually revolve around some form of unwelcome sexual advances or requests for sexual favors, or possibly verbal or physical conduct of a sexual nature. These types of conduct are illegal when they are made or attempted as a condition of employment, or used as a basis for employment decisions affecting the employee. Also, when sexual misconduct creates an intimidating or hostile working environment, a violation may have occurred.

It should be noted that an employer will usually be held liable for sexual harassment even if it had specifically directed the individual employee accused of sexual harassment to stop. The employer will also be held liable if it knew of the ongoing conduct that constituted sexual harassment, unless the employer can prove that it took immediate and appropriate action once it became aware of the illegal conduct.

Recent cases on this issue have established that an employee who suffers sexual harassment on a job does not necessarily have to incur any tangible monetary job loss. If the employee can establish that various acts created a work environment that proved to be consistently hostile and abusive to the employee, based on ongoing sexual harassment or innuendos, the aggrieved employee could recover for other forms of damage. Also, the acts involved do not necessarily have to be clearly sexual in nature, but may be geared toward or directed to members of the opposite sex that others would consider to be clearly out of place in a normal working environment.

COVENANTS NOT TO COMPETE

A *covenant not to compete* is defined as a legally binding agreement between an employer and an employee where, as a condition of employment or continued employment, the employee agrees, for a certain period of time, and usually within a certain geographic area, to refrain from any type of competition with his former employer. Covenants not to compete usually come into play after the termination of an employee or if an employee voluntarily leaves his place of employment.

Enforceability

Although local standards will vary in whether a covenant not to compete is enforceable, many courts look at the following factors to determine whether the contract is legally valid.

First, the court will determine if the restriction placed on the former employee is reasonably necessary to protect a legitimate business interest of the former employer. The court will also decide if the covenant not to compete unreasonably restricts the employee's right to further economic opportunity or employment. Finally, the court must see if the contract itself is prejudicial to public interest by potentially negating or limiting an individual's right to work. It is this last factor that often makes it difficult for employers to enforce covenants not to compete.

If an employer cannot demonstrate that his employee received certain specialized training or had access to or was given specific knowledge or information pertaining to the employer's business, it is not likely that the court will uphold a covenant not to compete.

Most covenants not to compete state a certain time frame in which the covenant is to exist after the employee has left his former employer. Generally speaking, the longer the duration of the covenant not to compete, the lesser likelihood the court will allow the enforcement of the agreement. Anything longer than one year is often difficult to enforce.

Also, if the covenant not to compete involves a specific geographic area the former employee cannot compete within, the broader the geographic area, the less likely the employer can enforce the agreement. This will, however, depend on the nature of the business and the geographic area in which the employer is currently conducting business. Public policy concerns make it difficult to enforce a covenant not to compete when the affected geographic area is so large that employment in the surrounding area is impossible.

Covenants not to compete are not to be used to keep a former employee from using any skill and general knowledge that he has acquired while on the job. The purpose of a covenant not to compete is to keep an employee from taking legitimate business information from his former employer and using it against him. Courts will not allow covenants not to compete to be used as a restriction on ordinary competition, but will only uphold the agreement if the terms are reasonable and necessary to protect an employer's legitimate business interest and good will. A sample covenant not to compete is found in the appendix.

WORKERS' COMPENSATION

Workers' compensation refers to laws that specifically provide for compensation for injured employees. In principle, workers' compensation is a no-fault system by which employers guarantee payments to employees injured on the job, and employees give up the right to sue employers for work-related injuries. Workers' compensation laws provide an economic and rehabilitation remedy to employees without the necessity of the injured employee proving that the employer was negligent in causing the accident or condition that led to his injury.

Aside from employment-related injuries, death or diseases that an employee incurs as a result of his employment is also subject to compensation without of proving the employer is negligent or otherwise liable, as would be the case under typical tort law. Most workers' compensation laws require that the injured individual actually be an employee as opposed to an independent contractor.

Most states have administrative bodies or specialty courts that deal exclusively with workers' compensation laws. Usually, workers' compensation procedures and hearings are somewhat more simplified and less formal than typical personal injury or negligence lawsuits.

Type of Injury

The key point in workers' compensation laws is that the injury must arise from the course of employment. Generally, the injury or disability must take place within the normal hours of employment, at the place where the employee performs his employment duties, and while the employee in fact carries out his job or some act directly related.

Damages

The amount of money recoverable for damages under injuries suffered by an employee under workers' compensation coverage will usually be determined by strict guidelines. For instance, if an employee suffers a 100 percent disability to his right arm, the amount the employee can recover for this type of permanent disability may be predetermined by the workers' compensation damage laws, and will take into consideration the employee's age, earnings, etc. These types of damages do not include any medical bills or therapy requirements that may be incurred as a result of a disability or injury. Most workers' compensation injuries will be covered by workers' compensation insurance that must be maintained on the employer's employees.

Third Party Injuries

On a somewhat related topic, and as was referred to in chapter six, an employer will usually be held liable for any injury to a third party that is caused by the negligence of his employee, provided the act occurred within the scope of the employee's job. That is, the liability of the employee will be passed to the employer without the injured party being required to show any negligence or wrongdoing on the part of the employer.

DRUGS IN THE WORK PLACE

In 1989, the Federal Drug-Free Work Place Act went into effect. This body of laws requires that employers who are recipients of federal contracts or grants must periodically certify to the federal government that it is making a good-faith effort in providing a drug-free work place.

To accomplish this goal, all employers who are subject to the Drug-Free Work Place Act must do the following:

• Publish and distribute a statement to each employee notifying them that the illegal manufacturing, distribution, possession or use of any controlled substance is prohibited in the work place and specific actions will be taken against any such employee in violation of these prohibitions.

• Establish a drug awareness program.

• Notify all employees that, as a condition of employment, they must abide by the terms of the Drug-Free Work Place Act and notify the employer of any criminal drug violation in the work place.

• Notify the federal government of any employee convicted of a drug violation.

• Impose a sanction or penalty against any employee convicted of a drug violation, including termination of the employee, or require him to participate in and satisfactorily complete a drug assistance or rehabilitation program.

If the employer does not meet these requirements, he will be considered guilty of making a false certification under the Drug-Free Work Place Act and any further payments under the federally awarded contract or grant may be terminated. The contract or grant may be terminated entirely. It is also possible that an employer who violates the certification requirements may be suspended from further participation in any federal contracts for five years.

Private Sector Employees

With regard to private sector employees, the amount of drug or alcohol testing allowed will depend somewhat on if the employee is an *at-will*, union or contract employee. The employee's right of privacy is at odds with the public policy of keeping employees off the job who are under the influence of drugs or alcohol. Employees who are required to take drug tests as a condition of employment will not succeed in alleging an invasion of right of privacy under the U.S. or state constitutions.

However, if an employee can show that the drug testing is an invasion of his common law or statutory right to privacy, he may prevail in successfully avoiding a drug or alcohol test as a condition of employment. Many states have specific laws in this regard, with some recognizing the common law right to privacy while others have ruled that such a right does not negate the employer's ability to test for drugs or alcohol as a condition for employment or continued employment.

Drug or alcohol testing of union employees is usually subject to the terms of the collective bargaining agreement between the employer and the employees. Any drug or alcohol testing program will usually result from negotiations or agreements with the employees' union.

Public Employees

With regard to public employees, the primary dispute with drug or alcohol testing is the employee's right to be free from unreasonable searches and seizures. The courts will usually determine the reasonableness of the testing in deciding whether the alcohol and drug testing methods and criteria are appropriate. Another factor is the type of job involved, with the more responsive jobs being less likely to successfully challenge reasonable testing for drugs or alcohol use. In some employment situations, individualized suspicion of a certain employee will be enough reason to justify an employer's testing for drugs or alcohol.

Other types of public employment jobs, such as public transportation, allow employers to implement random drug and alcohol testing. As a general proposition, then, public employers can implement drug and alcohol testing programs for both current and prospective employees, especially when safety or security concerns are a motivating factor.

Honesty Testing

On a somewhat related note, in 1988 the federal government passed the Employment Polygraph Protection Act. This body of laws limits the use of devices designed to determine the honesty or dishonesty of an employee. These devices usually include polygraphs or voice stress analyzers.

The Employee Polygraph Protection Act mandates that an employer engaged in or affecting interstate commerce is prohibited from requiring or suggesting that any current or prospective employee submit to an honesty or lie detector test. The act further provides that an employer shall not discharge, discipline or discriminate against any employee, including the denial of potential employment, based on a refusal to take, or the results of, an honesty or lie detector test. A penalty of up to $10,000 may be ordered against an employer who violates the act.

All covered employers are required to post a summary of the act in a conspicuous location in the work place. Certain limited exceptions to the act do exist, and usually revolve around jobs of national security or jobs involving nuclear power plants or public water supply facilities.

AMERICANS WITH DISABILITIES ACT

Based on findings showing that discrimination against individuals with disabilities existed in the work place, the Americans With Disabilities Act was drafted and took effect in July 1992. The act provides certain accommodation laws to the disabled.

Employees Affected

The Americans With Disabilities Act applies to employers with fifteen or more employees for each working day in each of twenty or more calendar weeks in the current or preceding calendar year. In the first two years following its enactment, the Americans With Disabilities Act will apply only to private employers with twenty-five or more employees. After July 1994, the act will be applicable to all employers with fifteen or more employees. The major exceptions to the act are the United States government, Indian tribes and certain tax-exempt private membership associations.

Disability Defined

As stated, the act requires employers to make reasonable accommodations for disabled workers and disabled job applicants to avoid discriminating against them. Under the act, an employee or potential employee is considered disabled if he has a physical or mental impairment that substantially limits one or more of his major life activities, if the individual has a record of such an impairment, or if the individual is regarded as having such an impairment. The act does exclude users of illegal drugs from its definition of disability.

Who is and is not a qualified individual with a disability is defined by the act as any person with a disability who, with or without reasonable accommodation, could perform the essential functions of the employment position that he holds or desires and is applying for.

Prohibited Discrimination

The acts of discrimination by an employer prohibited under the Americans With Disabilities Act are broadly defined. In general, it states that an employer cannot discriminate against a qualified individual with a disability because of the disability. The discrimination is not to occur in either the job application procedure, the hiring or discharge process, the compensation of a disabled employee, the potential advancement of disabled employees, or job training or privileges of employment.

Employer Requirements

The Americans With Disabilities Act requires an employer to reasonably accommodate the condition of the disabled employee. Although judicial interpretations of the requirements of Americans With Disabilities Act are just beginning, the term *rea-*

sonable accommodation usually means that the employer must make existing facilities at the work place accessible and usable by individuals with disabilities. It also means that the employer must, within reasonable means, restructure the job or modify work schedules, or make other appropriate adjustments or modifications to accommodate individuals with disabilities.

The Americans With Disabilities Act also states that an employer must make these reasonable accommodations without *undue hardship* to the employer's business. Again, what constitutes undue hardship is going to be open for interpretation for years to come. However, some factors that will probably be looked to when determining whether undue hardship exists will be the size of the business, the financial resources of the employer, and the type of business in which the employer is engaged.

As can be seen, the Americans With Disabilities Act greatly increases the duty of an employer to accommodate a handicapped or disabled current or potential employee. The basic premise of the act is to apportion a degree of responsibility and cost of accommodating disabled employees to the private business sector.

Chapter Nine

Business Law

The chief business of the American people is business.
    — *Calvin Coolidge*

This chapter will focus on the different types of business organizations and the legal effects and ramifications of each.

SOLE PROPRIETORSHIPS

A *sole proprietorship* is a type of business entity in which one individual owns all (or substantially all) of the business assets. If the business is fairly stable without the prospect of immediate or rapid growth, the sole proprietorship is the form generally used. Typical sole proprietors are individuals working or practicing a trade or craft on behalf of himself, usually with very few employees or independent contractors working for him.

Creation and Effect

There is generally no formal requirement for becoming a business entity operating as a sole proprietor. Generally, the sole proprietor will be *operating as*, for example, Bob Jones doing business as Jones Construction Service. If a checking account or banking account is maintained by the sole proprietor for business purposes, it will be held under this name.

Since the sole proprietor's business is merely an extension of himself as an individual, business debts and individual debts are often commingled. The law will not consider the sole proprietor's business assets as separate and distinct from his personal life. Accordingly, debts of the sole proprietor, whether personal or business, are subject to any assets the sole proprietor may own, whether they be individual or business.

Taxation

There is no separate tax on the sole proprietor's business. Rather, all income earned by the sole proprietor is taxed as self-employed income to the sole proprietor, subject to all applicable business expenses and deductions.

Name Usage

In many states, if the sole proprietor is using the words *corporation*, *incorporated* or *company* in his business name or dealings, he could be subject to certain state fines based on an unfair trade practice violation, because the usage of such words may lead a customer to believe he is dealing with a corporation rather than a sole proprietorship.

As mentioned, most states require no formal filing or legal action to create a sole proprietorship. Instead, the individual operating his business as a sole proprietor merely conducts his business without the formality of a partnership agreement or incorporation of a business. However, if the sole proprietor wants to use a particular trade name, any such trade name (if available) could and should be registered with the secretary of state or applicable state office to ensure that the sole proprietor is not using the corporate or trade name owned by another individual or entity.

PARTNERSHIPS

A business relationship created by a *partnership* is a legally binding voluntary contract between two or more persons or entities. These individuals agree to contribute either money, time, labor or all of these things to the business into which they have decided to enter. Further, an arrangement for distributing any profits the partnership may realize is also contained within the partnership agreement.

Creation

Most states have adopted the Uniform Partnership Act, which specifically provides the necessary procedures for the creation and registration of a legally created partnership. This will entail drafting and signing a partnership agreement and filing a certificate of partnership with the county clerk's office where the partnership is going to do business.

General Partnership

A *general partnership* is a business relationship in which the general partners are equal in the sharing of profits and are equally liable for any business losses. Also, general partners are usually considered equal in managing the business, even though capital or labor contributions may not be equal.

Limited Partnership

A *limited partnership* is a legal relationship consisting of at least one general partner and one or more limited (or special) partners. The limited partners will generally contribute only cash to the partnership, without being involved in the active management or the day-to-day operation of the business. Limited partners are usually liable only up to the amount of money that they have contributed to the partnership.

Partner Authority

Any partner can legally bind the partnership because most partners will be assumed by others to have the necessary authority to enter into transactions that will render the partnership responsible. In essence, every partner of the partnership acts as an agent for the partnership and the other partners.

Partnership Agreement

When a partnership is created, the most important aspect is the partnership agreement. This is a document outlining the type of business the partnership has agreed to pursue, including any necessary permit or license needed to pursue that type of business.

Some partnership agreements state the specific periods of time that the partnership is to exist. However, most partnership agreements are created to last in perpetuity, unless otherwise agreed on between the partners. Also, some mention should be made of the procedure in admitting a new partner, whether special or general.

The partnership agreement should also contain a provision

that states what exactly the general partners are expected to contribute to the business, whether it is a cash contribution, labor contribution, or both. Most partnership agreements state that all general partners agree to give their full-time attention and efforts to the success of the business. Also, how the partnership is to be managed, including the voting rights of any and all general partners, should be set forth in the agreement.

Other factors considered in the partnership agreement are the way any compensation is to be determined, the sharing of profits and losses, if any, and the effect on the partnership of any death or withdrawal of a partner. It should be specifically stated that unless agreed on to the contrary, all property acquired by the partners with partnership funds, assets or efforts will become partnership property.

If the partnership agreement entails limited partners, it should specifically state that these partners are liable only up to the amount of capital they have contributed to the partnership. Limited partners are rarely given any rights or control over partnership affairs. This is in the limited partner's interest, because without such a clause, his potential inability rises to that of general partner.

Taxation

Partnerships are treated as a *pass through* entity by the I.R.S. and are not subject to taxation as a separate legal body. Any profit earned by the partnership is divided equally among the general partners and taxed as income to the general partners under the taxation rules for self-employed individuals. General partners will be taxed on their respective proportionate shares of partnership income, whether or not any of the money is actually distributed to the partners. Although the partnership does file a tax return, it is only for information purposes as the partnership itself pays no income taxes.

Liability

Regarding liability to partnership creditors, as previously alluded to, the general partners will be individually liable for all partnership obligations. Limited partners will, under most circumstances, be responsible only for debts of the partnership up to the amount of any money contributed by them to the partnership. Accordingly, any individually owned assets of the general partners can be subject to partnership debts.

Name Usage

As with sole proprietorships, if a partnership openly does business including the words *corporation, company, incorporated* or *Inc.*, the partnership could potentially be fined or penalized for using a name that would lead its customers to believe they are dealing with a corporation as opposed to a partnership. Also, as with sole proprietorships, business partnerships can own and register tradenames that can be used by the partnership in their business. A check with the secretary of state or commerce in that particular state will allow the partners to discover whether their desired tradename is available, and the necessary procedures involved in registering it.

CORPORATIONS

A *corporation* is a legal entity that is usually created for the purpose of conducting business. The creation and perpetuation of a corporation must be done in accordance with the state in which the corporation is doing business or has its registered office. The creation of a corporation creates a new legal entity that is legally treated as separate and distinct from the individuals who own it (the shareholders).

Closely Held Corporation

General Motors, IBM and Ford Motor Company are all examples of large, widely held American corporations. The type of corporation that this book is concerned with, however, is the type commonly known as a *close corporation* or *closely held corporation*.

A closely held corporation is a corporation whose shares of stock are usually held by one or two stockholders (also known as shareholders). There are usually no public investors and the stockholders are active in the day-to-day business operations. Usually the board of directors, the corporate officers, as well as the shareholders are all the same people. In many states, it is possible for one person to be the sole corporate stockholder, the only individual on the board of directors, the president, vice-president, secretary and treasurer. Nevertheless, the corporation will be considered a separate legal entity from the individual who wears all these corporate hats on behalf of the corporation.

Creation of a Corporation

The procedure used to create a corporation is called *incorporating*. Typically, an individual will contact an attorney and proceed with having the desired corporate name checked to see if it is still available in the state where the corporation will do business. If the corporate name is available, or no other person or entity has registered the name as a tradename, *articles of incorporation* are then drafted.

Articles of incorporation are the papers that formally set out the person who is creating the corporation, the purpose of the corporation and the various annual meeting requirements that will be met under applicable state law. These articles of incorporation are then filed with a central state office (such as the secretary of state) so that the creation of the corporation becomes a matter of public record. Any state corporate taxes, typically called *state corporate occupation taxes*, can then be levied.

Once the articles of incorporation are filed, a copy is also filed in the county clerk's office where the corporation will have its main location. Also, some type of notice of incorporation publication requirement is often necessary to complete the process.

After these incorporating formalities are taken care of, an initial meeting of the incorporators takes place. At this meeting, shares of stock are sold or transferred and the stockholders of the corporation then elect the *board of directors*. The board of directors are the individuals who elect the corporate officers, such as the president, vice-president, secretary and treasurer. These corporate officers are responsible for the day-to-day operation of the company. The board of directors has the power to hire and fire corporate officers.

Keep in mind that the majority of corporations, and almost all closely held corporations, will be operating with only one or two stockholders, one or two board of directors members, and usually only one or two people who are corporate officers. Thus, the procedures described in the preceding paragraphs are fairly easily satisfied.

Effect of Corporation

Once the corporation has been created, it is the corporation, and not the stockholders, board of directors or the corporate officers, that conducts business with the public. One of the most important reasons for creating a corporation to conduct business is to negate any personal liability that the stockholders or corporate officers may otherwise have regarding corporate debts or liabilities. Only the corporation, by being a separate legal entity, will be responsible for any debts or liabilities that it may incur.

However, in many instances, the people involved in the day-to-day operation of the corporation do not make it clear to the general public or to the corporation's creditors that they are, in fact, operating under a corporation. By not making it obvious that they are a corporation, it is possible that the corporate officers, stockholders or board of directors can be personally liable for what would otherwise be a corporate debt. This obviously negates one of the reasons for creating a corporation, the inherent limitation of liability that goes with it.

Maintaining the Corporate Shield

As alluded to, any time a corporation is created for business purposes, anybody who is working for or operating the corporation must always make it clear that he is an agent or representative of the corporation and is not operating as an individual. This is usually accomplished by maintaining a corporate bank account under the corporation's name, always using corporate stationery or documentation in dealing with the public or creditors, and making it obvious in any way possible to all people coming in contact with the business that they are dealing with a corporation and not an individual who is doing business as a particular tradename or company.

Any time an individual signs a document on behalf of the corporation, he should sign it as a representative. The corporation name should first be placed on anything that needs to be signed by the company, followed by a reference to the capacity of the individual who is actually signing. For example, if an individual signs a contract on behalf of a company, he should sign it as follows: "Bob Jones, on behalf of Jones and Company, Inc."; or, if the individual is a corporate officer, he should sign as follows: "ABC, Inc. by Arnie B. Coolidge, President."

Personal Liability

An individual may become personally liable for a corporate debt if he signs as an individual to guarantee a corporate debt. Generally, a newly organized corporation will require personal guarantees by certain individuals, whether the stockholders or the board of directors, before any type of financing will be extended to the newly formed corporation, unless it can be demonstrated that the corporation is adequately capitalized.

Personally guaranteeing a corporate debt cannot be strictly avoided, in fact it is often a necessary evil in the creation of any new business corporation. Nevertheless, when the corporation is dealing with the public or with creditors who have not required a personal guarantee, these procedures make sure that the corporation, and not the individual, is the responsible party.

As with other types of guarantees, an individual guaranteeing a debt of a corporation can be liable based on a guarantee of payment or collection. A guarantee of payment creates an absolute liability on the guarantor to pay any debt of the corporation, if and when the corporation fails to make the required payment. A guarantee of collection, however, is a promise by the guarantor that if the creditor cannot collect from the corporation, the guarantor is liable. The creditor must exhaust any remedies it has against the corporation before it can pursue the guarantor for payment. This usually means that the creditor must file suit and obtain a judgment against the corporation, and prove to the satisfaction of the court that the judgment is uncollectible, before the guarantor can be held liable.

Piercing the Corporate Veil

Do not presume that the creation of a corporation will absolutely absolve the stockholders or corporate officers from debts of the corporation. Creditors have been successful in going after the individuals behind the corporation for what would otherwise be a corporate debt by *piercing the corporate veil*. The individuals behind the corporation become responsible for corporate obligations, despite any nonguarantee of these debts by the individuals involved.

In piercing the corporate veil, a creditor must prove that the corporate officers, stockholders or board of directors used the corporation merely as a shell or fraudulent device in an attempt to deceive creditors. The facts of each particular case must be taken into consideration in deciding whether the individuals can be held liable because of their actions in creating and maintaining the corporation.

Although the applicable law will vary from state to state, the following factors are usually considered in determining whether the corporate veil should be pierced and the individuals behind the corporation held personally liable:

- Insolvency of the corporation at the time the debt was incurred
- Failure of the corporation to conduct required annual stockholder or board of director meetings
- Failure to maintain adequate corporate records
- Removal of unreasonable funds from the corporation by a stockholder
- General commingling of activities and/or funds of a dominant and the corporation

A creditor attempting to hold individuals liable for a corporate debt will most likely file a lawsuit against both the corporation and the individuals. The creditor must first establish that a corporate debt exists, and then move that the individuals behind the corporation are liable.

It should be noted that, in most circumstances, the corporation's board of directors and corporate officers can be held personally liable for any unpaid corporate tax debts owed the federal government. This is true regardless of whether the corporate veil was adequately maintained.

Other Corporate Legalities

Some of the other general principles of law that apply to a business corporation are that a corporation will exist in perpetuity unless otherwise dissolved by law or by action of the owners of the corporation (the shareholders). As previously mentioned, the creation of a corporation establishes a legal entity that is separate from the corporate shareholders. The corporation can file a lawsuit or enter into an agreements with other corporations or individuals.

Although a corporation can establish and maintain its own credit and financial capabilities, when a new corporation is created, it usually will be the individual guarantors who create the financial bedrock of the company. However, theoretically a corporation has a financial history and credit rating distinct from its stockholders or corporate officers.

Taxation

Any net profit of the corporation is taxed as income to the corporation. Owners of the corporate stock will be taxed only on any dividends distributed to them. However, any compensation paid to a corporate officer is treated as typical income or wages earned. Also, most states will have corporate occupation taxes that require the corporation to pay a certain amount to the state yearly to perpetuate its legal existence.

Sub-Chapter S Corporation

Sometimes, for tax purposes, a closely held corporation will elect to become a *sub-chapter S corporation*. When the requirements of a sub-chapter S corporation are met, any undistributed taxable income to the corporation will be taxed to the stockholders. This way, a sub S corporation avoids any corporate income tax. Further, any corporate losses can be claimed directly by its shareholders. Accordingly, a sub-chapter S corporation, for purposes of income taxes, operates more like a general partnership than a true corporation. Usually small corporations or businesses are best suited to implement a sub S status to avoid double taxation on corporate and dividend income. An accountant or tax professional should be consulted if the stockholders believe that a sub S status for their corporation would be desirable.

Professional Corporation

Another type of corporation is called a *professional corporation*, also known as a *PC*. Professional corporations are organized by individuals who are selling personal services to the public. These personal services will usually require a specific license or legal authorization that could not be performed by a corporation, such as the practice of dentistry, law, medicine or accounting.

The election of a professional corporation status for a corporation is usually designed to take advantage of certain tax laws.

Understand that the general shield of liability that exists for a business corporation is modified somewhat for a professional corporation. The incorporation of a professional corporation does not alter the duty or privilege that is owed to the PC's patients or clients, and it does not insulate it from liability as to any malpractice committed by the PC's professional employees.

Dissolution

A corporation can be dissolved by different methods. Most states have definite procedures to follow when a corporation is legally dissolved. *Dissolution* usually involves written notice to any existing creditors of the corporation, including publishing a notice of dissolution. Any assets of the corporation must be sold to pay remaining corporate debts.

Another method of corporate dissolution is where it is deemed to no longer legally exist due to its noncompliance with state filing or tax laws. For example, if a corporation fails to pay its annual occupation tax, it will likely be considered dissolved by the secretary of state. Many businesses that no longer operate allow their corporations to dissolve in this manner. If a corporation consistently fails to have legally required annual shareholder and board of director meetings, dissolution may also occur.

FRANCHISES

A *franchise* is a business relationship where a local person, partnership or corporation (known as the *franchisee*) contractually agrees to conduct his business in accordance with methods, procedures and products prescribed by an established manufacturer or supplier (known as the *franchisor*). The franchisor may also assist the local franchisee with advertising, marketing or other advisory services. Many national fast-food restaurants are operated by way of franchise agreements.

Sometimes the franchise contract grants the franchisee only the right to use a particular tradename or trademark. Other times a more complex arrangement is made commonly referred to as format franchising.

Format Franchising

Format franchising is where the franchise contract involves an ongoing connection between the franchisor and franchisee. The franchisee is required to use only the products or services provided by the franchisor to maintain local quality control within the franchise chain. The costs or fees required of the franchisee in entering into a format franchise are often higher than with the other franchise arrangements.

Disclosure Statement

Whenever a franchise contract is offered, the Federal Trade Commission requires the franchisor to provide certain written information to the potential franchisee. This disclosure statement will contain a great deal of information about the background, legality and financial status of the franchisor. It also entails a synopsis of how the franchisor operates and maintains its franchise system, including a description of the franchiser's and franchisee's obligations and responsibilities to each other.

Although franchises can be advantageous to an individual just starting a business, they are no guarantee of success. Both the aforementioned disclosure statements and the prepared franchise contract need to be carefully reviewed and analyzed before any commitments of capital or labor are made.

SOME FINAL THOUGHTS

I trust that the information contained in this book has shed some light on the otherwise dark and misty world of consumer law. Always keep in mind that every law is designed to protect or promote certain rights and responsibilities that we have as citizens, as well as to enhance society's well-being. Our legal system exists to see that these laws are effectively and fairly enforced.

It has been stated many times in recent years that America has an abundance of attorneys. One of the advantages of being inundated with lawyers is the competition it brings to the marketplace. In many areas, initial legal consultations are typically free or offered at a minimal charge.

This being the case, if a person feels that his legal rights are being violated, or if he has a legal wrong that needs to be corrected, or if he needs to use the legal system to protect his personal or business interests, a "step through the legal looking-glass" is always available. Hopefully, this book will allow you to intelligently and confidently use our laws to your advantage without anxiety toward the legal unknown.

ATTORNEY FEE AGREEMENT

To:

Re:

1. <u>Agreement of Attorney</u>. Attorney agrees to provide legal representation to client, which will include all required telephone calls, correspondence, legal drafting and conferences, in connection with the following Issues:

_____

_____

_____

_____

_____

_____

_____

2. <u>Agreement of Client</u>. Client agrees to pay Attorney Fees and to advance Court Costs, as described below, and to cooperate with attorney requests for information and documentation.

3. <u>Attorney Fees</u>. The agreed upon Attorney Fee for professional services required concerning the Issues described is

$ _____.

_____

_____

In the event additional Issues (not described above) require additional Legal Representation, this Agreement may be modified.

4. <u>Court Costs</u>. Court Costs to be advanced by Client are as follows: _____

_____

_____

Client agrees to pay additional Court Costs when authorized by Client.

5. <u>General Agreement of Attorney and Client</u>. All payments are due on the 20th of each month. If payment is not received by the 30th of such month, a $5.00 rebilling cost will be charged to the account balance. Nonpayment by Client may result in withdrawal from representation by Attorney.

Dated: _____   _____
                                    Client

                                    _____
                                    Client

                                    _____
                                    Attorney

ATTORNEY CONTINGENT FEE AGREEMENT

THIS CONTRACT AND AGREEMENT made and entered into this _____ day of _____, 1993, by and between Latenser & Johnson, P.C., (hereinafter called attorneys), and _____, (hereinafter called client).

WITNESSETH:

Whereas, client suffered damages on or about the _____ day of September, 19 _____; and

Whereas, client wishes to retain attorneys to make claim for damages for personal injuries and property damages against _____.

Now, therefore, it is agreed by and between the parties as follows:

1. Attorneys agree to make any and all investigations, prepare and file any pleadings necessary, conduct all discovery required in order to protect the interests of client, try the case, if necessary, and perfect and litigate any appeal, if deemed necessary, and defend against any adverse appeal.

2. Client agrees to pay attorneys a sum of money equal to one-fifth ($\frac{1}{5}$) of any sums recovered by settlement within 90 days of the date of this Agreement, or a sum of money equal to one-fourth ($\frac{1}{4}$) of any sums recovered by settlement thereafter. In the event suit is filed, client agrees to pay attorneys a sum of money equal to one-third ($\frac{1}{3}$) of any sums recovered by settlement or judgment. In the event appeal is docketed, client agrees to pay attorneys a sum of money equal to two-fifths ($\frac{2}{5}$) of any sums recovered by settlement or judgment.

3. In the event that no recovery is had, client shall not be indebted in any sum whatsoever to attorneys for services rendered in this matter, but only for actual court costs or agreed upon expenses incurred by attorneys on behalf of client, including medical records and reports, expert witness fees, or other authorized expense.

_____
Client

_____
Client

_____
Attorney

DIVORCE PETITION

IN THE DISTRICT COURT OF
MAKE BELIEVE COUNTY, NEBRASKA

YOUR AVERAGE HUSBAND, Petitioner,	DOC. NO.
vs.	PETITION
YOUR AVERAGE WIFE, Respondent.	(Domestic Relations)

Comes now Your Average Husband, Petitioner, and for cause of action against Your Average Wife, alleges and states as follows:

I.

Petitioner presently resides at Corner of East and West Streets, Anywhere, Make Believe County, Nebraska, and has resided in Make Believe County, Nebraska, for more than one year prior to the date of filing of his Petition herein, with a bonafide intention of making this state his permanent home. Petitioner is represented in this action by Hot Shot Lawyer, Business District, Anywhere, Nebraska. Respondent resides at Corner of North and South Streets, Anywhere, Make Believe County, Nebraska, and has resided in Douglas County, Nebraska, for more than one year prior to the date of filing of the Petition herein, with a bonafide intention of making this state her permanent home.

II.

Petitioner and Respondent were married at Anywhere, Make Believe County, Nebraska, on July 4, 1980. One child has been born to Petitioner and Respondent as a result of said marriage, namely:
Your Average Child, born July 4, 1984.

Petitioner and Respondent are fit and proper persons to have custody of the parties' minor child awarded to them. It is in the best interest of said minor child that her care, custody and control be awarded to Respondent, subject to reasonable visitation by Petitioner. No other dependent minor children are affected by these proceedings.

III.

Neither Petitioner nor Respondent is a party to any other action pending for dissolution, separation or divorce.

IV.

Neither Petitioner nor Respondent is a member of the military services of the United States or of its allies.

V.

The marriage relationship of Petitioner and Respondent is irretrievably broken and no reasonable prospect remains for reconciliation. It is in the best interests of the parties that a Decree of Dissolution be entered.

VI.

During the course of their marriage, Petitioner and Respondent have acquired real and personal property and have incurred obligations. An equitable division of the parties' property and obligations should be made.

VII.

There is no adequate remedy at law.

WHEREFORE, Petitioner prays that this Court enter a Decree and orders providing for the following relief:

a) Decree of Dissolution of the marriage of the parties;

b) Orders awarding custody of the parties' minor child to Respondent; subject to the right of reasonable visitation by the Petitioner;

c) Orders providing for the award of child support to be paid by the Petitioner to the Respondent for the support of the parties' minor child as provided by Nebraska Supreme Court Guidelines;

d) Orders providing for the equitable division of property and obligations of the parties;

e) Such other and further relief as is just.

> YOUR AVERAGE HUSBAND,
> Petitioner,
>
>
> By: _____
> HOT SHOT LAWYER
> Attorney for Petitioner
> Business District
> Anywhere, Nebraska

DIVORCE DECREE

IN THE DISTRICT COURT OF
MAKE BELIEVE COUNTY, NEBRASKA

YOUR AVERAGE HUSBAND,
    Petitioner,

vs.

YOUR AVERAGE WIFE,
    Respondent.

DOC. 123   NO. 321

DECREE

On January 6, 1993, the above captioned cause came on for trial on the Petition of the Petitioner, Your Average Husband, for dissolution of the marriage of the parties and on pleadings. The Petitioner appeared in person and by counsel, Hot Shot Lawyer. The Respondent, Your Average Wife, appeared in person and by counsel, Smooth Talking Lawyer. The parties were sworn, evidence was adduced, arguments made, and the matter submitted for decision by the Court. The Court, having reviewed the evidence, final arguments, and law, finds as follows:

1. The parties have resided in the State of Nebraska for more than one year prior to the filing of the herein action; that the Petitioner was a resident of Make Believe County, Nebraska at the time this action was filed; that neither party is in the military services of the United States or any of its allies; that there are no other actions pending between the parties for divorce, dissolution or separation; and that the Court has jurisdiction of the parties and of the subject matter of this action.

2. That the parties have experienced marital difficulties and that efforts have been made to effect a reconciliation, that same have failed and any further efforts would be fruitless; that the relationship existing between the parties is irretrievably broken, and that the relationship should be dissolved.

3. The parties were married on July 4, 1980, at Anywhere, Make Believe County, Nebraska. One child has been born the issue of the marriage who will be affected by these proceedings, to wit: Your Average Child, born July 4, 1984. That both parties are fit and proper persons to be awarded the care, custody and control of the minor child. It is in the best interests of said minor child

that her permanent care, custody, and control be awarded to the Respondent, subject to reasonable visitation by the Petitioner, as hereinafter provided.

4. The Petitioner should be ordered to pay Respondent, through the office of the Clerk of the District Court of Make Believe County, Nebraska, child support in the sum of $600.00 per month, commencing on February 1, 1993, and a like sum on the 1st day of each month thereafter until such child reaches her majority under Nebraska law, becomes emancipated, self-supporting, married, dies, or until further Order of the Court.

5. The Petitioner should be ordered to pay Respondent, through the office of the Clerk of the District Court of Make Believe County, Nebraska, as alimony for the support and mainte-nance of the Respondent, the sum of $500.00 per month for sixty (60) months, commencing on February 1, 1993, and a like sum on the first day of each month thereafter for sixty consecutive months, said alimony to terminate upon the death or remarriage of the Respondent, the death of the Petitioner, or the passage of sixty months, whichever shall first occur.

6. That an equitable distribution and division of the real prop-erty, personal property and obligations of the parties should be made, as is hereinafter more specifically set forth.

IT IS THEREFORE ORDERED, ADJUDGED AND DECREED that the marriage of Your Average Husband and Your Average Wife, which marriage was entered into at Anywhere, Make Believe County, Nebraska, on July 4, 1980, is hereby dissolved and the dissolution and this Decree of Dissolution shall become final and operative except for the purpose of review by appeal, without any futher action of the Court on a) the date of death of one of the parties to the dissolution; or, b) six months after the Decree is rendered, whichever occurs first. If the Decree becomes final and operative upon the date of death of one of the parties to the dissolution, the Decree shall be treated as if it became final and operative the date it was rendered. For the purpose of review by appeal, the Decree shall be treated as a final order as soon as it is rendered. If an appeal is instituted within thirty (30) days of the date the Decree is rendered, such Decree shall not become final until such pro-ceedings are finally determined. Neither the Petitioner nor the Respondent may remarry anyone, anytime or anyplace until the expiration of said six month period from the time of the execution of the Decree by this Court, each of them being under a legal, total and complete disability to do so.

IT IS FURTHER ORDERED, ADJUDGED AND DECREED that the care, custody, care and control of the parties' minor child be and hereby is awarded to the Respondent, subject to the Petitioner's right of reasonable visitation with said minor child, which shall include the following as visitation rights:

1. The Petitioner is entitled to have visitation every other weekend and every Tuesday evening, along with Easter, July 4, Thanksgiving Day, Christmas Eve, and New Year's Day in the even numbered years, and Memorial Day, Labor Day, Christmas Day and New Year's Eve in the odd numbered years. Petitioner is granted visitation with said minor child on said minor child's birthday in the odd numbered years and on Father's Day, regardless of whether it is the Petitioner's weekend for visitation. Respondent is to have said minor child on Mother's Day, regardless of whether it is the Petitioner's weekend for visitation.

2. Respondent shall authorize the educational institution being attended by said minor child to provide Petitioner, at Petitioner's request and expense, copies of report cards, notices of open houses, notices of parent-teacher conferences and school programs.

3. Respondent shall authorize any attending physician or dentist treating said minor child to provide Petitioner, at Petitioner's request and expense, any medical and/or dental reports. Respondent and Petitioner shall advise each other should the said minor child become so ill as to consult a physician when said minor child is in their custody.

IT IS FURTHER ORDERED, ADJUDGED AND DECREED that the obligations and property of Petitioner and Respondent be and hereby are awarded and distributed as follows:

1. <u>Child Support</u>: The Petitioner is ordered to pay Respondent, through the office of the Clerk of the District Court of Make Believe County, Nebraska, child support in the sum of $600.00 per month child support for the support and maintenance of the minor child of the parties, commencing on February 1, 1993, and a like sum on the 1st day of each month thereafter until said child reaches the age of majority under Nebraska law, becomes

emancipated, self-supporting, marries, dies, or until further Order of the Court.

2. Alimony: The Petitioner is ordered to pay Respondent, through the office of the Clerk of the District Court of Make Believe County, Nebraska, as alimony for the support and maintenance of the Respondent, the sum of $500.00 per month for Sixty (60) months, commencing on February 1, 1993, and a like sum on the first day of each month thereafter for sixty consecutive months; said alimony to terminate upon the death or remarriage of the Respondent, the death of the Petitioner, or the passage of sixty months, whichever shall first occur.

3. Real Estate: The family residence, legally described as: Lot 10, Block 10, Sticks and Stones Addition to the City of Anywhere, as surveyed, platted, and recorded in Make Believe County, Nebraska, is awarded to the Respondent, free and clear of any interest of the Petitioner, subject, however, to Respondent's obligation to assume and pay any indebtedness thereon, holding Petitioner harmless from any liability therefor.

4. Household Goods and Personal Property: Petitioner is awarded the household goods, furnishings and personal items currently in his possession and Respondent is awarded the household goods, furnishings and personal items currently in her possession.

5. Motor Vehicles: Petitioner is awarded all right, title and interest in and to the automobile in his possession, free and clear of any interest of the Respondent. Respondent is awarded the automobile in her possession, free and clear of any interest of the Petitioner.

6. Obligations: The Petitioner shall pay all debts and obligations incurred by the parties subsequent to the date of the filing of the Petition herein, holding Respondent harmless from any liability therefor. Respondent shall assume and pay the indebtedness on the parties real estate awarded to her, holding Petitioner harmless from any liability therefor. Each party shall pay his or her own debts incurred subsequent to the date of filing of the Petition herein.

7. Bank Accounts:

A. The Petitioner shall be awarded all right, title and interest in all bank accounts owned by Petitioner or in which Petitioner has an interest, free and clear of any right, title, claim or interest of the Respondent.

B. The Respondent shall be awarded all right, title and interest in all bank accounts owned by Respondent or in which Respondent has an interest, free and clear of any right, title, claim or interest of the Petitioner.

8. Pension and Retirement Plans: Each party is awarded all interest in any pension or retirement plan in which they have an interest, free and clear of any interest of the other party.

9. Health and Accident Insurance: The Petitioner shall provide health and accident coverage on said minor child until said child reaches the age of majority under Nebraska law, so long as it is available through Petitioner's employer. Any medical, dental, hospital, orthodontia, eye wear, or health expense, including the examination of said minor child not covered by insurance, shall be paid for equally by the Petitioner and the Respondent. The Petitioner shall maintain the Respondent on his health and accident insurance policy during the interlocutory period.

IT IS FURTHER ORDERED, ADJUDGED AND DECREED that the Petitioner be and hereby is required to furnish to the Clerk of the District Court of Make Believe County, Nebraska, his address, telephone number, social security number, the name of his employer, and any other information the court shall deem relevant until any such judgment ordered to advise the Clerk of the Court of any changes in the aforementioned required information between the time of the entry of this Decree and the payment in full of any judgment entered herein. In the event Petitioner fails to pay any such child support payment as such failure is certified each month by the District Court Clerk in cases where court ordered support is delinquent in an amount equal to the support due and payable for a one month period of time, he shall be subject to income withholding and may be required to appear in court on a date to be determined by the Court and show cause why such payment was not made. In the event that Petitioner fails to pay or appear as so ordered, a warrant shall be issued for his arrest.

IT IS FURTHER ORDERED, ADJUDGED AND DECREED that should the parties or either of them fail, refuse, or neglect, within thirty (30) days from the date hereof, to execute and deliver any deed, conveyance, assignment, waiver, certificate of title, or other documents necessary or required to carry out and fulfill the terms and requirements hereof, then this Decree shall have the same operation and effect as any such deed, conveyance, assignment, waiver, certificate of title or other document.

Dated: _____

BY THE COURT:

_____

District Judge

Prepared and submitted by:

_____

HOT SHOT LAWYER
Attorney for Petitioner

Approved as to form:

_____

SMOOTH TALKING LAWYER
Attorney for Respondent

PATERNITY PETITION

IN THE DISTRICT COURT OF
DOUGLAS COUNTY, NEBRASKA

STATE OF NEBRASKA, on behalf of ELVIS BROWN, JR., Minor Child,	DOC. 007 NO. 007
vs.	PETITION FOR ESTABLISHMENT
ELVIS BROWN, Respondent.	OF PATERNITY AND SUPPORT

Comes now the State of Nebraska, on behalf of Elvis Brown, Jr., minor child in interest, Petitioner, and for its cause of action against Respondent, states as follows:

1. That Tiffany Jones is the natural mother and custodian of the child of interest.

2. That Tiffany Jones, mother, and said minor child in interest are residents of Douglas County, Nebraska.

3. That Respondent is a resident of Douglas County, Nebraska.

4. That Tiffany Jones and Respondent have never been married to each other.

5. That Petitioner and Respondent had sexual intercourse at various times between March, 1991, through May, 1992, as a result of which Tiffany Jones became pregnant.

6. That Tiffany Jones gave birth to the child in interest on December 1, 1992.

7. That Respondent is the father of the minor child.

8. That the child in interest is dependent upon and in need of financial support from the Respondent.

9. That Respondent has failed to provide adequate support for the child in interest.

10. That Respondent is capable of:

a) supporting the minor child by means of monthly payments;

b) paying the prenatal, delivery, and postnatal medical expenses incurred pursuant to the birth of said minor child;

c) paying the cost of providing for the physical needs of the child in interest since birth;

d) providing ongoing health and hospitalization insurance or health maintenance plan for the child in interest.

WHEREFORE, the Petitioner prays for a Decree determining that the Respondent:

1. Is the father of Elvis Brown, Jr., minor child in interest;

2. Owes a duty of support for the child in interest;

3. Should pay a sum certain each month to meet the duty of support;

4. Should pay for prenatal, delivery, and postnatal medical expenses incurred pursuant to the birth of the child in interest;

5. Should pay the cost of providing for the physical needs of the child in interest since birth;

6. Should provide ongoing health and hospitalization insurance or a health maintenance plan for the child in interest;

7. Should pay the cost of this action and such other relief as the Court may allow.

STATE OF NEBRASKA, on behalf of Elvis Brown, Jr., Minor Child, Petitioner

By: _____

DANIEL L. JOHNSON #16785 of LATENSER & JOHNSON, P.C.
Authorized Attorney,
Suite 201
14545 West Center Road
Omaha, Nebraska 68144
(402) 333-4026

LISTING CONTRACT

_____, 19____

IN CONSIDERATION of your agreement to list, and to offer for sale the property hereinafter described and to use your efforts to find a purchaser, I hereby give you the sole and exclusive right until _____ to sell _____

_____

_____

I agree to pay you a cash commission of _____ per cent of the gross sale price, said commission to be payable on the happening of any one or more of the following events, to wit:

If a sale is made, or a purchaser found, who is ready, willing and able to purchase the property before the expiration of this listing, by you, myself, or any other person, at the above price and terms or for any other price and terms I may agree to accept, or if this agreement is revoked or violated by me, or if you are prevented in closing the sale of this property by existing liens, judgments, or suits pending against this property, or the owners thereof, or if you are unfairly hindered by me in the showing of, or advertising to sell said premises, within the stated period, or if within three months after the expiration of this listing I made a sale of said premises to anyone due to your efforts or advertising done under this listing.

I hereby represent that to the best of my knowledge, information and belief, there are no termites in the buildings on the real estate hereinbefore described, and if termites are found in said buildings and it is known that such condition existed prior to the date of the closing of the sale thereof, I hereby agree to indemnify you and hold you harmless from any or all costs, damages or expenses to which you may be subjected arising in connection therewith.

In case of forfeiture, by a prospective purchaser, of any earnest money payment, upon the within described property, said earnest money, after expenses incurred by the agent have been deducted, shall be divided equally between the parties hereto, in proportion of one-half to the owner and one-half to the agent;

Provided, that in no event shall the agents share exceed the amount of the commission provided for in this contract.

In the event of sale, I agree to, without delay, furnish title insurance or a complete abstract, certified to date, showing good and merchantable title and to pay any expenses incurred in perfecting the title in case same is found defective, and convey the property within _____ from the date of sale, by warranty deed or _____ executed by all persons having any interest therein, clear of all encumbrances except _____ which encumbrances if assumed by the purchaser, shall be part of the agreed purchase price.

You are authorized to place a "For Sale" sign on the above property.

I agree to give possession within _____ from date of closing.

_____

_____
Owners

We accept the listing and agree to the terms thereof on this date and date above written.

_____
Agent

The owner acknowledges receipt of a copy of this listing contract as of the above written date.

_____

_____
Owners

AGREEMENT TO OCCUPY PRIOR TO FINAL CLOSING

The undersigned Seller and Purchaser, having executed a Purchase agreement dated _____ relating to the property located at:

Address _____

Legal Description _____
_____

and Purchaser, desiring to enter into possession of said premises prior to closing the sale and obtaining title thereto, the parties agree as follows:

1. In consideration of Seller's permission to Purchaser to take possession of the premises, Purchaseer agrees:
    a. To accept the premises in its present condition.
    b. To take responsibility for and maintain heating, sewer, plumbing and electrical systems and any built in appliances and equipment in normal working order, to keep the roof water-tight and to maintain the grounds.
    c. To have all utilities put in the name of the purchaser by the date of possession.
    d. To refrain from undertaking any alterations without prior written consent from the seller.
    e. To abide by all laws and governmental regulations with respect to the use or occupancy of the premises.
    f. To admit Seller, or his authorized agent, at reasonable times for the purpose of inspecting the premises until the final closing.
    g. To obtain and keep a homeowner's insurance policy in the name of the purchaser in effect for the entire time of occupancy before closing. Said insurance policy to be in the amount of $_____. *Note:* Possession of the Property by the Purchaser changes policy rights. Both Purchaser and Seller should consult their insurance agent prior to initial early occupancy date.

2. This agreement is not intended to create a relationship of landlord and tenant and the right of the Purchaser to occupy the

premises shall be on a day to day basis at _____ per diem. It is agreed that _____ will be paid in advance of initial occupancy by the Purchaser. In the event the Purchaser does not close as per the terms of this agreement or the Purchase Agreement, or in the event the Purchaser breaches either agreement, Purchaser agrees to vacate the premises within three days following written demand by Seller, personally delivered or mailed to the premises. Purchaser agrees to pay all cost of any legal action that may be instituted by Seller to enforce the terms hereof or for the eviction of the Purchaser from the property, including a reasonable attorney's fee.

3. Purchaser will pay any reasonable costs to restore the premises to the same condition as when the Purchaser took possession should the sale not close. The Purchaser acknowledges that if a sale should not take place that the retention of possession could seriously interfere with the subsequent sale of the property and that this agreement does not cause either party to waive their right to damages should the property sale not close.

4. Early occupancy per diem charges will commence on the _____ day of _____, 19 _____, and will terminate on the day of closing.

5. Occupancy date to be _____

_____	_____
Seller	Purchaser
_____	_____
Seller	Purchaser
_____	_____
Date	Date
Subscribed and sworn to be-	Subscribed and sworn to be-
fore me this _____ day	fore me this _____ day
of _____, 19_____	of _____, 19_____
_____	_____
Notary Public	Notary Public

102-REC

(This is a legally binding contract. If not understood, seek legal advice.)

PURCHASE AGREEMENT

_____, Agent   _____, 19_____

_____, Nebraska

I/We the undersigned Purchaser, hereby agree to purchase the property described as follows:

Address _____ Legal Description_____

_____

_____ including all fixtures and equipment permanently attached to said premises. The only personal property included is as follows: _____

Subject, however, and on condition that the owner thereof has good, valid and marketable title, in fee simple, and said owner agrees to convey title to said property to me or my nominees by warranty deed _____

free and clear of all liens, encumbrances or special taxes levied or assessed, except _____.
Purchaser shall be furnished a complete abstract of title, certified to date by a bonded abstractor, or a current title insurance commitment before closing

and a title insurance policy insuring marketability. The cost of title insurance shall be paid by: _____.Purchaser
agrees that should a valid title defect exist, that Seller shall have a reasonable period of time to correct such defect, not to exceed 30 days from the date
of the title opinion or title commitment. If the title defects are not cured within such time period, the Purchaser may declare this agreement null and
void, and obtain the return of the earnest money. The documentary revenue on the conveyence shall be paid by Seller.

I agree to pay for same _____ ($_____) DOLLARS,

on the following terms: $_____ deposited herewith as evidenced by your receipt attached below. Balance to be paid

as shown in Paragraph(s) #_____ following, which paragraph(s) numbered 1 to 5 inclusive as being applicable to this agreement.

#1 All Cash:
Balance of $_____ to be paid in cash or by certified check at time of delivery of deed, no financing being required.

#2 Conditional Upon Loan:

Balance of $_____ to be paid in cash or by certified check at time of delivery of deed, conditional however, upon my

ability to obtain a loan to be secured by deed of trust or mortgage on above described property, in the amount of $_____.

Said loan to be VA_____, FHA (Farmers Home Administration)_____, FHA (Federal Housing Administra-

tion)_____,CONVENTIONAL_____, M.G.I.C._____,or VA/FHA _____,

with terms providing for interest not exceeding _____%per annum, and monthly payments of approximately $_____

plus taxes and insurance. I agree to make application for said loan within _____ days from the date of acceptance
or this offer shall be null and void and the earnest money shall be forfeited. I agree to sign all papers and pay all costs in connection therewith, and to

establish escrow reserves as required. If said loan is not approved within _____ days from date of acceptance hereof, this offer shall be null and
void, and the money paid herewith to be returned to me. Provided, however, that if processing of the application has not been completed by the lending
agency within the above time, such time limit shall be automatically extended until the lending agency has in the normal course of its business advised
either approval or rejection. If the loan is not ultimately approved by the lending agency, this offer is null and void and the earnest money is to be
returned to the Purchaser.

#3 Assume Existing Mortgage:

I agree to assume and pay existing mortgage or deed of trust note balance in favor of _____ in the

approximate amount of $_____ and pay the balance in cash or by certified check at time of delivery of deed; it

being understood that present note terms call for interest rate of _____% per annum and payments of $_____ per

_____. Said payments includes _____ Interest on existing loan to be prorated to

date of closing. I also agree to reimburse the Seller for the amount in the escrow reserve account which is to be assigned to me. Buyer agrees to pay any

assumption fees. This agreement is □ or is not □ contingent upon the release of the liability of the Seller.

#4 Seller Financed:

Balance to be evidenced by _____ with Seller, providing for additional cash payment or certified check of $_____

at time of execution of the contract, and remainder of $_____ to be paid in monthly payments of

$_____, or more, which monthly payments shall include interest at the rate of _____% per annum computed monthly on

the unpaid portion of the principal, over _____ years with a balloon payment on _____, 19_____. Preparation of the instruments shall

be the responsibility of the □ Purchaser □ Seller and the cost of such preparation shall be paid by _____.

#5 Additional Terms: See reverse side.
Possession of said premises shall be delivered to me on or before _____, 19_____, or within _____ days after loan approval.
Possession shall be given to Purchaser on or before _____, 19 _____, but not prior to closing.
It is understood and agreed that this agreement shall in no manner be construed to convey title to said property or to give any right to take possession thereof.
Seller (Sellers) shall pay all taxes on and including _____. Taxes for the year _____, together with interest, rents and homeowners association dues, if any, shall be prorated to date of possession. Taxes shall be prorated based on the most recent assessed valuation and tax rate applicable to the property at the time of closing.
It is understood and agreed that in the event Sellers hold title to said property as joint tenants, they are contracting as joint tenants in their acceptance of this offer.
This offer is based upon my personal inspection or investigation of the premises and not upon any representation or warranties of condition by the Seller or his agent. Purchaser agrees to accept the property in its present condition, except as set forth in this agreement. Seller represents that there are no latent defects in the property of which Seller is aware except as noted in this agreement. Seller agrees to maintain, until delivery of possession, the heating, air conditioning, water heater, sewer, plumbing and electrical systems and any built-in appliances in working condition. If not already installed, Seller agrees to install any smoke detectors required by law.
It is understood and agreed that both parties retain their right to bring action for Specific Performance in the event the other party is in default in carrying out his obligations under this contract, or such other legal remedies which are available to either party.
Buyer requests a termite and wood destroying insect inspection of the property at Buyer's expense (except should Buyer obtain a VA loan, the expense shall be paid by Seller.) Should evidence of termites or wood destroying insects be found, the property shall be treated at Seller's expense. Buyer agrees to accept the treated property. If visible evidence of previously treated infestation which is now inactive is found, treatment shall not be required. Should damage from such insects be found, the damage shall be corrected at Seller's expense. However, if the cost required for repairs exceeds 1% of the purchase price, and Seller does not elect to pay the cost in excess of such amount, Buyer shall have the option of declaring this Agreement null and void and to the return of the earnest money.
Except for the costs required by the preceding two paragraphs, Seller's total liability for any costs for maintenance, repairs or replacements required

by terms of this Agreement or by Buyer's lender, shall not exceed $_____. Should maintenance, repairs or replacement exceed the
stated amount and Seller does not elect to pay the cost in excess of such amount, Buyer shall have the option of declaring this Agreement null and void
and to the return of the earnest money.
Any risk of loss to the property shall be borne by the Seller until title has been conveyed to the Purchaser. In the event, prior to closing, the structures on said property are materially damaged by fire, explosion or any other cause, Purchaser shall have the right to rescind this agreement, whereupon Seller shall then refund to Purchaser the deposit made hereunder.
It is understood that all real estate brokers and/or salespersons involved in this transaction are agents of, and are representing, the Seller.

BUYER_____ DATE_____ SS#/FedID#_____

BUYER_____ DATE_____ SS#/FedID#_____

ADDRESS_____Zip_____ Phone_____

Selling Agent Signature:_____ Listing Company:_____

Received from _____

$ _____ to apply towards the purchase price of the property under the terms set forth above.
In the event this offer is not accepted by Seller, or the conditions set forth in this agreement can not be met, this earnest money shall be refunded.

_____ Seller/Agent

By_____

Additional Terms:

_____
_____
_____
_____
_____
_____
_____
_____
_____
_____
_____
_____
_____
_____
_____
_____

Names for deed: _____

ACCEPTANCE

_____, 19_____

Seller accepts the Purchase Agreement on the terms stated and agrees to convey title to the Property, deliver possession, and perform all the terms and conditions set forth.

SELLER _____   SS#/FedID# _____

SELLER _____   SS#/FedID# _____

STATE OF _____)   STATE OF _____)
)ss.   )ss.
COUNTY OF _____)   COUNTY OF _____)
The foregoing purchase agreement was acknowledged before me on   The foregoing purchase agreement was acknowledged before me on

_____, 19_____, by _____   _____, 19_____, by _____

_____   _____

_____   _____
         Notary Public   Notary Public

Commission expires _____   Commission expires _____
(seal)   (seal)

RECEIPTS FOR FULLY EXECUTED PURCHASE AGREEMENT

Buyer acknowledges receipt of executed copy of this agreement.

_____   Date _____
              (Buyer)

_____   Date _____
              (Buyer)

PURCHASER PLEASE NOTE

In closing your purchase, we, as agents, are required to have cash, or its equivalent, upon conveyance of title. Please bring cash, certified check or cashier's check for the balance of your payment. This will permit us to deliver papers promptly.

SELLER PLEASE NOTE

Upon termination of Seller's insurance at closing, Seller should insure all personal property remaining on the premises prior to delivering possessions.

Note: While this form is acceptable to the Nebraska Real Estate Commission, its use is not mandatory and it will not be suitable for contracts having unusual provisions.

RESIDENTIAL LEASE

NOTICE: THIS IS A LEGALLY BINDING CONTRACT; IF NOT UNDERSTOOD, CONSULT A LAWYER.

This agreement made this ____ day of _____, 19____, by and between _____, hereinafter referred to as LANDLORD and _____ , hereinafter referred to as TENANT (whether one or more).

LANDLORD agrees to deliver possession of the following described premises, to wit: _____, occupancy to commence on the ____ day of _____, 19____, and to be continuous through the _____ day of _____, 19____. This agreement will terminate upon the date agreed, or upon ____ days notice in writing by either party, or upon breach according to the terms of this agreement.

LANDLORD agrees said premises are to be habitable and further agrees to keep common areas in reasonable clean and safe condition.

LANDLORD agrees to maintain in working order all electrical, plumbing, sanitary, heating, ventilating and other facilities which are supplied by LANDLORD except repairs necessary because of abuse or improper use by TENANT.

LANDLORD agrees to provide garbage facilities, facilities for running water and facilities for reasonable amounts of hot water, and reasonable heating facilities.

Electricity to be paid by: _____

Gas to be paid by: _____

Water to be paid by: _____

IN CONSIDERATION of the above, TENANT agrees to pay rent, in advance, without need for demand as follows:

$_____ on the ____ day of _____, 19____, and $_____ on the ____ day of each month thereafter.

Rent is to be paid to _____ at _____.

TENANT herewith deposits with LANDLORD the additional sum of $_____ as security which will be retained by LANDLORD to apply on any damage or loss other than ordinary wear occurring to said apartment or equipment therein, or for unpaid rent, or for failure to abide by the terms of this agreement. Under no circumstances can said deposit be applied by TENANT to pay rents due. Said deposit, less itemized deductions, will be returned within 14 days of demand and notice by TENANT of TENANT's forwarding address. An additional sum of $_____ is to be deposited as a pet deposit subject to the same conditions as the security deposit.

TENANT is fully responsible for all damage, other than ordinary wear, and agrees to pay for all damage in excess of damage deposit caused by TENANT, TENANT's family, guests, servants, pets or others permitted by TENANT to be on the premises.

TENANT further agrees to use said premises solely for living purposes as a private residence and shall not sell or assign this agreement, or sublet under this agreement, without written consent of LANDLORD.

TENANT agrees not to interfere, or allow any pet, guest, or family member of TENANT to interfere with the rights of peaceful enjoyment of other tenants occupying any building of which TENANT's apartment is a part, or do anything on the premises which would increase insurance rates or fire hazards or violate any municipal ordinances or codes or state laws.

That failure on the part of tenant to comply with any of the provisions of this agreement shall, at the option of the LANDLORD, constitute a forfeiture thereof.

TENANT agrees that LANDLORD shall have the right to enter said premises with notice at reasonable times and to post rental signs for the renting of said premises prior to the termination of this agreement and to enter without notice in case of emergency.

TENANT agrees to give prior notice of any intended absence in excess of seven (7) days; and any absence for seven (7) days, without notice, is cause for entry for reasonable purposes without notice. Absence of thirty (30) days, without notice, will be grounds for LANDLORD to retake possession of said premises.

TENANT agrees to be bound by all existing rules and regulations and all reasonable rules and regulations which may, from time to time, be adopted by said LANDLORD, and the same shall be construed to be conditions of this agreement.

The names of all persons living in said premises are: _____

TENANT agrees to notify LANDLORD of any additional persons living in said premises and LANDLORD may, at LANDLORD's option, refuse to allow said additional persons or raise the rental by $_____ per each additional person.

Any property of whatsoever description left in or about the premises shall, at LANDLORD's option, be stored in a public warehouse at the expense of and for the account of TENANT.

TENANT is urged to procure insurance on TENANT's personal property as LANDLORD assumes no liablity or responsibility for the personal property of TENANT.

Not alterations, remodeling or any fixtures or locks shall be made except as follows: _____

_____

or as subsequently agreed in writing by LANDLORD.

LANDLORD and TENANT agree that in the event said premises are totally destroyed by fire, rain, wind, or other causes beyond the control of LANDLORD, or are condemned and ordered torn down by any properly constituted authorities of the Federal, State, County, or City Governments, then in any of these events, this agreement shall cease and terminate as of the date of such destruction of said premises.

In addition hereto, the LANDLORD and TENANT make the following covenants and agreements:

It is agreed that the terms of this agreement are contractual and not mere recitals and are binding upon the parties hereto, their successors, heirs, personal representatives and assigns. Any breach thereof shall necessitate immediate correction, and if not corrected immediately, shall be grounds for termination upon thirty (30) days notice for a first breach or upon fourteen (14) days notice for substantially the same act within a six month period.

If rent is unpaid when due, LANDLORD may terminate this agreement after three (3) days notice and take action for possession as provided by the Uniform Residential LANDLORD and TENANT Act.

If any provision or paragraph of this agreement is unenforceable, the remaining provision or paragraphs shall nevertheless be carried in effect.

_____

LANDLORD

_____

TENANT

MOTION TO SUPPRESS EVIDENCE

IN THE DISTRICT COURT OF
DOUGLAS COUNTY, NEBRASKA

STATE OF NEBRASKA, Plaintiff,	DOC. 125 NO. 070
vs. LEFTY CARLSON, Defendant.	MOTION TO SUPPRESS EVIDENCE

Comes now Lefty Carlson, defendant herein, by and through his attorney, and moves the Court to grant a Motion to Suppress Evidence for the following reasons:

1. That defendant is charged with the offense of unlawful possession of a controlled substance.

2. That a preliminary hearing was previously held before the Court, whereupon defendant was bound over for trial on the above charge.

3. That the arresting police officer's conduct violated defendant's constitutional right to be free from unreasonable searches and seizures, as granted by the Fourth Amendment to the U.S. Constitution, and the Fourteenth Amendment to the U.S. Constitution.

4. That the evidence seized by the arresting police officer was a result of an illegal search and seizure.

WHEREFORE, defendant, Lefty Carlson, prays that the Court grant his Motion to Suppress Evidence.

DANIEL L. JOHNSON #16785
of LATENSER & JOHNSON, P.C.
Attorneys for Defendant
Suite 201
14545 W. Center Rd.
Omaha, NE 68144
(402) 333-4026

AUTOMOBILE NEGLIGENCE PETITION

IN THE DISTRICT COURT OF
DOUGLAS COUNTY, NEBRASKA

CHUCK CHEVY,
        Plaintiff,   DOC. 010   NO. 020

vs.

FRANK FORD,
        Defendant.   PETITION

Plaintiff, Chuck Chevy, for his cause of action against defendant, Frank Ford, states the following:

I.

Plaintiff is a resident of Omaha, Douglas County, Nebraska. Defendant is a resident of Omaha, Douglas County, Nebraska. The accident took place at approximately 210th Street and West Dodge Road in Douglas County, Nebraska, on October 15, 1992.

II.

At the time of the accident plaintiff was the owner and operator of a 1987 Chevrolet Camaro and was traveling northbound on a private road (approximately 210th Street) approaching its intersection with West Dodge Road. At the same time, defendant was operating a 1972 Ford Mustang, approaching the intersection from the west in the left hand eastbound lane of West Dodge Road.

III.

Said intersection is not controlled by traffic lights or signs. There is a hill crest on West Dodge Road a short distance to the west of the intersection.

IV.

As plaintiff reached the intersection, he stopped his automobile and looked both ways, observing all visible eastbound and westbound traffic. After determining that it was safe to do so, and while there was no eastbound traffic in sight, plaintiff entered the intersection, intending to turn left.

V.

As plaintiff entered the intersection, defendant drove over the hill crest at an extremely high rate of speed and collided with plaintiff.

VI.

The proximate cause of the accident was defendant's negligence. Defendant was negligent in the following particulars:

1. In failing to maintain a proper lookout;
2. In driving at a speed which was extreme and unreasonable under the circumstances;
3. In failing to yield the right-of-way;
4. In failing to keep his automobile under reasonable control.

VII.

As a proximate result of the negligence of defendant, plaintiff has suffered damage to his automobile in the amount of $7,000.00, destruction of tools of his trade in the amount of $1,600.00, undetermined lost income and medical expenses, temporary right leg paralysis, disabling right hip pain, headaches, back pain and mental anguish, and will continue to so suffer.

WHEREFORE, plaintiff prays for judgment against defendant for his special damages in the amount of $8,600.00, plus additional special damages as proven at trial, general damages as provided by law, and the taxable costs of this action.

CHUCK CHEVY, Plaintiff,

By: _____
DANIEL L. JOHNSON #16785
of LATENSER & JOHNSON, P.C.
Attorneys for Plaintiff
Suite 201
14545 W. Center Rd.
Omaha, NE 68144
(402) 333-4026

PREMISE LIABILITY PETITION

IN THE DISTRICT COURT OF
DOUGLAS COUNTY, NEBRASKA

JOE JONES, Plaintiff,	DOC. 123 NO. 321
vs. BOB SMITH, Defendant.	PETITION

The plaintiff complains of the defendant and for cause thereof alleges:

I.

That defendant is and was at all times relevant hereto owner of the residence located at 8500 Old Style Road, Omaha, Douglas County, Nebraska.

II.

That on or about January 1, 1993, defendant was negligent in that he failed to properly maintain his premises; specifically, but not by way of limitation, defendant failed to clear his front steps of ice and snow.

III.

That on or about January 1, 1993, as a result of the negligence of defendant, plaintiff was caused to slip and fall on defendant's front steps.

IV.

That plaintiff was seriously injured in the fall, suffered a severe fracture of his right ankle, contusions, abrasions, and other injuries.

V.

That as a result of the negligence of the defendant, plaintiff has in the past and will in the future continue to incur medical expenses and lost income.

VI.

That plaintiff's earning capacity has been impaired as a result of the injuries suffered because of defendant's negligence.

VII.

That plaintiff has suffered great pain and discomfort as a result of the injuries and will continue in the future to suffer pain and discomfort.

WHEREFORE, plaintiff prays for judgment against defendant in an amount in excess of Fifty Thousand Dollars ($50,000.00), together with his costs and disbursements herein.

_____

JOE JONES, Plaintiff,

By: _____
DANIEL L. JOHNSON #16785
of LATENSER & JOHNSON, P.C.
Attorneys for Defendant
Suite 201
14545 W. Center Rd.
Omaha, NE 68144
(402) 333-4026

LAST WILL AND TESTAMENT
OF MICKEY MOUSE

I, Mickey Mouse, being of sound mind and disposing memory, do hereby make, publish and declare this to be my Last Will and Testament, hereby revoking all former wills and codicils made by me.

I.

It is my intention by this will to dispose of all of my property, whether real, personal or mixed, including any and all property, of whatever nature, and wherever situated or acquired after the execution of this will.

II.

I direct that my Personal Representative, hereinafter named, pay all my just debts, funeral expenses and obligations existing against my estate.

III.

I may, from time to time, prepare a written document for the purpose of bequeathing part of or all of my tangible personal property at my death. Any such document shall specifically make reference to this will and shall further be dated and signed by me in order to be valid. Any such document shall be considered a part of this will as fully as if it were set forth herein and is incorporated as a part of this will by reference. If I shall make more than one such written document, only the most recent of such documents shall be valid and any earlier documents shall be deemed void.

IV.

I give, devise and bequeath the entire residue of my property, and estate, whether real, personal or mixed, of whatever nature, wherever situated, to my beloved wife, Minnie Mouse.

V.

Should my beloved wife, Minnie Mouse, predecease me, I give the entire residue of my property and estate, whether real, personal or mixed, of whatever nature, wherever situated, to my beloved children, in equal shares, share and share alike, or if any of them shall predecease me, to his or her issue, such issue to take per stirpes. All reference in this Will to my children includes any children that may hereafter be born or adopted.

VI.

In the event it should be necessary to appoint a Trustee for any of my children, I nominate and appoint, to serve as Trustee, Donald Duck. Should he predecease me or otherwise be unable to serve, I nominate and appoint, to serve as Trustee, Gladstone Gander. The Trustee is to serve without bond.

VII.

In the event it should be necessary to appoint a Guardian for any of my children, then I direct the County Court to appoint, to serve as Guardian, Donald Duck. Should he predecease me or otherwise be unable to serve, then I direct the County Court to appoint, to serve as Guardian, Gladstone Gander. The Guardian is to serve without bond.

VIII.

I nominate and appoint, to serve as my Personal Representative, my beloved wife, Minnie Mouse. Should she predecease me or otherwise be unable to serve, then, I appoint my father, Markie Mouse, as my Personal Representative. Should he predecease me or otherwise be unable to serve, then I appoint my mother, Mary Mouse, as my Personal Representative. My Personal Representative is hereby granted all powers set forth in Section 30-2476, R.R.S. Nebraska, and is specifically authorized and empowered by this will to sell any property of my estate, whether real, personal or mixed, or any interest therein, without a court order and notice. My Personal Representative is to serve without bond.

IX.

I hereby instruct and request the Court probating this Will to institute supervised proceedings pursuant to Section 30-2439, R.R.S. Nebraska, if my Personal Representative so requests.

X.

In the event that a beneficiary or beneficiaries under this will and I die as a result of a common accident or disaster, or under such circumstances that it is doubtful as to which of us died first, such beneficiary shall be deemed, for the purposes of this will, to have predeceased me.

I, Mickey Mouse, the Testator, sign my name to this instrument this ＿＿ day of ＿＿＿＿＿＿＿＿, 19＿＿, and being first duly sworn, do hereby declare to the undersigned authority that I sign and execute this instrurment as my Last Will and that I sign it willingly, that I execute it as my free and voluntary act for the purposes therein expressed and that I am eighteen years of age or older or am not at this time a minor, and am of sound mind and under no constraint or undue influence.

＿＿＿＿＿＿＿＿＿＿＿＿＿＿＿＿

MICKEY MOUSE, Testator

We, Santa Claus and EasterBunny, the witnesses, sign our names to this instrument, being first duly sworn, and do hereby declare to the undersigned authority that the Testator signs and executes this instrument as his Last Will and Testament and that he signs it willingly, and that he executes it as his free and voluntary act for the purposes therein expressed, and that each of us, in the presence and hearing of the Testator, hereby signs this will as witness to the Testator's signing, and that to the best of his knowledge, the Testator is eighteen years of age or older or is not at this time a minor, and is of sound mind and under no constraint or undue influence.

＿＿＿＿＿＿＿＿＿＿＿＿   ＿＿＿＿＿＿＿＿＿＿＿＿＿＿

Santa Claus, Witness   Easter Bunny, Witness
USA   USA
STATE OF NEBRASKA
                              SS
COUNTY OF DOUGLAS

SUBSCRIBED AND SWORN TO before me this ＿＿ day of ＿＿＿＿＿＿＿, 19＿＿, by Mickey Mouse, the Testator, and subscribed and sworn to before me by Santa Claus and Easter Bunny, witnesses, this ＿＿ day of ＿＿＿＿＿＿＿, 19＿＿.

＿＿＿＿＿＿＿＿＿＿＿＿＿＿＿＿

Notary Public

(Seal)

DURABLE POWER OF ATTORNEY

KNOW ALL MEN BY THESE PRESENTS:

That I, _____ , of _____ County, Nebraska, have made,

constituted and appointed, and by these presents do make, constitute and appoint _____

of _____ , _____ County, Nebraska, true and lawful attorney for me and in my name, place and stead, and on my behalf, subject to the provisions of Paragraph 13 hereof, to do and execute all or any of the following acts, deeds and things:

1. To receive debts, payments and property. To ask, demand, sue for, recover and receive all sums of money, debts, dues, goods, wares, merchandise, chattels, effects and things of whatsoever nature or description which now are or hereafter shall be or become due, owing, payable, or belonging to me in or by any right, title, ways or means howsoever, and upon receipt thereof, or of any part thereof, to make, sign, execute and deliver such receipts, releases or other discharges for the same respectively as my said attorney shall deem advisable.

2. To settle accounts. To settle any account or reckoning whatsoever wherein I now am or at any time hereafter shall be in any wise interested or concerned with any person whomsoever, and to pay or receive the balance thereof as the case may require.

3. To satisfy security interests and mortgages. To receive every sum of money which now is or hereafter shall be due or belonging to me upon the security or by virtue of any security interest or agreement, or mortgage, and on receipt of the full amount secured thereby to execute a good and sufficient release or other discharge of such security interest, or mortgage by deed or otherwise.

4. To compound, submit to arbitration, or otherwise settle or adjust differences. To compound with or make allowances to any person for or in respect to any debt or demand whatsoever which now is or shall at any time hereafter become due and payable to me, or by me, or upon my account, and to take and receive, or to pay and discharge (as the case may be), any composition or dividend thereof or thereupon, and to give or receive releases or other discharges for the whole of such debts or demands, or to settle, compromise, or submit to arbitration every such debt or demand and every other right, matter, and thing due to or concerning me as my attorney shall think best, and for that purpose to enter into and execute and deliver such bonds of arbitration or other instruments as my attorney may deem advisable in the premises.

5. To prosecute and defend. To commence, prosecute, discontinue, or defend all actions or other legal proceedings touching my estate or any part thereof, or touching any matter in which I or my estate may be in any wise concerned.

6. To manage real estate. To enter into and upon all and singular my real estate, and to let, manage, and improve the same or any part thereof, and to repair or otherwise improve, alter, or recontract, and to insure, any building or structures thereon, and further to contract with others for the management of such real estate, and to grant to such others all the powers with respect to such real estate usual in real estate management contracts, and granted to my said attorney herein.

7. To grant leases, receive rents, and otherwise deal with tenants and leased property. To contract with any person for leasing for or in such periods, including periods longer than my life, and without regard to the termination of this power of attorney, at such rents and subject to such conditions as my attorney shall see fit, all or any of my said real estate, and to let any such person into possession thereof, and to execute all such leases and contracts as shall be necessary or proper in that behalf, and to give notice to quit to any tenant or occupier thereof, and to receive and recover from all tenants and occupiers thereof or of any part thereof all rents, arrears of rent, and sums of money which now are or shall hereafter become due and payable in respect thereof, and also on non-payment thereof or of any part thereof to take all necessary or proper means and proceedings for terminating the tenancy or occupation of such tenants or occupiers, and for ejecting the tenants or occupiers and recovering the possession thereof.

8. To sell or exchange real or personal estate. To sell, either at public or private sale, or exchange any part or parts of my real estate or personal property for such consideration, payable immediately or upon such terms as my attorney shall think fit, and to execute and deliver good and sufficient deeds, bills of sale, endorsements, assignments, or other instruments for the conveyance or transfer of the same, with such covenants of warranty or otherwise as my attorney shall see fit, and to give good and effectual receipts for all or any part of the purchase price or other consideration.

9. To deposit moneys, withdraw, invest, and otherwise deal with tangible property. To deposit any moneys which may come to his hands as such attorney with any bank or banker in my name, and to withdraw any of such money or any other money to which I am entitled which now is or shall be so deposited, and either employ such money as he shall think fit in the payment of any debts or interest, payable by me, or taxes, assessments, insurance, and expenses due and payable or to become due and payable on account of my real and personal estate, or in or about any of the purposes herein mentioned, or otherwise for my use and benefit, or to invest such money in my name in any stocks, shares, bonds securities or other property, real or personal, as he may think proper, and to receive and give receipts for any income or dividend arising from such investments, and to vary or dispose of all and any such investments or other investments for my use and benefit as he may think fit.

10. To vote at stockholders' meetings, execute proxies, and otherwise substitute for owner. To vote at the meetings of stockholders or other meetings of any corporation or company, or otherwise to act as my attorney or proxy, with power of substitution, in respect of any stocks, shares, bonds, debentures, or other evidences of ownership, or securities, now or hereafter held by me and issued by or on account of said corporation or company and for that purpose to execute any proxies, limited to general, or other instruments.

11. To execute deeds, bills, notes, and similar instruments. For all or any of the purposes herein stated to enter into and sign, seal, execute, acknowledge, and deliver any contracts, deeds, or other instruments whatsoever, and to draw, accept, make, endorse, discount, or otherwise deal with any bills of exchange, checks, promissory notes, or other commercial or mercantile instruments.

12. To do all other things necessary in connection herewith. In general to do all other acts, deeds, matters, and things whatsoever in or about my estate, property, and affairs, or to concur with persons jointly interested with myself therein in doing all acts, deeds, matters, and things herein, either particularly or generally described, as fully and effectually to all intents and purposes as I could do in my own proper person if personally present, it being my intent to grant to my said attorney a general power to act for me and in my behalf, and not a limited or special power, limited to the specific acts herein described.

13. Power of attorney effective notwithstanding disability of principal; continues in effect after principal's death until notice. Pursuant to the provision of the Uniform Durable Power of Attorney Act, I declare that this power of attorney shall not be affected by my disability or incapacity, and that the authority granted herein shall continue during any period while I am disabled or incapacitated. Further, pursuant to said Sections, all such authority shall continue after my death, until notice of such death shall have been received by my attorney so that he has actual knowledge of the fact that I have died. Any action taken in good faith by said attorney during any period while is uncertain whether I am alive, before he receives actual knowledge of my death, or, in any event, taken during any period while I am disabled or incapacitated, shall be as valid as if I were alive, competent, and not disabled.

IN WITNESS WHEREOF, I have signed and acknowledged this instrument this _____ day of _____ , 19_____ ,

_____

STATE OF NEBRASKA)
) ss.
_____ COUNTY)

BE IT KNOWN, that on the _____ day of _____ , 19_____ , before me personally appeared

_____ above named, who is to me known to be the person described in and who executed the above Durable Power of Attorney, and acknowledged the same to be his or her voluntary act and deed.

IN TESTIMONY WHEREOF, I have hereunto subscribed my name and affixed my official seal, the day and year last above written.

_____
Notary Public

LIVING WILL DECLARATION

If I should lapse into a persistent vegetative state or have an incurable and irreversible condition that, without the administration of life-sustaining treatment, will, in the opinion of my attending physician, cause my death within a relatively short time and I am no longer able to make decisions regarding my medical treatment, I direct my attending physician, if so expressly directed or requested by my spouse, Minnie Mouse, to withhold or withdraw life sustaining treatment that is not necessary for my comfort or to alleviate pain.

Signed this _____ day of _____, 19_____

_____

MICKEY MOUSE

The declarant voluntarily signed this writing in my presence.

_____   _____

Witness   Witness

STATE OF NEBRASKA |
                                           | SS
COUNTY OF DOUGLAS |

The declarant voluntarily signed this writing in my presence.

_____

Notary Public

(Seal)

COVENANT NOT TO COMPETE

Employee agrees that at no time during the term of this Agreement, or for a period of one (1) year immediately following the termination of his employment hereunder, will employee, for himself or in behalf of any person or corporation other than employer, engage in the Widget selling business within the County of Douglas, State of Nebraska. Employee will not, directly or indirectly, solicit or attempt to solicit business or patronage of any person or corporation within such territory for the purpose of selling Widgets.

Employee will not, during the term of his employment or for one (1) year following the termination of such employment, service contracts and accounts from, or work in, the above-described territory for any person or corporation other than employer regarding the sale or service of Widgets.

_____

Employee

GLOSSARY

Abstract of Title. A summary of all conveyances, transfers or other facts of public records to determine ownership interests in real estate.

Acceptance. The unconditional acquiescence to the terms of an offer that results in a contract.

Addendum. A document added or supplemental to an original contract; usually used to clarify or add to the original terms of a contract.

Administrative Law. A body of law created by administrative agencies, typically in the form of rules and regulations specific to the particular agency involved.

Adoption. The legal procedure where the legal rights and duties of a natural parent to his child are terminated with similar rights and duties given to the child's adoptive parents.

Age Discrimination in Employment Act. The federal body of law that prohibits age discrimination against employees and job applicants. Generally, it prohibits discrimination against employees forty years of age or older, on account of age as to hiring, promotion, termination and compensation.

Alibi. A defense to a criminal charge used to prove that the accused was at a place other than the scene of the crime when it occurred, thus making it impossible for him to be guilty.

Alimony. Money paid from one spouse to another, usually husband to wife, to provide continued support of the recipient spouse during or after a divorce.

American Rule. The theory of American law that states that attorney fees are, with some exceptions, not awarded to the prevailing party in a lawsuit.

Americans With Disabilities Act. A federal body of law that requires employers to make reasonable accommodations for disabled workers and job applicants and prohibits discrimination against a qualified individual with a disability because of that disability.

Annulment. The legal procedure that establishes, for legal purposes, that a marriage never existed.

Antenuptial Contract. An agreement between spouses made prior to marriage, typically addressing the issues of support and distribution of wealth and property in the event of death, separation or divorce.

Appeal. The legal procedure where a losing party at trial requests a review and reversal of a decision (or verdict) by a higher court.

Arraignment. The legal procedure where a criminally accused is brought before the court and advised of the charges against him and then enters a response or plea to the charges.

Articles of Incorporation. The document filed with the appropriate governmental agency, such as the secretary of state, to initiate the incorporation of a business.

As Is. An expression used in sales agreements that indicates the buyer is assuming all risk of the condition of the property being purchased and that no warranties, expressed or implied, are given or made by the seller.

Assignment. The transfer to another of any interest in property, real or personal, or any right to possession.

Assumption of Risk. A theory that provides an injured person may not recover for his injuries when he voluntarily exposes himself to a known danger or dangerous situation.

At-Will Employees. An employee who has no employment contract and may be terminated at any time by his employer, without reason or cause.

Attachments. The procedure where personal property is taken by court officials following a court order or judgment.

Attractive Nuisance. The theory that provides that an individual who creates a condition on his premises that may be a source of danger to minors is under a duty to take all reasonable precautions to prevent injury to minors who the property owner may know would be attracted to or expected to play on the premises.

Automatic Stay. The stopping or immediate ceasing of any type of lawsuit activity, usually associated with a bankruptcy.

Bail. The procedure to release an individual who is charged with a criminal offense, usually requiring a certain amount of money to ensure his future attendance in court and/or making sure he remains within the jurisdiction of the court during the proceedings.

Bankruptcy. The procedure where an individual is declared unable to pay his debts and have them discharged or, in some instances, repays his debts under a court-supervised plan.

Bench Trial. A trial conducted without a jury in which a judge resolves all issues of fact and law and ultimately decides the case.

Beneficiary. One who receives a benefit from another, usually under the terms of a will or probate proceedings.

Board of Directors. The governing body of a corporation elected by the stockholders.

Bond. *See* Bail.

Breach of Contract. The failure, without legal justification, to perform any promise or obligation that is part of a contract.

Brief. The written argument used in a legal proceeding, generally used to summarize pertinent factual issues and applicable law.

Business Invitee. An individual who is implicitly invited onto certain premises, such as a store, for transacting business, is owed a duty of care by the owner.

Caveat Emptor. A Latin phrase meaning let the buyer beware, generally used to summarize the rule that a purchaser must examine and judge for himself the quality of an item being purchased without relying on any statements or comments by the seller.

Child Custody. The care, control and maintenance of a child who is awarded by a court to one of the child's parents after a divorce or separation proceeding.

Child Support. The obligation of a noncustodial parent to contribute to the economic support of a child, usually by way of periodic payments to the custodial parent.

Civil Rights Act of 1964. A federal body of law enacted to further guarantee and enforce the personal rights provided for by the United States Constitution, such as the prohibition of discrimination based on race, color, age and religion.

Closely Held Corporation. A corporation whose shares of stock are owned by a single shareholder or a closely knit group of shareholders, such as a family.

Closing. The final settlement of a real estate sale where the purchase price is given for the deed to the property being transferred; may include the execution of loan documents by the purchaser.

Closing Costs. The various charges and fees involved in closing a real estate transaction, such as filing fees, escrow fees, title insurance and attorney fees.

Co-Signer. One of two or more individuals who obligate themselves for a particular debt.

Codicil. A document that acts as a supplement or an addition to a will, usually designed to explain or modify an existing term of the will.

Collateral. Property that is given or used by a creditor as security for the repayment of a debt.

Common Law Marriage. A nonceremonial marriage that is created by an agreement to marry, followed by cohabitation between individuals sufficient to warrant a fulfillment of necessary relationship of spouses, including an assumption of marital duties and obligations.

Community Property. Property owned by spouses where each has an undivided one-half interest in each other's property solely by reason of their marital status, including one-half of any money earned by either spouse during the marriage.

Comparative Negligence. The theory of law where negligence is measured in terms of percentage, depending on the actions or inactions of the individuals involved in a negligent act; accordingly, any damages are allowed or dismissed in proportion to the amount of negligence attributable to the person sought to be held liable.

Condemnation. The prodecure where a privately owned parcel of real estate is taken and transferred to a government entity under the power of eminent domain.

Conditional Sales Contract. A type of installment sales contract where the seller reserves or maintains title to the property until the buyer pays the purchase price in full.

Conservatorship. The procedure where a court appoints another to manage the financial affairs of a minor or incompetent individual.

Consortium. The conjugal fellowship of spouses, including the right of each to the company and affection of the other.

Construction Lien. A claim on real estate stemming from labor or materials provided for the permanent improvement of the real estate involved, operating as security for the money owed.

Contingency Fee. A type of attorney fee that allows an attorney to retain or collect a portion of any money received by the client; typically used in collection or personal injury representation.

Contributory Negligence. The act or omission to act by an injured party that contributes to the negligence involved and, accordingly, contributes to his own injury.

Corporation. The legal entity created by state procedure that operates as an association of individuals doing business as the corporation; owned by shareholders and operated by a board of directors that appoints the corporate officers.

Counterclaim. A legal filing by a defendant in a civil lawsuit where he is seeking some form of damages or relief from the plaintiff, rather than just denying the plaintiff's claim.

Court. An entity created by law to adjudicate disputes pursuant to the applicable law.

Court Costs. The amount of money involved in filing a lawsuit and pursuing a legal claim, such as a filing fee or money paid to a sheriff for the service of a summons.

Court of Appeals. A court with jurisdiction that is limited to hearing appeals from other courts.

Covenant Not to Compete. A contract entered into by an employee whereby the employee agrees not to compete with his employer during or subsequent to his period of employment, usually involving a particular geographical area and set period of time.

Crime. An act in violation of the applicable criminal code or ordinance.

Crossclaim. A claim made by a defendant against a co-defendant in the same lawsuit.

Damages. Any loss that may be recovered in the judicial system that is suffered by an injured party.

Debtor's Exam. The judicial procedure whereby a defendant is ordered to appear in court and give testimony as to any assets or means of satisfying a judgment against him.

Deed. A written document used to convey real estate.

Deed of Trust. A deed transferred by a home buyer by which title of the home is placed in the name of a trustee to secure repayment of a loan; a security device used by lenders making loans for home purchases.

Defendant. The party against whom a lawsuit is filed.

Deficiency Balance. The amount of money left owing a lender subsequent to the lender enforcing its interest in real estate, such as a mortgage foreclosure or deed of trust.

Discharge. The term used in a bankruptcy court to negate or dissolve an otherwise valid debt.

Discovery. The legal procedure whereby parties to a lawsuit learn as much about the opposing parties' case as possible, usually by way of depositions, interrogatories and request for production of documents.

Divorce. The legal separation of spouses, usually accompanied by the apportionment of property and debts, child custody and support obligations.

Divorce Decree. The document signed by the judge stating that the parties to the divorce are no longer married and setting forth the obligations of the divorced parties subsequent to the divorce pertaining to child custody, alimony, child support, property division and debt allocation.

Double Jeopardy. The prohibition against being tried for the same crime or same set of facts allegedly constituting a crime on two separate occasions.

Due Process of Law. A constitutional guarantee of a course of legal proceedings that must be established and followed to allow for the enforcement and protection of private rights and property.

Early Occupancy Agreement. A contract between a home seller and home buyer where the home buyer is allowed to occupy the home prior to closing.

Earnest Money Deposit. The money used as a down payment by the buyer of real estate as evidence of good faith and serious intention; usually forwarded to the seller at the time the purchase agreement is made and credited to the buyer at the time of closing.

Easement. A nonpossessory interest in real estate that allows an individual to use another's property for a limited or predesignated purpose.

Elective Share. A widow's election to receive a portion of her deceased spouse's estate as opposed to what she would otherwise receive under the terms of his will.

Eminent Domain. The power of the government to take private property for public use; entails the obligation to reimburse the owner the fair value of the property taken.

Employment Contract. A contract between an employer and employee that sets forth the specific duties and obligations of each during the term of employment, including any grounds for termination.

Entrapment. Any act by law enforcement officials that induces a person to commit a crime that he would not otherwise commit.

Equal Credit Opportunity Act. A federal law prohibiting a creditor from discriminating against any applicant for credit on the basis of race, color, religion, national origin, age, sex or marital status.

Equal Pay Act. A federal law that requires employers to pay the same amount of wages and compensation to all individuals who do the same work in the same manner and in the same capacity without regard to sex, age, color, race, religion or national origin.

Equitable Title. The type of ownership rights that a purchaser of real estate has who is buying property by way of a land install-ment sales contract.

Escrow Agent. The neutral third party to a real estate transfer who is obligated to carry out the provisions of a purchase agree-ment, usually involving the receipt of funds to purchase the prop-erty in exchange for the deed.

Eviction. The legal procedure where an owner or landlord of a piece of property obtains a court order to have a tenant forcibly removed for violation of the lease agreement, usually the nonpay-ment of rent.

Evidence of Title. An obligation of a seller of real estate to show or prove to the buyer that the real estate being transferred is legally his and that he has the legal right to transfer it; evidence of title is usually provided by way of title insurance or attorney's opinion.

Exclusionary Rule. A rule of criminal law that any evidence obtained illegally cannot be used in the criminal prosecution of an individual.

Executor. An individual who is legally obligated to carry out the terms of another's will; also known as an executrix or personal representative.

Express Warranty. An expressed promise or guarantee of quality or condition of property being purchased, usually made in writing.

Fair Credit Reporting Act. A federal law that regulates the consumer reporting industry to ensure that consumer reporting activities are conducted in a manner that is fair and equitable to the affected consumer, including the consumer's right to privacy as against the informational demands of others and the right of the consumer to correct any erroneous information that may be the basis of a denial of credit, insurance or employment.

Fair Credit Billing Act. A federal law that contains procedures with regard to the settlement of billing disputes and requires credit card companies to be more responsible for the quality of merchandise purchased by their card holders.

Fair Debt Collection Practices Act. A federal law that sets forth the allowable and prohibited procedures with regard to the collection of a debt by a third party on behalf of a creditor.

Fair Housing Act of 1968. A federal law that makes it unlawful to discriminate on the basis of race, color, religion, sex or national origin with regard to the sale or leasing of real property.

Family Purpose Doctrine. A legal theory that the owner of a motor vehicle who allows a family member to use it is liable for any injuries inflicted upon a third party while the vehicle was being operated by that family member.

Federal Drug-Free Work Place Act. A federal law requiring that any employer that is a recipient of federal contracts or grants must certify to the federal government that it is making a good faith effort in providing a drug-free work place for its employees.

Federal Tort Claims Act. A federal law that states that the United States may not be sued in a tort action without its consent, thus preserving its traditional governmental immunity with respect to a certain category of torts.

Felony. A criminal offense that is typically more serious in nature than other types of crime.

Fiduciary Duty. The legal duty owed from an agent to a principal pursuant to an agency relationship in which the agent is obligated to promote and protect the interests of his principal.

Fixtures. Items of personal property that are permanently attached to real estate and, by means of such attachment, are considered part of the real estate.

Flat Fee. A type of attorney fee in which the attorney charges a specific amount of money for a particular legal job, such as a will or divorce.

Foreclosure. The legal process by which a lender (known as a mortgagor) obtains a foreclosure decree and proceeds with the forced sale of real estate that was used as security for a loan.

Franchise. A business device where a privileged right to use the trade name of license is given to another, usually accompanied by a franchise agreement setting forth the obligations and rights between the party granting the franchise (franchisor) to the party receiving the franchise (franchisee).

Garnishment. A proceeding where an individual's property or money that is in the possession of another (such as a bank or employer) is required to be transferred to an individual who has obtained a money judgment in his favor; a means of collecting on a judgment.

General Damages. The type of damages that the law presumes an injured party has incurred as a result of an injury, such as pain and suffering or loss of enjoyment of life.

General Partnership. The type of partnership in which the partners, known as general partners, equally share any profits as well as the management of the partnership, and bear equal responsibility and liability for partnership debts and obligations.

Grand Jury. A jury of inquiry where the individuals making up the jury have the duty to receive complaints and accusations in criminal cases and decide whether enough evidence exists to issue an indictment or formal criminal charge.

Gross Negligence. A type of negligence where an individual or entity is deemed to have acted in total or reckless disregard for the consequences of another; considered more difficult to prove than ordinary negligence.

Guarantee. An agreement to answer for payment of a debt or performance of an obligation of another.

Guardian Ad Litem. A person appointed by a court to prosecute or defend a lawsuit on behalf of an infant or incompetent individual; is obligated to promote and protect the rights of said person.

Guardianship. The procedure where a court appoints an individual to provide general care and control over another who is otherwise unable to manage his own affairs.

Habeas Corpus. The phrase used to define a procedure in which a criminal defendant is challenging the legality of his detention or imprisonment; the right of habeas corpus is guaranteed by the U.S. Constitution.

Holographic Will. A last will and testament drafted by and written in the handwriting of the deceased.

Implied Warranty. A type of warranty given by the seller of property that, by the nature of the property and by what it was designed to do, is implied by law.

Imputed Negligence. A legal doctrine that transfers to one person the responsibility for the negligence of another; typically used between husband and wife, employer and employee, and parent and child.

Independent Contractor. An individual who is hired to do a particular job or obtain a specific result, without being instructed as to the procedure or process of how the task is accomplished.

Intestate Laws. State laws that provide for the apportionment of a deceased's estate when he dies without a will.

Irrevocable Living Trust. A type of trust that may not be revoked after its creation.

Joint Custody. When both separated or divorced parents have an equal say in how their child is to be raised, even though actual physical possession of the child is with one parent.

Joint Will. A type of will that is used by married persons and, through one document, provides for the distribution of their assets and other bequests at the time of their respective deaths.

Judge. An individual appointed or elected as an officer of the court who conducts hearings and trials, and generally presides over any proceedings in his court.

Jurisdiction. The authority by which courts and judicial officers, such as judges, take control of and have the power to decide various cases within their power.

Jury. A certain number of individuals selected according to legal procedure to inquire or decide matters of fact brought before them pursuant to legal disputes or potential criminal charges.

Land Installment Sales Contract. A contract for the sale of real estate in which the seller does not convey full title to the property until all of the purchase price is paid by the buyer, usually in installments over an extended period of time.

Last Clear Chance Doctrine. A doctrine of law with regard to automobile collisions that states that if the injured party had the last opportunity to take some affirmative action to avoid the accident, and does not do so, he is prevented from recovering against the party who otherwise caused the accident.

Last Will and Testament. An instrument by which a person provides for the disposition of his property and affairs after his death, and that is generally revocable during his lifetime.

Latent Defects. A hidden or concealed defect of property that is not ordinarily discoverable or apparent upon a reasonable inspection.

Law Firm. A group of attorneys that practice law together as a business entity, such as a partnership or professional corporation.

Law Suit. A formal legal action brought against another requesting that the court adjudicate a dispute and issue an order or judgment in favor of one of the parties.

Lease. A contract where one party transfers the right of property possession to another, usually for a specific time and for specific consideration.

Legal Description. A precise description of real estate by either a government survey or lot number of a prerecorded plat map.

Legal Separation. A legal procedure where spouses seek a decree of separation that sets forth their obligations to each other, including their children, and marital estate; usually used if the parties do not wish to obtain a formal divorce or where other requirements of a formal divorce are not yet met.

Lemon Laws. A body of laws available in many states pertaining to motor vehicles, where constant and chronic problems not remedied by the manufacturer or dealer allow the purchaser to obtain a substitute vehicle.

Levy. To obtain money or property through seizure and sale, usually pursuant to court order or a judgment.

License. An individual who has been given the authority, either expressed or implied, to enter upon another's land; the owner of the land owes the licensee a duty of reasonable due care and must provide a safe environment for the licensee's occupancy.

Lien Waiver Affidavit. A document signed by the seller of real estate stating that no permanent improvements have been made on the property that may give rise to a construction lien being filed after the property is sold.

Limited Partnership. A partnership where certain individuals, known as limited partners, are not bound by the obligations of the partnership as they would otherwise be if they were general partners; limited partners are only liable for partnership obligations up to the amount of capital or money that they have specifically invested or placed with the partnership.

Listing Agreement. An employment contract between a home seller and a real estate agent whereby the agent is directed to find a ready, willing and able buyer for the home at terms acceptable to the seller.

Living Trust. A type of trust that is only in effect during the lifetime of the creator of the trust, also known as an active or intervivos trust.

Living Will.   A document that provides that if no reasonable expectation exists of recovery from a mental or physical disability, then the person signing the document be allowed to die and not be kept alive by artificial means or measures; not considered a legally binding document in the majority of states.

Magnuson-Moss Act.   A federal law that requires written warranties on consumer products be fully and conspicuously disclosed in clear language, including any terms and conditions of such a warranty.

Malpractice.   Professional misconduct or unreasonable lack of skill; usually applied to attorneys, physicians and other professionals.

Miranda Rights.   Specific rights that must be given to a criminally accused; unless these rights are sufficiently given, no evidence obtained in any questioning or interrogation thereafter may be used against the accused.

Mechanic Lien.   *See* Construction Lien.

Misdemeanor.   A type of criminal offense that is considered lesser in severity than a felony.

Mortgage.   A document granting an interest in real estate from an owner/borrower to a lender as security for a loan.

Motion to Suppress.   A criminal defense procedure used to eliminate any evidence that may be used against a criminally accused that has been obtained illegally or in violation of the accused's constitutional rights.

Negligence.   The failure to use such care as a reasonably prudent person would use under similar circumstances.

No Contest.   A type of plea given by a criminally accused that acts as a guilty plea for purposes of sentencing, yet does not require the defendant to actually plead guilty or acknowledge guilt of a criminal act.

No Fault Divorce.   A divorce that may be obtained without having to prove that one of the spouses was guilty of some type of marital misconduct.

Nonconforming Use. The use of real estate in nonconformance with existing zoning requirements, but is allowed due to its lawful existence prior to the enactment of the applicable zoning provision.

Notice to Quit. Written notification given by a landlord to a tenant that formally notifies the tenant that he has a certain period of time to pay any past-due rent or remove himself from the premises; often a prerequisite of filing an eviction action.

Offer. A proposal, whether verbal or written, to do something or pay a certain amount and, when coupled with an unconditional acceptance, creates a binding contract.

Option to Purchase. A contract where an individual is given the right to buy a certain piece of property within a particular time frame.

Pardon. An act by a governor or other empowered official to negate a penalty for a conviction and/or restore any rights and privileges previously removed from a convicted criminal.

Parole. The reduction of a criminal sentence by a parole board using the supervision of the defendant for a certain period of time by a parole officer.

Partnership. An agreement between two or more individuals or entities with regard to a particular endeavor or concern, such as a business or professional relationship.

Patent Defect. A type of defect in property, whether real or personal, that is plainly visible or can be readily discovered by an ordinary person using typical care and prudence.

Paternity Suit. A legal action to establish that a particular person is the natural father of a child and to establish child support obligations.

Periodic Tenancy. A type of landlord/tenant relationship that continues for successive periods, such as weekly, monthly or annually, and continues to exist unless terminated by either party at the end of each particular tenancy period.

Personal Guarantee. A type of guarantee of a debt or obligation that is made by an individual, usually stemming from a debt incurred by a corporation or other entity.

Personal Representative.   The individual or entity, also known as an executor or executrix, appointed to carry out the terms of an individual's last will and testament.

Plaintiff.   The party who brings or commences a lawsuit.

Plea.   A statement of guilt or innocence, or no contest, entered by a criminally accused to establish his formal response to charges against him.

Plea Bargain.   The procedure where a criminally accused and prosecutor agree to a disposition of the charges, subject to court approval; usually entails the defendant pleading guilty to an offense lesser in degree than the charges against him.

Pleadings.   The written documents filed with the court to establish the parties' positions and allegations in a lawsuit.

Postconviction Relief.   A procedure that allows a convicted prisoner to challenge the constitutionality of his conviction or sentence.

Power of Attorney.   The transfer of power from one individual to another allowing the recipient to dispose of any property or handle any affairs of the donor, depending upon the breadth of power given.

Preliminary Hearing.   A hearing in a criminal matter where the judge determines whether enough evidence exists to establish that a crime has been committed and that the defendant committed it; if such facts are established, the defendant is ordered to stand trial.

Prenuptial Agreement.   *See* Antenuptial Contract.

Preponderance of Evidence.   The evidentiary standard that is used in most civil cases; provides that whichever evidence is of the greater weight or more convincing shall dictate the outcome of the trial.

Pro Bono.   Legal services or work done free of charge.

Pro Se.   When an individual appears for himself in a court proceeding.

Probable Cause.   Also known as reasonable cause; having more evidence than not, the basis for obtaining a criminal search warrant or allowing an officer to arrest an individual or conduct a reasonable search of an individual thought to have committed a crime.

Probate.   A court-supervised procedure in which a will is determined to be valid and the terms thereof carried out.

Probation.   A type of criminal sentence in which the defendant is released into the community under the supervision of an officer of the court and reports periodically with regard to his conduct and whereabouts.

Product Liability.   The legal liability of manufacturers and sellers of products to compensate buyers for any damages or injuries suffered because of defects in the items purchased.

Promissory Note.   A written promise to pay a specific sum at the end of a certain period of time.

Property Settlement.   The portion of a divorce or separation decree that sets forth the division of property and allocation of debts between ex-spouses.

Proximate Cause.   An element of proof used in negligence actions that alleges that a particular injury is caused by an unbroken series of events commenced by the negligent party.

Punitive Damages (also known as Exemplary Damage).
Damages awarded to an injured party in a lawsuit that go beyond compensation; used to punish the wrongdoer for acts or omissions so as to provide further deterrence to any such future acts.

Quit Claim Deed.   A deed that conveys any interest that the seller or transferor may have in a parcel of real estate, without making any guarantees or promises whatsoever.

Reaffirmation Agreement.   Used by a debtor in the process of bankruptcy; the debtor reaffirms a debt with a particular creditor and continues payment on the debt during and after the bankruptcy.

Real Estate Settlement Procedures Act (RESPA).   A federal law that requires that lenders involved in federally related mortgage loans must make certain disclosures and provide certain information to loan applicants and borrowers.

Replevin.   A lawsuit used to recover specific items of personal property that are unlawfully held or taken, usually filed by a creditor to recover secured property.

Res Ipsa Loquitor.   A legal theory that creates a rebuttable presumption of inference that an individual was negligent by causing a certain injury, if it is established that the cause of the injury was in the defendant's exclusive and total control and that the accident involved does not happen in the ordinary course of events.

Rescind.   To cancel or annul an otherwise binding contract.

Restrictive Convenants.   A private agreement between homeowners of an area or subdivision that creates certain use restrictions on the area so as to maintain acceptable standards of conduct and/or usage of the property; typically used in newer residential subdivisions.

Revocable Living Trust.   A type of trust in which the settlor (creator of the trust) reserves unto himself the right to revoke the trust at any time.

Search Warrant.   A court order directing a public official to seize property that may constitute evidence of the commission of a crime, or other criminally possessed items, or property designed or used for the commission of a crime.

Security Deposit (also known as Earnest Deposit).   Money used as a down payment made by a purchaser of real estate, used as evidence of good faith in proceeding with purchasing the property pursuant to the terms of a purchase agreement.

Security Interest.   An interest in property that is pledged to a creditor by a buyer so as to enable the buyer to purchase the property over an extended period of time.

Self-Incrimination.   Statements or acts by a criminally accused that implicate him in a crime; federal and state governments are prohibited from requiring a person to incriminate himself or be a witness against himself in a criminal matter.

Settlor. An individual or entity who creates a trust.

Soldiers and Sailors Civil Relief Act. A federal law that suspends or modifies certain civil liabilities of persons who enter the military; also requires individuals who have sued a military person to follow a certain procedure so as to adequately protect the rights of military personnel.

Sole Proprietorships. A type of business in which one individual owns all the assets of the business and is personally liable for all business debts and obligations.

Special Damages. Damages resulting from an injury that can be specifically identified and itemized, such as lost wages or medical bills.

Specialty Courts. Courts that have specific jurisdiction over particular matters, e.g., divorce court, workers' compensation court and small claims court.

Stare Decisis. The policy of courts to follow and stand by previous decisions in similar cases, thus establishing legal precendent.

Statute of Limitations. The applicable law that provides for the amount of time in which a lawsuit must be filed after the cause of action arises.

Statute of Frauds. A law that requires certain agreements to be in writing before they can be legally enforced.

Statute. A written law enacted by a legislature or governing body.

Strict Liability. A legal theory in which a seller of a product is liable for all resulting damages stemming from the use of a product that is determined to be inherently dangerous or ultra-hazardous.

Subchapter S Corporation. A small business corporation that, under tax law, is permitted to be taxed as if the corporation were an individual proprietorship.

Sublease.   Where a tenant transfers an interest in his leased premises to another person or entity.

Subrogation.   A substitution of one person in the place of another with reference to a particular lawsuit or legal claim; typically utilized by insurance companies who attempt to recover benefit proceeds paid to their insured.

Sudden Emergency Doctrine.   A theory of negligence that states that when in individual finds himself confronted with a sudden emergency situation that was not brought upon by his own negligence, that person has the legal obligation to do what is necessary to protect himself to avoid injury prior to being able to recover for such a loss.

Summary Judgment.   A rule of civil litigation where one party establishes that no material issue of fact exists and that he is entitled to a judgment as a matter of law, thus negating the necessity of a trial.

Supreme Court.   A court that hears appeals from other lower courts, usually the court of last jurisdiction or last resort pursuant to an appeal.

Tenancy.   The transfer of a possessory interest in real estate for a certain or undetermined period of time from the owner (landlord) to the tenant.

Testamentary Trust.   A type of trust that takes effect upon the death of the settlor (creator of the trust).

Testator.   A man who dies leaving a will.

Textatrix.   A woman who dies leaving a will.

Time Share.   An ownership in real estate that involves an undivided interest in a piece of property only during a specific predetermined period of time; often used as vacation or resort property.

Title Insurance.   Insurance against the loss or damage resulting from defects in the ownership rights to a particular piece of real estate.

Tort.   A private wrong or injury stemming from a violation of a duty imposed by one individual to another, which is breached, such as the negligent driving of one individual that causes injury or damages to another; necessary elements of all torts include the existence of a legal duty from one party to another, the breach of that duty, and damages that result therefrom.

Tort Feasor. An individual who commits a tort.

Trespass. The illegal interference, occupancy or usage of another's real property.

Trial. The determination by judge or jury of a particular issue of guilt or innocence in court, based upon the evidence.

Trust. A legal arrangement between the creator of the trust (settlor) who transfers property or assets to a third party (trustee) who is directed to manage or maintain such property subject to instructions or guidelines.

Trustee. The person or entity obligated to hold or manage property subject to a trust.

Trustor. One who creates a trust, also called the settlor.

Truth in Lending Act. A federal law that mandates various disclosures to applicants of consumer credit so as to provide the applicant with all relevant information as to the cost and ramifications of the loan.

Uniform Commercial Code. A uniform body of law applicable in most states setting forth rules governing commercial transactions involving the sale of goods, commercial paper, bank deposits and secured transactions.

U.S. Constitution. The written instrument agreed upon by the people of the United States of America establishing the fudamental law of the country upon which all other laws in the country are based.

Usury. A law that makes it illegal to charge an interest rate above a certain amount.

Venue. The geographic location of the court where a particular lawsuit can be heard.

Ward. An individual, often a child or incompetent person, placed by the court under the care of a guardian or other court official.

Warranty.   A statement or representation made by a seller of property with regard to the quality, character or condition of the property that is relied upon by the buyer at the time of purchase.

Warranty Deed.   A type of deed that contains within it certain implied promises that provide the buyer with various remedies in the event that the transfer of property or ownership rights in the property is not total and complete.

Will.   *See* Last Will and Testament.

Workers Compensation.   State laws that provide for predetermined fixed awards to employees (or their dependents) in the event of employment-related accidents or injuries; often dispensing with any establishment of negligence by the employer.

Zoning.   The division of real property into prescribed geographical areas wherein various types of activities are allowed, such as residential, industrial or commercial.

INDEX

More Great Books for Smart Money Decisions

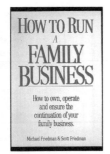

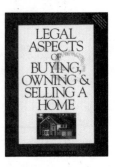

Homemade Money — With this all-new edition, you'll be up to speed on the legal matters, accounting practices, tax laws, and marketing techniques sure to make your home-based business a success! *#70231/$19.95/384 pages/paperback*

How to Run a Family Business — To ensure your family business stays afloat, you need sound advice. You'll find everything you need to know, from forming a board of directors, to setting salaries in this indispensable resource. *#70214/$14.95/176 pages/paperback*

Mortgage Loans — Don't make a big-money mistake signing for the wrong mortgage! Find the facts on the types of mortgages perfectly suited to your needs and financial situation. Plus get information on caps, margins, points, and more! *#70242/$14.95/144 pages/paperback*

Legal Aspects of Buying, Owning, & Selling a Home — In this easy-to-read guide you'll find the answers to all your legal questions concerning buying, selling, and occupying a home. *#70151/$12.95/176 pages/paperback*

The Complete Guide to Contracting Your Home — This all-in-one guide covers everything from site selection to financing your new home. Plus, you'll get a crash-course on dealing with suppliers, subcontractors, building inspectors, and more! *#70025/$18.95/288 pages/paperback*

The Small Business Information Source Book — Find the specialized information you need to be a success in the world of small business. This all-in-one guide covers everything from absenteeism to wholesaling. *#70097/$7.95/136 pages/paperback*

Becoming Financially Sound in an Unsound World — In this strategic guide, you'll find financial security while you improve your personal well-being with a positive outlook. *#70140/$14.95/240 pages/paperback*

Surviving the Start-Up Years in Your Own Business — It's a fact — most small businesses fail in the start-up years. This guide — chock full of sound advice and concrete examples — will help you make successful decisions. *#70109/$7.95/172 pages/paperback*

Use the order form below (photocopy acceptable) and save when you order two or more books!

- -

☐ **Yes!** I want the following books to help me make smart money decisions:

Book #	Brief title	Price
_____	_____	_____
_____	_____	_____

Credit Card Orders Call TOLL-FREE 1-800-289-0963

Subtotal _____

Tax (Ohio residents only, 5½%) _____

*Please add $3 for shipping and handling for one book; shipping is FREE when you order 2 or more titles.

Shipping* _____

Total _____

Check enclosed $ _____   ☐ Visa   ☐ MasterCard

Acct # _____ Exp. _____

Name _____ Signature _____

Address _____

City _____ State _____ Zip _____

Stock may be limited on some titles; prices subject to change without notice.

Mail to: Betterway Books, 1507 Dana Ave., Cincinnati, OH 45207

Write to this address for a catalog of Betterway Books, plus information on *Writer's Digest* magazine, *Story* magazine, Writer's Digest Book Club, Writer's Digest School, and Writer's Digest Criticism Service.